LEARNING PROBLEMS IN THE CLASSROOM

PREVENTION AND REMEDIATION

D0101684

MARIANNE FROSTIG, PH.D.

Founder, Executive-Director Emeritus, and Consultant,
The Marianne Frostig Center of Educational Therapy;
Professor of Education, Mount St. Mary's College,
Los Angeles, California

PHYLLIS MASLOW, M.A.

Research Consultant,
The Marianne Frostig Center of Educational Therapy,
Los Angeles, California

GRUNE & STRATTON *New York and London*
A Subsidiary of Harcourt Brace Jovanovich, Publishers

Library of Congress Cataloging in Publication Data

Frostig, Marianne.
    Learning problems in the classroom.

    Includes bibliographies.
    1. Child Study. 2. Handicapped children—Educa-
tion. 3. Remedial teaching. I. Maslow, Phyllis,
joint author. II. Title.
LB1117.F74   370.15'2   73-1578
ISBN 0-8089-0783-2

Grune & Stratton, Inc.
111 Fifth Avenue
New York, New York 10003

Library of Congress Catalog Card Number 73-1578
International Standard Book Number 0-8089-0783-2

Printed in the United States of America

*This book is dedicated to all
those who spend their lives
in the service of children
and to the children themselves.*

AUTHORS' NOTE

Because these chapters contain practical suggestions for teaching, with particular reference to children with learning difficulties, it is hoped that this book will serve not only as a textbook but also as a practical handbook for use in the classroom.

CONTENTS

FOREWORD

The last two decades have shown a phenomenal increase in the concern for the child with special learning problems. This concern seems to represent a juncture point between two major groups of professionals. The first group has been interested in the developmental consequences of organic insult on the child and are represented by many different disciplines producing books referring to the "brain-injured child" or the child with "minimal brain dysfunction." The second group, composed mainly of educators, have always sought the Holy Grail of individualization of instruction.

The work by pioneers such as Strauss, Kephart, Kirk, Cruickshank, Lehtinen, and Dr. Frostig herself have provided a rich background of clinical experience in providing for individualization of educational programming for the handicapped child.

In a rather specific way, this particular book signifies a shift in the strategy and approach that has been taking place in the last decade. Originally, many of these investigators focused on the training of specific mental functions and concentrated on such issues as visual-perception problems or attentional difficulties. There now is emerging a broader perspective of the child with learning problems. Instead of the identification of a specific deficit and the design of specific exercises to deal with that deficit, the child and his total developmental status are being reviewed. His overall motivation and social environment are reviewed and included in the planning.

Another dramatic change in the remedial strategy has been at least a broadening of the clinical approach. The clinical approach assumes that whenever the child is having school problems, there must be a specific deficit in that child, and therefore all efforts are concentrated on providing remedial instruction for that child. Yet it is quite clear that the child exists in a social envelope and that the portrait of the child interacting with adults, family, and peers can reveal that the problem is influenced significantly by one of the other components in that system of interactions.

To provide a crude example, if a child is crying all the time, it may be because he is being physically abused by his parents. In such an instance, it seems hardly wise to focus all of the efforts on trying to help the child to learn how to smile. Similarly, the child may show manifest unhappiness and lack of motivation for school and school-related activities. However, this may be due to inappropriate educational programming or lack of sympathy on the part of the teacher for a youngster who isn't learning as quickly or responsively as she feels is required. Dr. Frostig does not agree with those who search for an optimum reading method. The wide diversity of skills brought to the situation by the child, but also of the predisposition of individual teachers to more effective use of certain methods than of others, argue for flexibility rather than universality.

In short, the social sciences have abandoned the search for general principles that can apply in all situations with all kinds of subjects. Instead, they are reluctantly exploring an incredibly complex set of interactions that defy easy generalizations such as "frustration breeds aggression," or "positive reinforcement will cause behavior to be repeated."

As we look at this broader portrait of the life environment of the child with learning problems, we can review the broad strategies for remediation within an educational framework. Three major dimensions can be influenced from the standpoint of the teacher. First, the *content* of the material can be modified. The most dramatic illustration of this would be the transformation of the standard Dick and Jane readers into readers whose content has interest to particular cultural minority groups or volumes that have themes of interest to older children even if the difficulty level is that of the first or second grade. A second example would be the development of the new math curricula, which provide for a different set of experiences and different objectives for the mathematics program. For children with learning problems, one of the questions that the remedial specialist must ask then is, Is the content of the material or lesson or curriculum itself appropriate for this particular child?

The second major area of possible modification lies in the *style of presentation* itself. In particular, the remedial person, as Dr. Frostig and Ms. Maslow appropriately point out, needs to have a vast array of remedial techniques available and a psychological disposition flexible enough to use any combination of these that seems appropriate in a given circumstance. Examples of the modification of teaching style might be the use of a sand table to help youngsters trace out letters, or the use of phonics in reading if the "look and say" method did not seem appropriate, or the adaptation of a specific set of reinforcement schedules to eliminate undesirable behavior or encourage desirable behavior.

The technique of behavior modification deals not so much with content as with attempts to change the hierarchy of response patterns on the part of the child himself when nonproductive learning strategies are at the top of that hierarchy. Behavior modification has received such eloquent praise and violent attack that one suspects it is going through a fad stage where its supporters overgeneralize its usefulness, while its critics fail to see its true worth. One undeniable fact based on the evidence already available is that it is a technique that clearly works for rather limited, but nevertheless useful, behavior changes on the part of the learner. In that sense, it takes a legitimate place in the total array of techniques and methods that any good clinician should have available for proper application to attain specific objectives that respond to this kind of approach.

The third major remedial dimension is the *learning environment* itself. Here, instead of having thirty youngsters in a classroom with one teacher the whole day long, one can modify that environment by establishing a resource room where the youngster leaves the regular program for a period of time and receives more individualized or tutorial kinds of work. It could mean the design of special individual carrels in the regular classroom where a youngster who is over-stimulated or distracted by social interaction or general noise level can retreat to a more serene learning environment. Since the teacher is an integral part of any learning environment, it can also mean the insertion of specially trained persons who can do adequate psychoeducational diagnosis and design of treatment programs for individual children.

What Dr. Frostig and Ms. Maslow present in this volume is a new portrait of the therapeutic environment and the therapeutic personnel who should occupy that environment. They have gone beyond the usual identification of a specific learning deficit, and the planning of remedial exercises to meet that deficit, and view the whole developmental spectrum of the child's situation. And that environment includes the essential social interactions of the child with the significant people in his environment.

One remaining needed area of emphasis is that of evaluation. The clinician must state his clinical objectives in such a way that he can check whether or not he has attained his goal. The clinician is susceptible, as are all human beings, to self-deception that provides false comfort and justification. Evidence beyond that of the clinician's own opinion should be present to demonstrate child growth, and this requires both a remedial plan with specific objectives and some form of objective testing of the child to see if he has reached the goal.

This volume represents one more contribution of a distinguished clinician who has already enriched our understanding of young children with learning problems and provided us with that special degree of human understanding and perceptivity that allows us to plan constructively to help other children out of their learning difficulties and into a more competent learning and life style.

James Gallagher, Ph.D.
Director, Frank Porter Graham Child Development Center,
and Kenan Professor of Education,
University of North Carolina,
Chapel Hill, North Carolina

ACKNOWLEDGMENTS

A central theme of this book is interaction, e.g., between genetic endowment and environmental events, among brain structure, body physiology, and impinging stimuli, and between the child's pattern of psychological abilities and optimum teaching methods.

Interaction in a more personal sense was instrumental in creating this book, interaction between and among the staff of the Marianne Frostig Center of Educational Therapy, its Fellows and graduate students, and the participants in the many seminars and workshops led by the Center's staff—the educational therapists, school psychologists, principals, reading and speech therapists, concerned parents, and above all, public school classroom teachers, who have taken part in choosing the topics, tested teaching and training methods, and clarified and expanded the points of view discussed.

The authors have been fortunate in their opportunity to interact with colleagues who have reviewed portions of the manuscript and who have made specific suggestions: Jean Adams, Senior Editor, Early Childhood Education, Follett Publishing Company (movement education and visual perception); W. Ross Adey, M.D., Professor of Anatomy and Physiology, School of Medicine, University of California at Los Angeles, and Director of Space Biology Laboratory, Brain Research Institute, UCLA (neurophysiology); A. Jean Ayres, Ph.D., Associate Professor of Occupational Therapy, University of Southern California (movement education); Charlotte Bühler, Ph.D., clinical and developmental psychologist (humanism); Michael D'Asaro, Ph.D., Chief, Speech Pathology and Audiology, Kennedy Child Study Center, Saint John's Hospital, Santa Monica (auditory perception); Steven Forness, Ed.D., Special Education Director, Mental Retardation Center, UCLA (behavior modification); Leo J. Henderson, Project Director, Los Angeles Urban League Head Start (economically deprived); Dr. Marina Krause, Assistant Professor of Elementary Education, California State University at Long Beach (math); Maria Lymberis, M.D., psychiatrist and Medical Director, Frostig Center, and Assistant Clinical Professor of Psychology, UCLA School of Medicine, (psychoanalysis);

C. E. Meyers, Ph.D., Department of Educational Psychology, School
of Education, University of Southern California (developmental point
of view, comparison, and Part III); Kenneth Nighman, M.A., psychologist, Frostig Center (programming); R. E. Orpet, Ed.D., Professor
of Educational Psychology, California State University at Long Beach
and Research Director, Frostig Center (Part III); Patricia Parnell,
Ph.D., speech therapist, Frostig Center (language training); Jo Stanchfield, Professor of Education, Occidental College, Los Angeles (reading).

The authors, of course, remain fully responsible for the contents as
published.

The authors wish to thank the University of Illinois Press for permission to reprint the clinical model of the ITPA from *Psycholinguistic
Learning Disabilities* by Kirk & Kirk; the International Reading Association for permission to reprint excerpts from "Corrective Reading in the
Classroom" by Marianne Frostig, Ph.D., *The Reading Teacher*, 1965;
and to Follett Publishing Company for permission to reprint excerpts
from Teacher's Guide to *Pictures and Patterns* (by M. Frostig, D.
Horne and A. Miller), revised edition, 1972, and from *Movement Education: Theory and Practice* by Marianne Frostig, Ph.D.

The authors also wish to thank Mary Cox, Managing Editor, and
Sue Watts, Staff Editor, Grune & Stratton, Inc., for their outstanding
cooperation and patience and for their invaluable professional
assistance.

Bruce Buckingham, Director, Curriculum Materials Center, Frostig
Center, not only drew the illustrations, but helped to clarify their presentation. Felicia Thomas Bernstein and Victoria Klein helped with
references. The manuscript was typed and retyped with patience (and
on Sundays, with determination) by Freda Shapiro, Nina Judd, and
Phyllis Gedge. To Phyllis Gedge, the senior author's secretary, go
special thanks not only for carrying the primary typing responsibility,
but also for all her personal efforts in helping bring the manuscript to
completion.

INTRODUCTION

This book is concerned with the needs of the teacher, as well as with the needs of the child. It discusses the *why*, the *what*, and the *how* of education—of education in general, and of education in relation to the child with learning difficulties in particular.

This book represents an attempt to summarize those ideas, opinions, and facts that are presently influential in education, to compare and evaluate them on the basis of present-day knowledge and the authors' personal experiences in the classroom. The authors build on humanistic ideas that have survived the changes of time and are therefore applicable to any educational endeavor in every part of the globe. They explore basic knowledge, such as the known facts about child development, and compare the findings and opinions of various scholars.

Presentation of a multiplicity of theories and ideas has been necessary because in surveying existing knowledge and the trends in education based on this knowledge, it has become obvious that there is no royal road to the solution of educational problems. Every educator must have, however, the background to make wise choices from a wide range of approaches and techniques in the day-to-day encounters with students. Some of that necessary background is given here. The choices themselves, of course, rest with the educator.

Dr. James Gallagher, in his preface to Volume 2 of *Educational Therapy* (1969), writes that there are two major professional approaches discernible in the attempts to help those children who need special care through education. One is the *mental-health approach*, which places a great deal of emphasis on the youngster's self-image and ego structure. The mental-health approach is primarily concerned with the problem of the individual's personal relationships to others and the world around him. The educational philosophies and techniques described later in the chapters on humanistic and psychoanalytically oriented education in this book are based on the mental-health approach.

The second approach is the *psychoeducational approach*, which focuses on the diagnosis and remediation of learning problems, whether

1

due to sociocultural experience, mild neurological injury, poor educational facilities, or other factors. This approach is concerned with adapting the educational task so that the youngster is able to progress in his learning. Gallagher mentions that these two approaches can be combined and that there are programs based on both.

Classroom practices must be derived from a theoretical framework. Gallagher cites the growing tendency to use developmental theory as a basis for designing remedial programs. This book discusses developmental theory, but not as the *sole* theoretical basis of education. Various theories, approaches, and points of view are compared and their relationships to education explored.

One field of study that has recently made enormous strides is neurophysiology, the study of the functions of the central nervous system. This branch of natural science is especially important for understanding and helping children with learning difficulties, because their problems can often be directly linked to brain dysfunction. Understanding the deficiencies with which these children have to struggle assists the teacher in choosing teaching methods; it also greatly enhances the teacher's respect for the children.

Theoretical considerations will always influence education in general, but they are of particular significance in the prevention and remediation of learning problems. The key word here is *prevention*. It is far better to be able to prevent most classroom problems, learning problems, and behavior problems that make learning difficult and disrupt the classroom than to have to attempt to ameliorate them.

The methods described are designed not only for children whom school authorities have identified as having learning problems, but also for those who may later develop learning and behavior problems when faced by tasks or stresses beyond their ability. Most of the suggestions therefore apply to all children.

The belief that learning problems can be prevented and ameliorated is based on the tacit assumption that the abilities necessary for learning can be improved.

The authors will not enter into the debate regarding the relative contributions of the child's environment (learning) and of his genes to his intelligence. They do not believe that this relationship can be expressed in percentages, as Jensen (1969) and others have attempted to do. They interpret growth as a result of interaction between the environment, inborn abilities, and maturational trends, as a single dynamic process in which at any given time any of the components may provide the major force, depending on the child's fund of experience, availability of energy, neurological functioning, and openness to new experiences. On a theoretical basis these factors, and many others, can be isolated; in actuality they constitute an indivisible matrix of ever-changing relationships.

All these factors are of significance in choosing teaching methods and curricula. At any given time the teacher has to decide what, how much, by what methods, in what environment, and with what kind of supporting relationships a particular child can learn best.

Psychometric tests are of great assistance in making these decisions, but evaluation must continue in the classroom on a day-to-day basis to ensure that instruction remains precisely geared to the individual's needs as he progresses. A child's responses in the classroom will indicate whether or not his physiological, emotional, social, and cognitive needs are being satisfied. If he shows behavior difficulties and resists learning, then some need is not satisfied, and the teacher must make adjustments. These may be of a variety of kinds—a child tends to have problems in behavior and learning quite as much if he is ill, hungry, lonely, angry, or sad as if he has perceptual disabilities or a problem with memory for sequences. A division between physiological, affective, social, and cognitive considerations must be avoided.

Gallagher believes that education is advanced significantly when school personnel themselves undertake diagnostic evaluation and prescribe appropriate corrective teaching. The expert called in from another profession often writes reports that are of little help to the educator. Teacher-training institutions must help the educator gain the skills necessary for individualizing the curriculum according to each child's needs and carrying out the program. This book attempts to contribute to the goal of providing the teacher with the skills required for diagnosis and remediation.

It is suggested that one of the major goals of education should be to help children to learn to respect the needs of each other and of people all over the world, and to serve those needs. As an expression of these humanistic values, it should be realized that the child who functions with difficulty in school or elsewhere should be helped by his peers rather than ridiculed or despised, and treated with dedicated attention by the teacher rather than with sarcasm, punishment, or indifference. When such principles are observed in the classroom, the nurturing atmosphere helps the child with learning problems to learn with greater ease, and assists both him and his classmates to become constructive rather than destructive adults.

Phyllis Greenacre (1952) has pointed out that after some children with minimal brain dysfunction, who so often suffer from learning difficulties, have reached adulthood, they may be better able to serve others because of their greater sensitivity and insight into others' feelings. They certainly may become quite as worthwhile members of society as those who progress through childhood with ease. Children with learning difficulties can also be of value to their class in school. If children learn to respect and help each other, they can experience the fulfillment that is achieved through caring for and assisting another human being.

The ultimate goals of education can be reached by almost all children provided their own needs are satisfied. The child with learning difficulties will rarely be unaware of his deficiencies. He will tend to have a poor self-image and may react with anger, despair, or apathy to his frustrations. Such feelings may interfere with both cognitive improvement and the ability to care for others, and the teacher's first task may be to focus on ameliorating the child's poor self-concept.

The choice of program for a child will be influenced by the educator's theoretical leaning as well as by the child's specific deficits. Some groups of educators (including Delacato [1963], Ayres [1967], and Kephart [1971]) ascribe problems in learning to deficits in sensory-motor functions, and they therefore emphasize remediation of these functions; while educators working with "perceptually handicapped children" (such as Strauss and Lehtinen [1947], Getman [1962], and their many followers) emphasize the training of visual-perceptual functions. Others —such as Susan Gray (Klaus and Gray, 1967), Vera John (1963), and many more—emphasize the importance of language. Montessori (1965) and subsequently Piaget (1966), Bruner (1962), Aurelia Levi (1966), and others have emphasized cognitive functions—categorizing, classifying, comparing, and evaluating.

The point of view of the authors is that the emphasis needs to shift from child to child, and from age level to age level. The best approach is probably the one that takes into account the child's total characteristics, the circumstances of his life, and his classroom situation. Taking the circumstances of a child's home life into account suggests that the teacher should involve the parents in the child's educative process. This need not necessarily be done by suggesting involvement in homework or other scholastic activities, but by helping the parents to understand and enjoy their child.

The school environment is equally important for the child with learning difficulties. A classroom in which the child feels serene and successful may forestall or ameliorate the emotional disturbances that so often accompany learning difficulties, and thus remove the worst block to learning.

Whatever training* programs are initiated should promote every skill

---

* The word "training" is often regarded as implying a very mechanistic approach, and the word "educating" is assumed to have a broader, more

that the individual child requires. Early training in gross motor skills and manipulatory activities will prevent or ameliorate deficits in visuo-motor functions, in laterality and directionality, and in the ability to follow a plan and concentrate on an activity. Training in auditory perception will facilitate reading and various language functions; it will also help the child's understanding of language and therefore indirectly facilitate communication. Visual-perceptual training will promote spatial orientation, the reading of maps and graphs, and the learning of academic skills. Equally important, visual-perceptual training helps the child to become more attentive to features of his environment and thus enhances visually mediated experiences. Training in language and thought processes will also influence the total characteristics and adjustment of the child.

The attainment of these objectives can only be accomplished if various educational viewpoints are understood and related to each other. At first sight, many current educational trends seem contradictory and confusing. But a more careful study reveals that they can be consolidated and fused into a unified theory of instruction. Such a unified theory can provide the basis for setting up definite goals (the *why* of education), curricula (the *what* of education), and teaching methods (the *how* of education). It is hoped that this book will further that aim, though its final attainment still lies in the future.

WORKS CITED

Ayres, A. J. Sensory integrative processes and neuropsychological learning disabilities. In J. Hellmuth (Ed.), *Learning disorders*. Vol. 3. Seattle: Special Child Publications, 1968.

Bruner, J. A *study of thinking*. New York: Science Editions, 1962.

Delacato, C. *The diagnosis and treatments of speech and reading problems*. Springfield, Ill.: Charles C Thomas, 1963.

Gallagher, J. J. Preface. In J. Hellmuth (Ed.), *Educational therapy*. Vol. 2. Seattle: Special Child Publications, 1969, pp. 7–11.

---

humanistic connotation. We commonly refer to *training* an animal, but *educating* a child. "Training," is, however, often used with reference to the development of specific personal skills; we speak, for example, of training pilots or physicians. In this book the word "training" is used to refer to the training of specific abilities—training in agility, for instance, or training in the perception of form constancy. It is used interchangeably with the word "educating" for broad areas of development, and should not be taken to imply more mechanistic procedures than the word "educating" does.

Getman, G. N. *How to develop your child's intelligence.* Luverne, Minn.: Author, 1962.

Greenacre, P. *Trauma, growth, and personality.* New York: Norton, 1952.

Jensen, A. R. How much can we boost IQ and scholastic achievement? *Harvard Educational Review,* 1969, 39(1), 1–123. See also the replies in the same journal, 39(2), 273–356.

John, V. P. The intellectual development of slum children: Some preliminary findings. *American Journal of Orthopsychiatry,* 1963, 33, 813–822.

Kephart, N. *The slow learner in the classroom* (2nd ed.). Columbus, Ohio: Charles E. Merrill, 1971.

Klaus, R. A., & Gray, S. W. The early training project for disadvantaged children: A report after five years. *Monographs of the Society for Research in Child Development,* 1968, 33, No. 4.

Levi, A. Remedial techniques in disorders of concept formation. *Journal of Special Education,* 1966, 1, 3–8.

Montessori, M. *Dr. Montessori's own handbook.* New York: Schocken, 1965.

Piaget, J. *Psychology of intelligence.* Totowa, N.J.: Littlefield, Adams, 1966.

Strauss, A., & Lehtinen, L. *Psychopathology and education of the brain-injured child.* Vol. 1. New York: Grune & Stratton, 1947.

PART 1

1
CAUSES
OF LEARNING
DIFFICULTIES

Scientists agree in general that there is a wide range of possible causes for learning difficulties. But they do not agree on which causes are primary and which are contributory. In the Soviet Union, for instance, all psychiatric disorders, including learning deficits, are ascribed to physical causes. Psychiatrists in the United States give far greater weight to psychodynamic explanations of learning difficulties, stressing the influence of personal relationships. Neurologists look mainly for changes in brain functions to explain learning difficulties, while sociologists stress the social and economic circumstances that lead to deviations in the individual's adjustment and his ability to profit from the school situation.

It would be of no appreciable help to the teacher to discuss at length all the possible causes of learning difficulties, because many of the causes cannot be influenced by educational intervention. Glandular deviations or metabolic disorders, such as phenylketonuria, are medical problems outside the teacher's province. Such medical problems, nevertheless, influence the functioning of the nervous system, and the resulting functional deviations require an adjustment in teaching methods, even when medical treatment has been indicated, if optimum learning and progress are to take place.

The organic disturbances causing learning deficits are many and diverse. (See selected references at the end of this chapter.) The same is true of the social and economic conditions that can enhance or disturb a child's ability to learn. It is not only the underprivileged child who has feelings of inferiority, helplessness, and despair in the classroom. The middle-class child whose parents submit him to too much pressure to achieve may be similarly afflicted. A child of any social class, race, or economic level may feel confused, frightened, anxious, or angry because he is mistreated, neglected, or ignored by his parents, or is aware that his parents are in conflict, or feels that he is not as gifted or as good-looking as his parents wish, or that his siblings are preferred over him. A family tragedy, bullying by another child, an inability to please the teacher—any of these environmental influences and many others can

9

arouse feelings and create circumstances that negatively affect the child's ability to learn.

It is impossible to discuss specifically in the framework of this book all the many causes of learning difficulties. The authors have chosen instead to exemplify the treatment of environmentally caused learning difficulties through a discussion of educational approaches to socio-economically deprived children, a very large group in this country. In regard to the other factors mentioned, the reader is again referred to the works listed at the end of this chapter.

That the causation of a child's learning problems is frequently multiple must again be stressed. The child who is less intelligent than his siblings may be further handicapped by feelings of inferiority. The child with a slight physical deformity or a neurological dysfunction may be rejected by other children and excluded from their play. Any deficit or defect usually affects the child's adjustment and leads to further deficits. Fortunately the reverse process also holds true: amelioration of one deficit often leads to the establishment of a better emotional and physical balance, to access to new energy, and to improvement in other deficits. The child who learns to read may become better able to handle his squabbles with his siblings. The child who improves in verbal expression may find more acceptance among his playmates. The child who improves in auditory functions may show a spurt in reading and in learning content subjects. The child who learns to control impulsivity caused by neurological dysfunction may improve in his behavior, in school learning, and in his ability to maintain good relationships.

One explanation for this phenomenon is that certain brain functions are common to various tasks. It is therefore no wonder that improvement in learning deficits has been reported to have resulted from such diverse causes as psychotherapy, eyeglasses, improved nutrition, greater attention paid to the child by the parents, and a teacher's ability to make the child feel successful. Whenever stress is alleviated in an over-stressed child, over-all improvement may result.

Some General References Concerning the Organic Causes of Learning Difficulties

Chalfant, J. C., & Scheffelin, M. A. *Central processing dysfunctions in children: A review of research.* NINDS Monograph No. 9. Washington, D.C.: U.S. Department of Health, Education, and Welfare, 1969.

Cravioto, J., Birch, H. G., de Licardie, E., Rosales, L., & Vega, L. The ecology of growth and development in a Mexican preindustrial community. *Monographs of the Society for Research in Child Development*, 1969, 34 (Serial 129, No. 5).

Levine, S. Stress and behavior. *Scientific American*, 1971, 224(1), 27–31.

Lipton, E. L., Steinschneider, A., & Richmond, J. B. Psychophysiologic disorders in children. In L. W. Hoffman and M. L. Hoffman (Eds.), *Review of child development research.* Vol. 2. New York: Russell Sage Foundation, 1966. Pp. 169–220.

Luria, A. R. *Human brain and psychological processes.* New York: Harper, 1966.

Masland, R. L., Sarason, S. B., & Gladwin, T. *Mental subnormality: Biological, psychological, and social factors.* New York: Basic Books, 1958.

McClearn, G. E. Genetic influences on behavior and development. In P. H. Mussen (Ed.), *Manual of child psychology.* Vol. 1. New York: Wiley, 1970. Pp. 39–76.

Pan-American Health Organization. *Deprivation in psychobiological development.* Science Publication No. 134, 1966, 55.

Richter, D. (Ed.). *Biochemical factors concerned in the functional activity of the nervous system.* New York: Pergamon, 1969.

Scheibel, M. E., & Scheibel, A. B. Some neural substrates of postnatal development. In M. L. Hoffman & L. W. Hoffman (Eds.), *Review of child development research.* Vol. 1. New York: Russell Sage Foundation, 1964. Pp. 481–519.

Some References Concerning the Environmental Causes of Learning Difficulties, Other than Socioeconomic Deprivation

Anthony, E. J. The behavior disorders of childhood. In P. H. Mussen (Ed.), *Manual of child psychology.* Vol. 2. New York: Wiley, 1970. Pp. 667–764.

Bowlby, J. *Maternal care and mental health.* Geneva: World Health Organization, 1952.

Caldwell, B. M. The effects of infant care. In M. L. Hoffmen & L. W. Hoffman (Eds.), *Review of child development research.* Vol. 1. New York: Russell Sage Foundation, 1964. Pp. 9–88.

Escalona, S., & Heider, G. *Prediction and outcome.* New York: Basic Books, 1959.

Glueck, S., & Glueck, E. *Unraveling juvenile delniquency.* Cambridge, Mass.: Harvard University Press, 1950.

MacFarlane, J. W., Allen, L., & Honzik, M. P. *A developmental study of the behavior problems of normal children.* Berkeley: University of California Press, 1954.

Rosenthal, R., & Jacobson, L. *Pygmalion in the classroom.* New York: Holt, 1968.

Sears, R. R., Maccoby, E. E., & Levin, H. *Patterns of child rearing.* New York: Harper, 1957.

Winnicott, D. W. *The maturational processes and the facilitating environment.* New York: International Universities Press, 1965.

2
APPLICATIONS
OF NEUROPHYSIOLOGIC
RESEARCH

It may seem obvious and trite to say that the brain is an essential organ of the body, and that the way the brain functions regulates all behavior. It is not, however, always recognized that conditions (genetic, nutritional, hormonal, metabolic, and so on) that affect the body also affect behavior. It is a mistake moreover to treat behavior as a byproduct of the brain, as if the functioning of the brain and behavior were not completely interdependent. Behavior has a reciprocal influence on the structure and functioning of the brain.

Conditions affecting the physical state of the child have not usually been considered concerns of the educator. It is true that the genetic endowment of a child cannot be changed. But the intrauterine environment of the embryo, birth stress, nutrition, infection, and injury, all of which have an enormous influence on the child's growth and intelligence (Birch and Cravioto, 1968), can be changed. As a member of society, the teacher may be interested in promoting arrangements to ensure that every child is conceived and born receiving the best care to help him reach his potential; but professionally the elementary-school teacher deals only with children five years old or older. With what aspects of the child's physical well-being must the teacher be directly concerned in the classroom? Can findings from the study of the functioning of the nervous system help her to choose the best methods of teaching and classroom management?

Temperamental Deviations

Kretchmer (1925), Sheldon (1942), and others have referred to the expression of personality in all aspects of behavior as temperament. Thomas, Chess, and Birch (1968, p. 4) view temperament as the *how* of behavior. Two children may be able to do something equally well, and have the same motives for doing so, yet differ in the intensity and rate with which they act, their expression of mood, their readiness to shift to a new activity, and the ease with which they approach a new toy, situation, or playmate.

Although types of temperament can be identified at birth, temperament is modifiable and must always be considered in relation to abilities and motives, environmental opportunities and stresses. The child responds selectively to his environment according to his temperament.

Gross deviations in behavioral style, which are often evident in children with learning difficulties, may be called temperamental deviations: if these deviations are very great, the total behavior of the child is disturbed. Such children may be exceedingly hyperactive or very withdrawn and lethargic. Children with volatile temperaments often answer before they have heard the question. Hyperactive children may engage in incessant activity and not listen to the question. Hypoactive children may daydream and not hear the question.

Educational measures discussed in the chapter on movement education will often promote the ability to delay responses in the hyperactive child and speed them in the hypoactive one. The teacher can also help a child establish behavioral control in the classroom by using such tactful cues as a glance, nod, or word to check his manner of responding. The impulsive child may be taught to count to three before answering. The slow child may be helped by self-pacing devices (stop watches, metronomes, egg-timers, tachistoscopes, reading pacers, and so on). Desired behavior should be promptly rewarded.

Shifting from one task to another may be difficult for children with temperamental deviations. Such children need to be alerted in advance, and guided through the act of changing activities. For example, the teacher may say, "In two minutes the bell will ring for recess. When it does, put your pencils down. Row One will line up at the door. Row Two will get out the play equipment. . . . Remember, line up quietly." Such cues to shift activity are necessary even in free or open classrooms, where some children may initially need help in changing from one area to another. Temperamental deviations are due in part to variations in the balance of arousal and habituation, discussed below.

Functioning of the Brain

Modern research has established that learning occurs as a result of the *interaction* between (1) environmental stimuli, (2) existing (internal) states of the brain, and (3) actions (internal or external) of the organism.

The findings of both neurophysiological and behavioral studies indicate that the child's nervous system does not passively reflect the outside world, but integrates stimuli actively. Thus each classroom situation provides a different learning experience for each child.

Subsystems of the Brain

Research has shown that learning is not stored in any single localized group of cells in the brain. Neurophysiologists have surgically or chemically destroyed various groups of brain cells in animals and found that the animal could still remember what it had learned before the operation (Lashley, 1950; Pribram, 1971). It is now believed that memory of a single experience is represented in many different neurons (nerve cells) in many different parts of the brain (Hebb, 1968; Pribram, 1971). Likewise perceptions and other functions simultaneously involve several subsystems (parts) of the brain.

As more has been learned about the subsystems of the brain, increasing emphasis has been given to its total functioning. For instance, if memory is not stored in particular locations, it must be the *pattern* of the electrical and chemical states of the brain that calls forth the image of an earlier experience.

Brain cells are extremely sensitive to their chemical environment, and sensitively reflect this in their patterns of electrical rhythms and impulses. These electrical patterns persist day and night, whether the person is asleep or awake. Brain cells are changed by as little as one part in a billion of LSD, for example, and are even more sensitive to some hormones. Learning and behavior are thus dependent not only upon the anatomy of the brain but also upon its physiology, and this in turn depends on the entire physiological state of the body. Thus a child who is overtired, hungry, too cold or too hot is a poor learner. Optimum learning is only possible when a child feels comfortable. Children do not always tell about their needs. The teacher must judge by observation.

The senior author of this book, while teaching a fourth-grade class in a public school in which some of the children were economically deprived, discovered that classroom morale and learning ability improved remarkably after she invested in a box of crackers and had it make midmorning rounds among the children. The success of this procedure made the small cost highly worthwhile.

Effects of Stress and Fatigue

Our current knowledge of the functioning of the brain indicates that the brain operates more or less efficiently according to many factors, some of which are temporary. "Disturbed brain functioning" or "minimal brain dysfunctioning" may apply to many states of the normal child or adult. Variations in brain functioning may be observed in daily life. We all know that there are certain times of the day when we work best and others when we have difficulty in doing a complicated task. Any stress, physical or emotional, can lead to temporary variations from normal brain functioning in anyone. In many persons more permanent slight variations occur from causes that are sometimes known, sometimes not. These variations may not affect adjustment. A child with minimally disturbed brain functions, whether gifted or of low general ability, may be only occasionally somewhat erratic or always be extremely disorganized. Children who show more permanent variations from the norm are strongly influenced by stress. They are more labile in their behavior and are more easily thrown off balance. A well-planned school day and an orderly classroom are essential for them. The teacher must also remember to adjust her* demands to each child's ability to concentrate on his work. Children with neurophysiological dysfunctions often tire very easily. A sizable number of children with reading difficulties improved "miraculously" after the teacher had them read only alternating paragraphs, taking turns herself with the children or having two children alternate.

Neurophysiological research has given scientific support to an optimistic view of the possibility of ameliorating disturbing symptoms in children with neurological dysfunctions. But because brain function is influenced by health, nutrition, motivation, previous learning, and so on, neurophysiological research also underscores the necessity of considering the functioning of the total child when amelioration is attempted.

Memory

The number of neurons in the brain does not increase after birth. How then are learning and development represented in the brain? Experiments in animals show that increased learning capacity during growth is correlated with the growth of certain projections from the nerve cell; these growth changes are mainly in the greatly branched dendrites, which extend as branches from the smaller nerve-cell body. The dendrites of one cortical neuron come to be intertwined with those of other cells, and as the dendrites mature, tiny spikes appear on them. Learning can also increase the number of cells that nourish the neurons (neuroglia) (Adey, 1967). Rosenzweig, Bennett, and Diamond (1972) have found a measurable thickening and increase in weight in the cortex

---

* Throughout the book and purely as a matter of convenience, the authors have used the pronouns she and her to designate the teacher, he and his to designate the student.

of rats reared in a stimulating environment as contrasted with rats reared in a restricted environment. Learning may also lead to changes in the production or storage of chemicals that transmit messages (Hyden, 1967). It may well be that several processes are involved, which occur in a definite temporal order. Long-term memory may be represented by changes in the growth of dendrites and/or changes in the protein at the surface membranes of nerve cells, while short-term memory may be represented by transient chemical changes.

It is evident that most changes in the brain will not be sudden, although memory of an experience that occurred only once is possible. Most school learning has to be repeated before it can be remembered, and overlearning (i.e., repeated review of what has already been learned) is necessary, and seems to be of even greater importance in children with learning problems. The transfer from immediate short-term memory to long-term memory appears to be severely impaired in many of these children.

The transfer of experience to long-term memory storage may be particularly vulnerable to chemical effects in children with learning difficulties. Strong emotions can trigger chemical changes in the blood, and both directly and indirectly distort the underlying pattern of electrical interaction and transmission in the brain. The constant admonitions to the teacher to maintain a calm, warm, emotional climate have, therefore, a neurophysiological as well as a philosophical basis.

Time is required for a memory to be consolidated. The teacher should ensure that a child experiences a few quiet moments after a new concept is presented. The child should also learn to rehearse (review) what he has been taught (Estes, 1970, pp. 9-10), using three different steps: 1) giving verbal labels; 2) describing the sequence of events in his own words; and 3) making mental pictures of what happened. From the behavioral evidence of monkeys with brain lesions, Pribram (1971, p. 146) believes that rehearsal distributes the new material to other groups of brain cells and forms associations with previously stored experiences. Children with learning difficulties may need to be taught rehearsal techniques that other children use automatically, without being fully aware of them.

A child who cannot remember that two pints equal one quart should watch the teacher pour a quart of colored liquid into two pint containers and then pour it back again as the teacher describes what is going on; the child should then pour it himself while describing it in his own words; he should draw the container; he should write: "two pints are one quart"; he should close his eyes and picture the action of pouring the liquid. The material to be remembered has then been represented by movement (the act of pouring), symbol (language), and imagery (the drawing and the mental picture). The associations thus formed can be recalled in many different ways.

The teacher should help the child to become very conscious of rehearsal techniques. "You can remember things much better if you put the information in your own words, draw a picture or diagram, and try to see it happen in your mind." All rehearsal techniques involve the child actively: he himself does something. This may be an important cue when a child habitually forgets his homework, for example. If an adult takes the responsibility for remembering it, the child will not bring it when the adult is away. Instead the child should suggest ways in which he can remind himself, such as putting it in his lunchbox the night before or writing a note to himself.

Guarding Against Habituation

When a person becomes aware of a change in his environment, new patterns of electrical discharges appear in his brain, and certain other physiological changes occur in the rest of his body. These changes are called the *orienting reflex*.

When the same pattern of stimuli is continuously repeated, the orienting reflex no longer occurs. *Habituation* takes place. If a person constantly works in a room to the sound of background music, it is doubtful if the worker is at all aware of the music; he is habituated. To keep the child alert, habituation has to be avoided.

The reticular formation (Magoun, 1964), lying at the base of the brain, and certain regions of the temporal lobe (limbic cortex) connected to the reticular formation are involved in orientation and habituation. (See Figures 1 and 2.) Luria (1970) identifies the reticular system as the part of the brain that "tunes" the general pattern of ongoing electrical activity. Magoun (1969) reports that the cortical responses to transient stimuli double or triple in amplitude when the reticular system is activated.

Varied stimuli and a changing rate of presentation can help the child remain alert. Many children with learning difficulties are highly attracted to movement, and movement is a very effective device to ensure an orienting reflex; for example, writing words on the chalkboard or on cards while the child watches is better than presenting new material already prepared. Changes in light intensity are also potent alerting stimuli; very highly distractible children may be helped by focusing a bright light on the material to be learned, while the surrounding space is diffusely lighted. All children become rapidly accustomed to a monotonous voice; variations in the teacher's tone of voice help them to

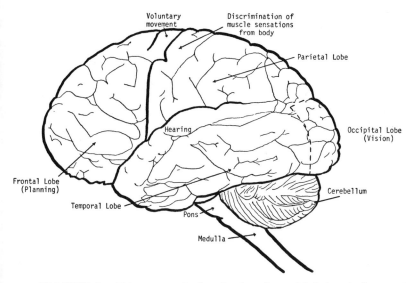

Voluntary
movement

Discrimination of
muscle sensations
from body

Parietal Lobe

Occipital Lobe
(Vision)

Hearing

Cerebellum

Frontal Lobe
(Planning)

Temporal Lobe

Pons

Medulla

FIGURE 1. Diagrammatic sketch of surface of left hemisphere.

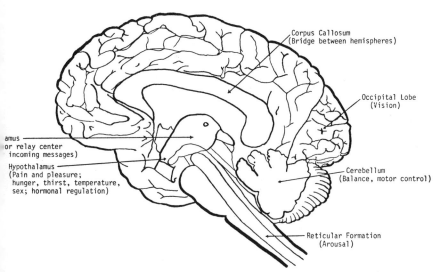

Corpus Callosum
(Bridge between hemispheres)

Occipital Lobe
(Vision)

amus
or relay center
incoming messages)

Hypothalamus
(Pain and pleasure;
hunger, thirst, temperature,
sex; hormonal regulation)

Cerebellum
(Balance, motor control)

Reticular Formation
(Arousal)

FIGURE 2. Diagrammatic sketch of brain as if cut in half at the midline of the body. *Note*: The allocation of functions to certain brain areas is broad and imprecise. In most cases, the regions indicated are critical, but not the only areas concerned.

pay attention. A teacher who is interested in what she is teaching does this automatically.

Various experiments have shown that emotions affect the brain's alerting mechanism (Gordon, 1969). John and Killam (1959) demonstrated that reinforcement* prevents habituation and increases the alerting responses. Such findings have important implications for teaching. A positive emotional tone and an expectation of pleasure and success directly stimulate the brain's capacity to discriminate, learn, and remember.

Perception

Neurophysiologists have found that certain cell groups in the brain analyze specific information about the environment, such as color, contour, and direction (Hubel and Wiesel, 1962; De Valois and Jacobs, 1968). They call these cells feature analyzers. The feature analyzers are, however, insufficient to account for percepts, because the electrical discharges from these cells interact with the ceaseless pattern of electrical activity in surrounding cortical regions, the so-called association areas. These areas respond sensitively to changes in blood chemistry brought about by nutritional, hormonal, and pharmacological factors, as well as to arousal states and expectations.

Disturbances in perception may therefore result from injury to brain cells (the feature analyzers), from strong emotion, fatigue, drugs, and so on, and from inadequate or inaccurate learning.

Children who are brain-injured show as a group a high percentage of perceptual deficits. For instance, in a diagnostic survey of a sample of 117 children enrolled at the Marianne Frostig Center of Educational Therapy, there were 54 children with learning difficulties in whom organic etiology apparently played a decisive role (Frostig, 1967), and over three-quarters showed a perceptual deficit. The report of Task Force 1 of the United States Public Health Service (1966) mentions perceptual impairment as one of the most frequent handicaps found in children with minimal brain dysfunction.

Perceptual ability also tends to be impaired in cases of neurosis and schizophrenia (Davis and Cullen, 1958; Ornitz and Ritvo, 1968). In the sample of 117 children at the Frostig Center referred to above, 34 children were found in whom emotional disturbances were thought to

---

* Reinforcement may be represented in the brain by patterns of electrical discharges in the "old brain," or limbic area, stimulation of which induces the organism to feel pleasure or pain (Olds and Milner, 1954).

play the major causative role in their learning disabilities, and most of them showed perceptual impairment. Again we can infer that the emotional tone of the classroom is as important in treating perceptual deficits as specific perceptual exercises.

Diagnostic Labeling and Learning Difficulties

A symptom (such as visual-perceptual disability) may result from many different factors; on the other hand, any specific medical diagnosis (such as brain damage) may result in widely varying symptoms. A label (brain syndrome, for example) does not give any indication of a particular child's behavior.

Much behavior that seems to be very primitive and simple is in reality highly complicated and is therefore likely to become disturbed, even in minimal disturbances of brain function, while behavior that seems more complicated may remain intact. For example, many children with learning problems may be unable to recognize such a simple pattern as a square, which children can normally recognize in spite of differences in presentation, in size, color, distance, or the angle from which it is viewed. Perceptual tasks such as the recognition of a geometric figure under varying circumstances are really enormously complicated. To simulate the solution of such a task by computers, huge instruments with most complex circuitry have to be built (Broadbent, 1965).

Another task of the utmost difficulty, although it seems to be easy for the so-called normal child, is understanding spoken language regardless of variations in pronunciation, voice quality, intensity, and so forth. The child who suffers from minimally disturbed brain function may have difficulty in understanding a teacher who is new to him or who comes from a different region of the country or who is talking in a noisy room in a quiet voice. (In the chapter on auditory perception, remedial procedures are discussed.)

Many different parts of the brain are involved in a particular behavior, and disturbances in any one of them may disrupt a particular behavior. On the other hand, as Luria (1970, p. 78) points out, "behavioral processes that seem to have nothing in common may actually be related through dependence on a particular brain factor." He found, for example, that a lesion in one area affected spatial orientation, arithmetical computations, and verbal logic. Luria's explanation was that the destroyed brain area had had the function of processing information about spatial relations, a common underlying ability in all three tasks. The teacher will note that these research results indicate that perceptual training may improve a variety of functions, and so may training in arithmetic or verbal skills.

Understanding the many possible relationships between brain function and behavior, and knowing that brain functions vary in normal children as well as in those designated as neurologically handicapped, the teacher will seek to individualize and personalize instruction. She will know that each child learns best in his own way. She will also know that improvement in one area of learning may cause substantial "fringe benefits."

Multisensory Presentation

One of the most complicated tasks of the brain is that of processing information received simultaneously from different sense channels. The integrative functions of the brain are very often disturbed in children with learning difficulties (Ayres, 1968). A teacher will observe that most children seem able to learn only when material is presented through several sense channels; but that in some children multisensory presentation produces complete confusion and disorganization.

Neurophysiological research suggests that this selective function may normally be carried out by inhibitory influences on the reticular formation descending from the cortex. These controls are apparently lost in many brain-damaged children.

Children who have difficulty in attending to a relevant stimulus may find multisensory presentation confusing. Such children can be helped to pay attention by accentuating a stimulus and by strengthening the perceptual contrast* between the stimulus and its background, using such devices as lighting, framing (presenting a problem or paragraph within a wooden box frame or colored outline), enlarging (e.g., using large size type like that designed for the visually handicapped), spacing (presenting very few problems or statements on a page), and coloring (tracing important facts or elements of a problem in a bright color). Irrelevant stimuli can be reduced by maintaining diffuse lighting, a quiet room with bare neutral walls, cubicles (Cruickshank et al, 1961), and so on. As children learn to become more selective in their attention to stimuli, a more satisfying classroom environment can be instituted in which they can move freely and exchange information. The authors' clinical experience indicates that even very highly distractible children can pay attention in a crowded, cluttered, noisy classroom if

* This contrast is represented in the nervous system by inhibition of electrical discharge by cells surrounding the excited, or firing, cells (Bekesy, 1967).

relevant stimuli are accentuated, if the child's attention is directed to them, and if the emotional climate is positive.

Although multisensory presentation may lead to overloading, as has been pointed out, children who have difficulty in directing their attention are usually helped when the same information is presented through two or more sense channels. Studies have shown that when stimuli are presented simultaneously to the auditory and visual channels, recognition is enhanced in both (Smith, 1965). This is true when the *meaning* of the stimuli is the same. Compatible stimuli are more easily integrated. For example, it is easier for a child to point to the big block every time the word *big* is said than to point to the small block, and vice versa. Speech is more easily understood when the hearer can observe the person's lips (Sunby and Pollack, 1964).

Research has shown that learning through the use of a strong sense modality may very well enhance the functioning of a weaker one. Learning should therefore not be delayed until the child is adequate in a lagging auditory or visual-perceptual function.

Semmes (1966) suggests that an understanding of spatial functions may depend on the convergence of stimuli from visual, kinesthetic, vestibular, and auditory channels, whereas understanding of language depends on familiar stimuli reaching a more localized area of the brain. These findings lend support to educators concerned with visualization and visual perception who stress multisensory methods.

Another line of evidence supporting multisensory methods for teaching tasks requiring spatial cognition comes from people who, because of epileptic seizures, have had surgery separating the two hemispheres of the brain. Their postsurgical pattern of spatial defects suggests that the two hemispheres normally work together to integrate different parts of the total spatial picture (Sperry, Gazzaniga, and Bogen, 1969).

Russian neuropsychologists (e.g., Luria, 1966, 1970) also advocate a multisensory approach, because they too believe that learning deficits can be remediated by associating a weak sense modality with a more efficient one. Luria postulates that in this way a real change occurs in the functioning of the nervous system. He would teach spelling to a child who is strong in the visual modality by having him look at a word, perhaps trace it with his fingers, and say the word aloud to integrate the visual, auditory, and kinesthetic modalities.

The Role of Movement

Movement integrates the simultaneous experience of spatial and temporal dimensions, and is therefore a powerful tool in promoting the integrative processes of the brain.

Ajuriaguerra, an internationally known neurophysiologist who works in Geneva, is among those neurologists who have introduced systems of movement education for the remediation of learning deficits, because he believes that movement influences brain functions concerned with attention, integration, and control.

Summary

There is an ever-increasing body of knowledge relating brain functions and behavior. The brain is no longer a completely unknown "black box," and though neurophysiological findings have had as yet very limited application in the classroom, they have validated many class-room practices.

Modern neurophysiological research has demonstrated that experi-ences do change both the physical structure and the functioning pat-terns of the human brain. Educators can no longer consider any child unteachable. The research emphasizes the multiplicity of connections and interdependence of feedback mechanisms among the various re-gions of the brain, so that educators are no longer justified in modeling instructional procedures on a simple stimulus-response paradigm. Both neurophysiology and education have advanced most when they have studied interactions rather than narrowed their fields of research.

Teachers often use correct teaching techniques and methods of class-room management intuitively. Several of these methods have been dis-cussed in the light of brain functioning, especially amelioration of hyperactivity and hypoactivity, the avoidance of habituation, use of rehearsal techniques in learning, and the accentuation of relevant stimuli to direct attention. Neurophysiology points to the importance of physical well-being for learning (including the importance of nutri-tion and avoidance of fatigue and stress), the influence of physical well-being and emotional tone in perception, and the role of movement in helping children with learning difficulties. Study of the central nerv-ous system emphasizes the interrelatedness of brain functions which is frequently reflected by improvement in several areas when the focus has been on the training of one. It has also stressed the importance of multisensory presentation for improving integrative functions, the ad-vantage of pairing strong and weak modalities, and above all, the neces-sity of individualizing instruction.

WORKS CITED

Adey, W. R. Intrinsic organization of cerebral tissue in alerting, orienting, and discriminative responses. In G. C. Quarton, T. Melnechuk, & F. O. Schmitt (Eds.), *The neurosciences*. New York: Rockefeller University Press, 1967.

Ayres, A. J. Sensory integrative processes and neuropsychological learning disabilities. In J. Hellmuth (Ed.), *Learning disorders*. Vol. 3. Seattle: Special Child Publications, 1968.

Bekesy, G. von. *Sensory inhibition*. Princeton: Princeton University Press, 1967.

Birch, H. G. & Cravioto, J. Infection, nutrition and environment in mental development. In F. H. Eichenwald (Ed.), *The prevention of mental retardation through control of infectious diseases*. Public Health Service Publication No. 1962. Washington, D.C.: U.S. Government Printing Office, 1968.

Broadbent, D. E. Information processing in the nervous system. *Science*, 1965, 150 (3695) 457–462.

Cruickshank, W. H., Bentzen, F. A., Ratzeburg, F. H., & Tannhauser, M. F. *A teaching method for brain-injured and hyperactive children*. Syracuse, N.Y.: Syracuse University Press, 1961.

Davis, D. R., & Cullen, J. H. Disorganization of perception in neurosis and psychosis. *American Journal of Psychology*, 1958, 71, 229–237.

De Valois, R. L., & Jacobs, G. H. Primate color vision. *Science*, 1968, 162, 533–540.

Estes, W. H. *Learning theory and mental development*. New York: Academic Press, 1970.

Frostig, M. *Movement education: Theory and practice*. Chicago: Follett Educational Corporation, 1970.

Frostig, M. A treatment program for children with learning difficulties. In M. Bortner (Ed.), *Evaluation and education of brain-injured children*. Springfield, Ill.: Charles C Thomas, 1967.

Gordon, M. W. Neuronal plasticity and memory. *American Journal of Orthopsychiatry*, 1969, 39(4), 578–595.

Hebb, D. O. Concerning imagery. *Psychological Review*, 1968, 75, 466–477.

Hubel, D. H., & Wiesel, T. N. Perceptive fields, binocular interaction and functional architecture in the cat's visual cortex. *Journal of Physiology*, 1962, 160, 105–154.

Hyden, H. Biochemical changes accompanying learning. In G. C. Quarton, T. Melnechuk, & F. O. Schmitt (Eds.), *The neurosciences*. New York: Rockefeller University Press, 1967. Pp. 765–771.

John, E. R., & Killam, K. F. Electrophysiological correlates of avoidance conditioning in the cat. *Journal of Pharmaceutical Experimental Therapy*, 1959, 125, 252–274.

Kretchmer, E. *Physique and character.* New York: Harcourt, 1925.

Lashley, K. S. In search of the engram. In Society for Experimental Biology, (Great Britain), *Physiological mechanisms in animal behavior.* New York: Academic Press, 1950.

Luria, A. R. The functional organization of the brain. *Scientific American,* 1970, 222(3), 66–78.

Luria, A. R. *Higher cortical functions in man.* London: Tavistock, 1966.

Magoun, H. W. Advances in brain research with implications for learning. In K. H. Pribram (Ed.), *On the biology of learning.* New York: Harcourt, 1969.

Magoun, H. W. *The waking brain* (2nd ed.). Springfield, Ill.: Charles C Thomas, 1964.

Olds, J., & Milner, P. Positive reinforcement produced by electrical stimulation of septal area and other regions of rat brain. *Journal of Comparative and Physiological Psychology,* 1954, 47, 419–427.

Ornitz, E. M., & Ritvo, E. R. Perceptual inconstancy in the syndrome of early infant autism and its variants. *Archives of General Psychiatry,* 1968, 18, 76–98.

Pribram, K. H. *Languages of the brain.* Englewood Cliffs, N.J.: Prentice-Hall, 1971.

Rosenzweig, M. R., Bennett, E. L., & Diamond, M. C. Brain changes in response to experience. *Scientific American,* 1972, 226(2), 22–29.

Semmes, J. Hemispheric dominance: A possible clue to mechanism. Paper presented at the Annual Meeting of the American Psychological Association, New York, 1966.

Sheldon, W. H. *The varieties of temperament: A psychology of constitutional differences.* New York: Harper, 1942.

Smith, W. M. Visual recognition: Facilitation of seeing by saying. *Psychonomic Science,* 1965, 2, 157–158.

Sperry, R. W., Gazzaniga, M. S., and Bogen, J. E. Interhemispheric relationships: The neocortical commissures syndromes of hemisphere deconnection. In P. J. Vinken & G. W. Bruyn (Eds.), *Handbook of clinical neurology.* Vol. 4. Amsterdam: North Holland Publishing Co., 1969.

Sunby, W. H., & Pollack, I. Visual contribution to speech intelligibility in noise. *Journal of the Acoustical Society of America,* 1964, 26, 212–250.

Thomas, A., Chess, S., & Birch, H. G. *Temperament and behavior disorders in children.* New York: New York University Press, 1968.

U.S. Public Health Service. *Minimal brain dysfunction in children: Terminology and identification.* NINDB Monograph No. 3. Washington, D.C.: U.S. Government Printing Office, 1966.

3
TEACHING
THE ECONOMICALLY
DISADVANTAGED CHILD

The Role of the School with Culturally Different Children

More children with learning problems are found among culturally different and economically deprived children than among any other subgroup in public school classrooms, and teaching these children involves special problems.

The attitude of the significant persons in a child's environment, as well as his whole way of life, may influence the child's school progress positively or negatively. Environmental factors must be taken into account not only in working with the underprivileged child, but also in working with the privileged or "overprivileged" child. The so-called privileged or overprivileged child who is left in the charge of a maid speaking a foreign language during most of the day, the child who is not permitted to touch anything in the beautiful country home of his parents and is relegated to a room without playmates, are as deprived of the stimulation necessary for normal development as the economically deprived child in the inner city. But the inner-city child suffers as a rule from other adverse influences. He lives in a crowded, noisy environment, and even in the case of very concerned and loving parents, he may often be felt to be underfoot. Greater conflict with adults and siblings can result, so that he is more frequently punished than the child who has ample play space assigned. In certain areas he is attacked by other children, especially those from different social, religious, or ethnic groups, and he learns to be wary and defensive, and to attack in turn.

The school environment is rarely designed for the lower-class child. In fact, it often causes more harm than good, as evidenced by the diminished self-concept that such children frequently acquire as a result of their continual experience of failure in academic tasks. Feelings of hopelessness, alienation, and hostility are nourished by school authorities, who frequently have no expectation of the lower-class student and lack respect for him. (See, for example, Rosenthal and Jacobson, 1964; Leacock, 1969; Stein, 1971.)

27

Beginning School

The young socioeconomically deprived child comes to school ill prepared. He has usually not had toys or arts and crafts materials to handle
and play with. The objects on the shelves in the schoolroom may seem
strange and threatening. Even when they appear desirable and the child
gains the coveted scissors or crayons or pencils or puzzles, he may find
himself uncertain how to use them.

Such a child is probably confronted by a teacher who speaks differently from his parents and the other people he knows. He quickly
discovers that there are many strange rules to follow, and it may be
difficult for him to remember them all—to run in the playground but
not in the hall; to raise his hand when he wants to go to the toilet or
ask for something or respond to a question. All this is bewildering and
rather frightening. He is expected to pay attention to the teacher, but
he often finds he can not because paying attention is difficult when one
is puzzled and afraid. He is afraid—afraid of the teacher, afraid that he
will make a mistake; he is also afraid of the walk home and what some
older child may do to him. As the days go by, he may become more
and more anxious and talk less and less, or he may become over-
aggressive because he decides that it is better to beat than be beaten.

Yet there are schools in low socioeconomic areas where the children
look and seem happy, are eagerly engaged in multifaceted activities,
and make progress in their learning as indicated by behavior observations and test results. They talk, laugh, play, and work, and are always
busy. A school principal in Washington, D.C., has just such a school.*
He was asked what he did to enable the children in his school to
function at their grade level, although fourth and fifth graders in surrounding schools were at second-grade or third-grade level in achievement. He explained that all entering children were first helped to
achieve optimum performance in the basic skills they needed for academic learning—sensory-motor and perceptual skills and the ability to
express themselves orally—and they were also taught school know-how
(the behavior expected of them in school) before they were confronted
with academic tasks.

To prepare culturally different and economically deprived children for
school learning, it is indeed necessary to introduce a readiness program
that includes ability training and instruction in school behavior.** Abil-

* Oral communication from a psychiatrist working in the school system.
** Descriptions of such programs are given in Bereiter and Engelmann
(1966), Blank and Solomon (1968), Weikart (1967), Klaus and Gray
(1968), Hellmuth (1968), Karnes (1968), Maccoby and Zellner (1970),
and by many others.

ity training refers to readiness training in sensory-motor functions, language, perception, and thought processes, as well as temperamental characteristics that affect learning, such as self-control, paying attention, and reacting adequately to environmental stimuli. It must also be remembered that the negative experiences to which the young child from a depressed or rejected area has often been exposed have almost surely affected his self-image.

Open classrooms* may make it far easier for the culturally different or economically deprived child to adjust to school. Such a classroom is designed to meet the needs of the child and not have the child meet the needs of the classroom. Young children feel more comfortable and secure when they can enjoy freedom of movement, and can change their position at will, sit on the floor, lie on a rug, or stand at a table, instead of always sitting in a little chair and only moving at the teacher's command. Another common characteristic of equal benefit in the open classroom is the contact with children of different age levels. This enables the children to assume diversified social roles, with a consequent increase in self-regard and the desire to communicate.**

In summary, the young economically deprived or culturally different child needs to be prepared for school through ability training, with emphasis on language and perceptual skills (Farnham-Diggory, 1970). He also needs more freedom to move around, to choose activities, and to become comfortable. Equally important are the goals of helping him develop a positive attitude toward school, of having him mingle with both younger and older children, and of giving him the opportunity to communicate freely, in order to enrich his life through multiple experiences and, most of all, to develop a positive self-concept. It is also most desirable to establish an effective liaison with the parents and the community based on an understanding of their problems.

The Middle Grades

The tasks of the teacher shift from about the third or fourth grade on. By this time the child should have acquired "school know-how." His anxiety in relation to his home and school environment has probably diminished. But it is still necessary for the teacher to adapt the curriculum and methods of classroom management to the economically deprived child because of his specific needs, and to concentrate on

* See, for example, Weber (1971), who describes the open classroom in England. Her descriptions of such classes in the London slums, where for many children English is a second language, are particularly vivid.
** For example, see Goodlad (1966) and Gartner, Kohler, and Reissman (1971).

enhancing his self-image. The methods for accomplishing these goals often differ from those needed with middle-class white suburban children.

The senior author's experiences date back to a time when she taught Mexican-American children in the fourth grade. After a short time the youngsters became so involved in studying Mexico and their own heritage that they would work for hours in small groups with minimal supervision. The need to use maps and dictionaries, to find information, and to make notes, led to academic improvement and a greater knowledge of the English language. The children's enthusiasm created excellent school adjustment, which made teaching a pleasure.*

The only drawback to such methods is that they involve much preparation and much in the way of collecting materials and resource units, but that is compensated for by the ease with which the children are motivated and the enthusiasm they have for their tasks.

A teacher who teaches Mexican-American children cannot teach Mexican culture to the children year after year. She has to proceed by slowly enlarging the children's interests as well as her own. For example, comparing the art, religions, and customs of Indian cultures may get the children acquainted with the various South American countries; or a discussion of how the Indians obtained food may lead to a discussion of agriculture, irrigation, food supply, conservation, ecology, and so on. Similarly the study of African cultures may lead to topics involving the geography, ecology, history, folklore, and religions of the African continent, and a comparison of its physical features and cultural manifestations with those of other continents.

Fifth Grade and Up

From the fifth and sixth grades on, teachers will often find that many children seem disaffected and have difficulty becoming interested in their work. But the teacher may also find that certain subjects, such as automobiles, are of quite universal interest in this culture. These interests can be used as the nucleus for a wider variety of experiences.

A group of boys in a detention ward for delinquent youths was fascinated to learn how to repair a car, including learning the oral and written vocabulary; the teacher then involved them in the study of geography by having them imagine that they were driving a car that

---

* These children were tested with the Stanford-Binet test at the beginning and end of the school year. The average gain was 10 points. This change is mainly ascribed to their improved use of the English language.

competed in a long-distance race; and finally the boys turned to a study of the people and customs in the various locations visited on a leisurely imaginary motor trip through the United States.

The interest in cars, which is universal among American boys, can be at least partly explained by the symbolic significance of cars. Cars mean speed, wealth, status, freedom. Most boys are reluctant to talk about their worries, difficulties, and defeats; but the choice of subject matter can at least afford them symbolic gratification.

The Role of the Peer Culture

The current rapid changes in our culture necessitate a change in the role of the school. The powerful influence of the family has greatly diminished, and the peer group has taken over part of the family's former function of shaping the character and behavior of the child. Urie Bronfenbrenner, in his book *Two Worlds of Childhood*, is of the opinion that the school itself strengthens the influence of the peer group. He writes (1970, p. 100) ". . . homogeneous grouping—and more recently by ability—has set the pattern for other activities, so that from preschool days onward a child's contacts with other children in school, camp, and neighborhood tend to be limited to youngsters of his own age and social background."

Even those children who seek other contacts often give up because they are actually pushed into peer groups by the adults responsible for them, who sometimes feel that if children are not peer-oriented they are introverted and therefore asocial. It seems that parents often withdraw from their children and vice versa. Bronfenbrenner continues (p. 102), "The vacuum left by the withdrawal of parents and adults from the lives of children is filled with an undesired—and possible *undesirable*—substitute of an age-segregated peer group."

What is the relevance of this trend for the school? The school can counteract the deleterious effects by providing adult leadership and fellowship that may help to bridge the generation gap. This is important because groups of young people, seeking identity and pleasure, if not given direction by adult leadership, seem to intensify any antisocial tendencies in individual members, as the prevalence of gangs and juvenile delinquency attests. Young people are especially vulnerable to social contagion, embracing ideas and performing actions condoned by a group without examining them critically.

For at least part of the day, children should not be grouped by age. The older child is gratified and gains in maturity if he has the opportunity to assist a younger child by tutoring or helping him in sports and games or arts and crafts. The younger child gains by feeling more protected and secure. Both may improve in academic achievement. Gartner, Kohler, and Riessman (1971) cite statistics from Mobilization for Youth, a New York City antipoverty program, that show that over a five-month period the children being tutored gained six months in school achievement while the student-tutors gained 3.4 years!

The authors have no proof but believe that street behavior becomes less hostile when children learn to assist and protect each other in the classroom.

The Role of Television*

Television has often been blamed for contributing to the unrest and even delinquency of young people. An abundance of research has shown that viewing violence and painful punishment in a film or on television enhances the aggressive and sadistic tendencies of both adults and children. Examples are the research of Albert Bandura (1963) and his students at Stanford University, and that reported by Singer (1971).

Recently, however, a few very good regular television programs have become available, especially for younger children, among them "Mister Rogers' Neighborhood," "Sesame Street," and "Electric Company." The latter can also be enjoyed by the fifth and sixth grader.

There is now also available a marvelous selection of films, slides, records and tapes that can be used to enlarge the interests of this young public. Full acceptance of their use is much easier if a group of older children forms a committee with the teacher to select films, slides, and other such material, not only for themselves but for the younger and even the youngest children. This is another way to bridge a "generation gap."

Teaching Self-Respect

Several specific methods that may help the teacher to develop the child's positive self-concept include:

1. The child is given only work at which he can succeed. There is no positive reinforcement more effective than success.

* It should be emphasized that the discussion here and in the previous section of this chapter applies to all children. The effects of commercial television, for example, or of age segregation are not confined to inner-city children.

2. Favorable comment and notice by the teacher is usually helpful at all age levels (e.g., "What a lovely dress you have on today!"). But social approval (reinforcement) will not be useful with very hostile children who do not care about the teacher's opinion. Such children need to be left alone until they themselves initiate contact and involvement.

3. Sharing success with the teacher and with classmates makes success doubly sweet. Displaying a good piece of work on the bulletin board, having a role in the class play, or for a little child, showing a new hair ribbon during sharing time, are examples of ways in which a child may be helped to feel important.

4. The teacher should show the child what he has accomplished, using concrete examples together with explanation. A booklet that documents each child's progress should be kept. Students who are unable to accept the teacher's approval will often show pride when the teacher helps them to evaluate their accomplishments for themselves.

5. The teacher helps the child to feel more secure when she connects current school tasks with the "real" tasks that the child has to meet at home or in the community, and also connects them with future aspirations. With younger children this can be done through such methods as dressing-up and role-playing—"I am a nurse. When I grow up, I might be a nurse." With older children the teacher should point out how a piece of work might help later on; for instance, learning to compute percentages can be explicitly applied to problems of installment buying, mortgage payments, and so on.

6. Having one child help another makes the helper feel important. It is ego-building for older children to help younger ones, help in the community, and take part in the management of the school.

7. A child ought to be satisfied not only with his performance, but also with himself as a person, including his body image. With young children a hand mirror can be used to develop such ideas as "I look good" and "This is me." A larger mirror should be used with older children, so that the whole person can be seen. This is very necessary for girls.

8. A child's pride in his home culture is greatly enhanced when his culture is part of the curriculum. The history, accomplishments, and special characteristics of his culture should be taught, but only if the teacher is sincerely interested in learning about the culture herself, and able to enjoy at least the aspects she chooses to bring into the classroom. If cultural differences are accepted

as valuable, a great deal of enthusiastic mutual learning can take place. In fact, a classroom comprised of children from several different cultures and socioeconomic levels affords the best possible opportunity for true education in mutual respect and social commitment.

Educational Ecology

At times environmental factors may require the teacher's intervention: Sue is hungry because she is not given breakfast; Mary is always tired because she goes to bed late; Peter is afraid because his father often becomes angry without provocation; Jonathan is worried because his mother cries a lot; Maurice is anxious because he has experienced bombs and fires and shouting mobs; Estelle is heartbroken because her best friend has moved away. Such examples of children's reactions, familiar to every teacher in every school, are usually more frequent and severe in classrooms with economically deprived children. Such children may be able to achieve in school only if they receive help with their problems. For this purpose it may be necessary to utilize community resources.

Teaching Communication

To enhance a child's self-concept and to maximize school achievement, the teacher has to be aware of the child's feelings. She has to listen. But culturally deprived children often use little verbal language and may choose not to talk at all. No form of communication will happen unless the children trust the teacher.* Once trust is established the children may begin to use language for communicating past experiences or future hopes, for sharing a sequence of events, and for exploring cause-and-effect relationships.

A child can learn to use language adequately only when he has something to talk about. A child will only learn to communicate his

---

* Labov (1970, pp. 157–161) gives very vivid examples of the influence of the situation on the ghetto child's verbal expression. The child perceives even a friendly but strange adult of his own ethnic group as one who will hold anything he says against him. The testing situation, particularly with an Anglo-American examiner, often produces only defensive, one-syllable utterances. But in a relaxed, informal situation, in which there is opportunity for interacting with a friend, the same child can become quite verbal.

ideas, opinions, and feelings, if the teacher provides the child with a great variety of concrete experiences.

With many children it is a most helpful and necessary step to give special instruction in the use of standard English to enable them to communicate more fully and also use their workbooks and textbooks to advantage (See Part V; also Brottman, 1968). But no child should be made to feel that his own dialect is bad, only that he has to learn "book" English because it is needed for talking to people who speak differently and also for reading.

The Importance of Ability Training

Another very urgent need is for ability training. Research studies, foremost among them those of Farnham-Diggory (1970), show that black children frequently have visual-perceptual handicaps that require special training. The studies by Deutsch (1965), Vera John (1967), and others show that lags in various language functions are frequently present and retard school learning. The authors' own experience has been that integrated training in these two broad areas improves the child's abilities to handle concepts necessary for school learning.

The Role of the Teacher

The behavior of the teacher is of the utmost importance. (See the discussion on psychoanalysis in Chapter 7.) No lecture on good behavior, politeness, or kindness will have the slightest effect if the teacher is herself impolite, uses corporal punishment, or consistently hurts a child's feelings. The teacher should not only put herself forward as a model, but teach about models with whom the child can identify. An economically deprived child is usually uninterested in school, not because the parents are indifferent to the child's schoolwork, but because the parents do not provide models of intellectual mastery. If a teacher has a genuine interest in finding out facts, events, ideas, and relationships, a child may develop a similar interest.

Reinforcement as a method of influencing the behavior of children is more thoroughly discussed later in Chapter 5, "Behavior Modification." The teacher who rewards desired behavior in the classroom affects not only the child who is rewarded but also all the other children who observe the event.

The teacher must adjust the amount of affection she bestows to the real needs of the child. Unfortunately a growing number of children do not get affection from their families or foster families, and their only source of love, appreciation, and enjoyment lies in the teacher. For such children a more intense relationship is appropriate than with children who are more fortunate, provided that the deprived child is able to accept affection.

Unfortunately many children feel hopeless and helpless in their environment. They feel that they cannot change many of the disagreeable circumstances in their own lives, and this feeling breeds apathy, hopelessness, and a lack of self-respect. In addition to enjoyment, the teacher must give each individual child the feeling that he can learn and that he can solve problems, so that he gains hope for the future as well as satisfaction in the present. The most important means of achieving this is to provide the youngster with experiences of success.

Anger, aggressiveness, regressive behavior, and destructiveness on the part of a child can best be handled by redirecting the child toward a constructive goal chosen and approved by the group. The aggressiveness of a most "hopeless" group of delinquents was redirected into positive channels after they had seen their own bungalow go up in flames, and had to construct a new one together (August Aichhorn, personal communication).

Service to others provides the most promising antidote for social maladjustment. Involvement of pupils in tasks that help others within the classroom, the school, the neighborhood, and the community, must be encouraged.

Involvement of Parents and Community

Another necessary step in the education of the child from a different culture is the involvement of parents and the community. As long as the adults in the child's environment are hostile or aloof to his learning experiences, the child will not enter wholeheartedly into the life of the school.

In many communities parents are unfriendly and even actively hostile toward the school. Educators must do everything in their power to bring about mutual respect and cooperation. It has been mentioned at the beginning of this chapter that learning problems are very frequent in the lowest socioeconomic areas. Children cannot profit from the school experience when they are confronted with standards of beliefs, ethics, and mores that not only contradict those of their parents, but seem to demean them.

The teacher herself is often not free from such an attitude. She feels that she has achieved her position because she has upheld white middle-class ideals regardless of her race or class origin. She presents a clean, conventional, courteous front (the three c's of the middle class). Poverty-stricken parents—and there are millions of them in this country —have one goal: survival. Although most of them have the same values as the middle-class, including the desire for a better, more comfortable way of living, one cannot live according to middle-class standards if one is hard pressed for money.*

The teacher should also remember that no race or ethnic group can look back on its own history without finding cruelty, misconduct, deception, and avarice, but each group has also achievements that deserve the utmost respect.

Winning Parents' Trust

Poverty-stricken parents usually have a very strong desire for their children to succeed, which includes succeeding in school. At the same time they are often ill and depressed, and always harassed and uncertain about their ability to provide even the basic necessities of life. The teacher, by enhancing the parents' own self-respect, helps everyone— herself, the parents, and the child.

Classrooms should be open to parents, and the teacher will help the children optimally if she listens to the parents' communications—to their criticisms, wishes, worries, complaints, and ideas. She can help them experience shared pleasures with their children. Room parties, skits played by the children for the parents, a group meeting to make Christmas toys and decorations from discarded materials, and other similar activities will ease tension and bring shared pleasure. The teacher may have the children plant flower seeds in a pot, or plant radishes or other vegetables in the schoolyard, and have them take "the harvest" home. She can take a photograph of each child who can then frame it as a Christmas present, or have the children make other little gifts as an indication to the parents that the teacher cares about them too. Any such event may constitute a turning point in a child's school and even home life.

The teacher can be a model for the parents in helping them interact in a positive way with their children. To give an example, during one summer some college students majoring in drama offered to read stories

---

* No one who reads Robert Coles' continuing study of poverty-stricken children (1967, 1972a, 1972b) can fail to appreciate the strength, courage, and innate decency with which such families lead their lives, and their contributions to America, whose ideals they cherish.

to preschool youngsters in the ghetto. They met with small groups of mothers and children in the children's homes or backyards. The students' own enthusiasm and enjoyment were contagious, and soon the mothers joined in, at first providing the sound effects or refrains appropriate to the story, later telling or reading stories themselves. Everyone had fun, and the children benefited. An additional benefit from this experience was that use of the local library increased 300 percent!

The teacher in her work with parents will encourage them to help their children learn by stressing a few important principles: guide the child toward the solution of a problem, without solving the problems; discuss what is going on; foster curiosity; share positive expectations; reinforce the child's correct responses and overlook his errors.*

As the teacher becomes accepted by the community, she will become a resource person and a point of referral for all kinds of services. The teacher will find her own life expanding as she learns about community resources and responds to expressed needs with honest interest and concern.

A teacher who spends some time with parents, who gives an extra hour in the afternoon to lead a group of teen-agers in writing and acting a play that can be presented to the public, the music teacher who establishes a small band that can play for the public on various occasions, gains the interest of the family and of the community in the school. The teacher who helps a child to solve difficult problems, who lends a helpful hand in situations too difficult for one child to tackle alone, who gives support during a family tragedy—this is the person who helps children to gain in trust and in the ability to solve future problems. Such a teacher may at the same time help to ease social tensions. Such a teacher will never be forgotten by her charges, but she must be satisfied that this remembrance will probably be the only reward for many hours spent in others' service. It is to be hoped that communities and school boards will realize that what are often regarded as frills may be the most essential aspects of education, that a teacher needs time to gain acceptance in the community, and that overloading her with other duties limits her effectiveness.

---

* Beem *et al.* (1969) found that the middle-class mother allows the child to work at his own pace, offers guiding suggestions, and tells him when he is correct. The lower-class mother makes controlling and disapproving comments. Aside from any emotional effect, being told what is wrong does not give the child any positive direction.

WORKS CITED

Bandura, A., & Walters, R. *Social learning and personality development.* New York: Holt, 1963.

Beem, H. L., Van Egeren, L. F., Straissguth, A. P., Nymen, B. A., & Leckie, M. S. Social class differences in maternal teaching strategies and speech patterns. *Developmental Psychology*, 1969, 1, 726–734.

Bereiter, C., & Engelmann, S. *Teaching disadvantaged children in the preschool.* Englewood Cliffs, N.J.: Prentice-Hall, 1966.

Blank, M., & Solomon, F. A tutorial language program to develop abstract thinking in socially disadvantaged preschool children. *Child Development*, 1968, 39, 379–389.

Bronfenbrenner, U. *Two worlds of childhood: U.S. and U.S.S.R.* New York: Russell Sage Foundation, 1970.

Brottman, M. A. (Ed.) Language remediation for the disadvantaged preschool child. *Monographs of the Society for Research in Child Development*, 1968, 33 (Serial No. 124, No. 8).

Coles, R. *Children of Crisis.* Boston: Little, Brown, 1967.

Coles, R. *Migrants, sharecroppers, mountaineers.* Boston: Little, Brown, 1972a.

Coles, R. *The south goes north.* Boston: Little, Brown, 1972b.

Deutsch, M. The role of social class in language development and cognition. *American Journal of Orthopsychiatry*, 1965, 35, 78–88.

Farnham-Diggory, S. Cognitive synthesis in Negro and white children. *Monographs of the Society for Research in Child Development*, 1970, 35 (Serial No. 135, No. 2).

Gartner, A., Kohler, M., & Riessman, F. *Children teach children.* New York: Harper, 1971.

Goodlad, J. I. *School, curriculum, and the individual.* Waltham, Mass.: Blaisdell Publishing Co., 1966.

Hellmuth, J. (Ed.) *Disadvantaged Child.* Vol. 2. *Head Start and early intervention.* New York: Brunner/Mazel, 1968.

John, V. P., & Goldstein, L. S. The social context of language acquisition. In J. Hellmuth (Ed.), *Disadvantaged Child.* Vol. 1. Seattle, Wash.: Special Child Publications, 1967.

Karnes, M. B., Hodgins, A., & Teska, J. A. An evaluation of two preschool programs for disadvantaged children: A traditional and a highly structured experimental preschool. *Exceptional Children*, 1968, 34(9), 667–676.

Klaus, R. A., & Gray, S. W. The Early Training Project for Disadvantaged Children: A report after five years. *Monographs of the Society for Research in Child Development*, 1968, 33 (Serial No. 120, No. 4).

Labov, W. The logic of nonstandard English. In F. Williams (Ed.), *Language and poverty.* Chicago: Markham, 1970.

Leacock, E. B. *Teaching and learning in city schools.* New York: Basic Books, 1969.

Maccoby, E. B., & Zellner, M. *Experiments in primary education: Aspects of Project Follow-through.* New York: Harcourt, 1970.

Rosenthal, R., & Jacobson, L. F. Teacher expectations for the disadvantaged. *Scientific American,* 1964, 218, 19–23.

Singer, J. L. (Ed.) *The control of aggression and violence: Cognitive and physiological factors.* New York: Academic Press, 1971.

Stein, A. Strategies for failure. *Harvard Educational Review,* 1971, 41(2), 158–204.

Weber, L. *The English infant school and informal education.* Englewood Cliffs, N.J.: Prentice-Hall, 1971.

Weikart, D. P. Preschool programs: Preliminary findings. *Journal of Special Education,* 1967, 1, 163–181.

PART II

4

IMPLICATIONS
OF PSYCHOLOGICAL
THEORIES
FOR INSTRUCTION

Hopefully the time has passed when an educator who does not adhere to the point of view of a specific school of thought is scornfully termed an eclectic, meaning a person who does not have a unified point of view but indiscriminately uses the ideas or findings of others to give credence and scientific respectability to his own ideas and actions.

The time has come to begin building a unified theory of instruction. Such a theory will certainly be far from complete. There may be contradictions, and there will certainly be many observations for which there is no theoretical explanation. The ideas of many other disciplines and of many theoreticians and practitioners in education have contributed to present educational theories, and the behavior of children and teachers has become more meaningful in the light of these theories. But if the understanding of human behavior and of educational intervention is to be increased by theoretical considerations, then the ideas and findings used as a frame of reference need to be related to each other and fused into a whole.

The authors' point of view is best described by a quote from Bettye M. Caldwell (1968, pp. 71–72). "There have been [in my own work] flirtations with many theoretical positions. . . . [I am a] part of all theories that I have had and I am glad. My only regret is that I have not had meaningful encounters with still other theoretical systems."

Similarities Among Four Different Schools

Abraham Maslow (1969) once stated, "I am a Freudian, and I am behavioristic, and I am humanistic." This quotation suggests that different psychological viewpoints need not necessarily be contradictory. Indeed, when the implications for education of behaviorism, psychoanalysis, humanism, and the cognitive-developmental point of view are compared, these different schools of psychology, which seem so divergent at first glance, begin to reveal many similarities.

Most of the behavioristic, psychoanalytic, and cognitive-developmental theories are based on observation of children's behavior and analysis of these observations. It is therefore not astonishing that adherents of all three schools have often arrived at the same conclusions, although the focus of each varies and the application of their conclusions to practical problems shows wide diversity.

Moreover, all educators of whatever persuasion aim to bring about more or less identical results. In general, all educators hope that their efforts will contribute to the development of friendly, happy children, who will find life meaningful. The behaviorist, who usually avoids any discussion of long-range goals, believes that a child must master the skills of his culture and be able to work with others in order to preserve that culture under changing conditions. The cognitive developmentalist believes that a child must learn to decenter and learn to understand other viewpoints. The humanist believes that a child must feel himself to be a part of the world and therefore able and willing later to take the needs and existence of all humanity into account. The psychoanalyst believes that a child must overcome his childish egocentricity and become able to love and to work. Certainly all arrive at essentially the same definition of a complete human being.

It is therefore difficult to make clear practical distinctions between the adherents of any particular school of thought in education, and the problem is multiplied by the fact that within each group there are so many divergent viewpoints and so many philosophical differences that sometimes the differences within a group seem greater than those of the groups themselves. Moreover, many educators combine certain aspects of each approach, as Barbara Bateman (1971) does, for example, in attempting to combine the technology of the behaviorists with the long-range idealistic goals of the humanists.

Comparison of Points of View

The specific suggestions of each school of thought for achieving the friendly, outgoing, but not unruly behavior that every educator wants in a child are not contradictory.

The psychoanalysts and the behaviorists agree that suppression by punitive means is a very poor method of educating children. What then are the best ways to help a child adjust to the school routine and to society in general? The behaviorists advocate giving the child extraneous pleasures (rewards). The humanistic psychologists advocate assisting him to achieve self-realization through creativity, which includes creative relationships and heightened awareness of others, including the other children in the classroom. The cognitive developmentalists advocate helping the child to understand, to master, and to learn by diminishing his doubts and perplexities about the world around him, by helping him to perceive the constancies and laws that govern all existence and all events. The psychoanalysts advocate having the teacher become the ego-ideal of the child so that the child will learn to sublimate, not because he has to, but because he wants to become like the teacher (A. Freud, 1962). The teacher in his leadership role as the ego-ideal of the children can then combine the children into a group with the same goals.

In behavior modification the reward can be something that has in itself value for the child, such as a toy or food, or something with a wider, more social connotation, such as praise and approval. Such social reinforcements are less dependent on a close personal relationship in the view of the behaviorist than the psychoanalyst.* Cognitive-developmental psychologists are not primarily concerned with the child's personal relationship with the teacher. Humanistic psychologists regard such a relationship as only one of a number of deep, rewarding, and helpful experiences that every child should have; the teacher-child relationship is given no more emphasis than any other relationship.

The importance of the meaning of what is learned, in the sense of articulation and choice of subject matter, is stressed by adherents of all four points of view, although psychoanalysts, cognitive developmentalists, and humanists define "meaning" in a more personal sense than behaviorists do. All four schools of thought believe in the importance of the development of ego functions, in providing experiences of mastery and success, in a close monitoring of the child's progress, and in individualization.

Specific Emphases

In part, the differences between the groups rest in the questions they ask, rather than in the conclusions they draw. The emphasis of humanism is on the goals of education. The curriculum is considered impor-

* Some educators and clinicians who consider themselves behavioral modifiers believe that the success of their methodology depends on a close relationship between teacher and pupil; others do not consider it important or believe that such a relationship should be discouraged.

tant only so far as it is a means to achieve these goals. The emphasis of behaviorism is on the *how* of education—the methodology. The psychoanalytic and the cognitive-developmental viewpoints direct their attention equally to the *what* of education (the curriculum), the *how* of education (the methods), and the *why* or *what for* of education (the goals).

The cognitive-developmental educator takes into account the various stages of the child's growth (see also Chapters 8 and 9), and emphasizes that certain learning tasks can best be accomplished at certain stages of development. Facts, concepts, and generalizations are to be taught in a similar progression from the more concrete to the more abstract. The belief that a child's intellectual functions develop through his activity, and that he is intrinsically motivated by his natural curiosity, leads to emphasis on an open-classroom environment, in which the child has freedom to explore, manipulate, and have many concrete experiences. Cognitive developmentalists emphasize the importance of play, and creativity is regarded as a more important goal than the learning of skills, with the exception of note-taking. This latter skill is considered of great importance because it requires the child to translate whatever he learns into symbolic form.

The psychoanalysts share with the cognitive developmentalists an interest in the child's future development, and both are interested in exploring the ways in which the child develops internal mental structures that affect the way he interacts with his physical and social environment. The psychoanalytic focus, however, is on the child's changing social and emotional needs, rather than on his cognitive development. Psychoanalysts suggest that curriculum, discipline, and classroom management should take these emotional needs into account. They consider the relationships between the child and teacher and between the child and his peers to be of major importance. They agree with the cognitive developmentalists in stressing the value of play, considering it one of the teacher's tasks to assist the child to express his emotions through play and verbal expression.

Piaget's theory of cognitive development is complementary to psychoanalytic theory. The one focuses on the cognitive aspects, the other on the affective and social aspects. Their respective treatments of play and imagery illustrate this complementary relationship. Psychoanalysts are mainly interested in imagery—which includes fantasy—and play because of the relevance of these activities to mental health and the emotional and artistic development of the child, whereas Piaget's interest is centered upon the relationship of imagery to thought.

Psychoanalysts, humanists, and cognitive developmentalists alike agree that the child should be given some freedom to develop and follow his own interests, and that he should be permitted to play an active role in setting up the curriculum and providing much of his own discipline. The emphasis of all three groups is upon their respect of the child as an individual.

Another agreement among the different theories discussed is that personality theory, learning theory, and cognitive-developmental theory all postulate a certain sequence in child development. In essence, these theories state that psychological development is based on the interrelationship between maturation and experience, and that new forms of behavior are always based upon earlier stages.

Behaviorists are less interested in the child's developmental phases, and are not directly concerned with maturational readiness in the teaching situation. They emphasize that teaching should progress step by step and believe that with correct teaching, any child can learn anything.* They usually regard the teaching of academic skills as the principal function of the school; they do not specifically stress the cultural heritage, social interaction, social values, and humanitarian principles. The special contributions of the behaviorists are the development of a theory of instruction, and of specific methods and a technology for teaching subject matter and skills. Since behaviorists are concerned with a strict assessment of behavioral changes in order to evaluate each aspect of their program, they are more interested in those aspects of teaching that can be quantitatively evaluated. Behaviorists are not primarily interested in the causes of behavior** as psychoanalysts are, or in affecting the child's philosophy of life, as humanists are. In fact, the behaviorists have no philosophy about educational goals, but provide the methodology by which they claim such goals can be achieved.

The behaviorists have taken hold of the technology of our times—the computers and the teaching machines—and used them to advantage. They have developed many methods of evaluating the teaching and learning processes. While cognitive developmentalists, psychoanalysts, and humanists tolerate some failure, behaviorists state that

* Bruner, who is greatly influenced by both Werner and Piaget and emphasizes cognition, has nevertheless followed the lead of the behaviorists in this respect. He states that a person can be taught anything at any time of life if only the teaching is skillful enough. He advocates a very broad curriculum in science and the liberal arts and the teaching of academic skills.

** The concept of cause and effect in psychoanalysis has undergone significant changes in recent years. Behavior is now viewed as being multidetermined, and it is analyzed more from the point of view of understanding its meaning than finding its cause.

failure in learning can be avoided by the proper utilization of technology.

The important conclusion to draw from the discussions that follow is that the teacher can combine the theories of these different psychological schools and use them appropriately in different situations. Although research findings stem from various points of view, the different theories do not necessarily apply to the same aspects of educational practice, and are often more complementary than contradictory. A knowledge of each of these directions in research will help the teacher to enrich her concepts in regard to education, clarify her ideas about her own goals, and diversify her practical skills.

The reader is referred to Table 1 on pages 97–103, which attempts to summarize and compare the positions taken by these four psychological schools of thought in regard to important educational practices.

WORKS CITED

Bateman, B. *The essentials of teaching*. San Rafael, Calif.: Dimensions Publishing Co., 1971.

Caldwell, B. M. In R. D. Hess & R. M. Baer (Eds.), *Early education*. Chicago: Aldine, 1968.

Freud, A. *Psychoanalysis for teachers and parents* (2nd ed.). Boston: Beacon Press, 1962.

Maier, H. W. *Three theories of child development: The contributions of Erik H. Erikson, Jean Piaget, and Robert R. Sears and their applications*. New York: Harper, 1965.

Maslow, A. Toward a humanistic biology. *American Psychologist*, 1969, 24(8), 724–735.

5
BEHAVIOR
MODIFICATION

Introduction

Behavior modification has led to important advances in classroom management and teaching techniques and it has also been the focus of much controversy.

Modifying behavior through educational approaches is nothing new; education is by definition a form of behavior modification. It is only in recent years, however, that the process has been scientifically applied. (See Forness and Macmillan, 1970.)

The position that extrinsic reinforcement is needed to motivate learning derives from a view of motivation which states that the organism always tries to maximize pleasure and minimize pain (Skinner, 1950). The behavior of human beings as well as animals is seen solely or primarily under the control of environmental stimuli.

It is not difficult to prove that extrinsic motivation is efficient in promoting learning. Animals learn to perform complicated tasks for rewards, and children who can not be motivated to learn in the usual classroom situation often learn when extrinsic motivation is introduced. Children may learn for high grades, or they may learn because they want to receive gold stars, food, their parents' affection, the teacher's attention, the privilege of erasing the blackboard, or any other of a great variety of tangible and intangible pleasures.

Because of the emphasis on rewards and the broad range of reinforcing (rewarding) measures that behavior modification makes possible, it is of special importance in teaching children who may need the extra incentive of a tangible reward—children with learning problems (e.g., Hewett, 1968; Gaasholt, 1970), children with emotional disturbances (e.g., Haring and Phillips, 1962; O'Leary and Becker, 1967), and economically deprived children who perceive the classroom structure as hostile or alien (e.g., Risley and Hart, 1968). (For reviews of research using token-reinforcement programs in the classroom, see Axelrod, 1971, and O'Leary and Drabman, 1971.)

A teacher may believe that rewards should not be given because she considers them bribes, but they are bribes only in the sense that an adult's salary is a bribe. They tell a child that his effort has a value and that he and his work are considered worthy of recompense. If a child's motivation depends on gaining satisfaction through receiving a reward, the measure should not be spurned. Operant conditioning is a legitimate method for motivating a child to learn—although by no means the only one.

This discussion may seem clearer if a differentiation is made between *motivation* and *reinforcement*. Reinforcement refers to stimulus-response sequences. In motivation the stimuli may be unknown or have occurred far back in the child's life, and the responses also may be unknown, as well as internal and unobservable. The teacher has taken no part in arousing the motives the child brings to school, and is unaware of their origin. Reinforcement, in other words, is a particular aspect of motivation—motivation brought about consciously through manipulation of stimulus-response sequences.

Methods of Modifying Behavior

According to behavior modification, any response (behavior) of an animal or person is more likely to occur if that response has been previously followed by a positive consequence (a reward) (Ullman and Krasner, 1965, p. 29).* (See also Skinner, 1963.) Modifications of this basic model may differ in:

1. **Types of reward**
   Primary (e.g., food for a hungry child)
   Social (e.g., mother's approval)
   Intrinsic (e.g., joy of mastery)

2. **The frequency (rate) at which these rewards are given**
   Continuously (after every response)
   At certain times (interval schedule)
   After so many responses (ratio schedule)
   Consistently or intermittently

3. **The method of giving the reward**
   To individuals (based on specific responses of each individual)
   To groups (based on response [achievement] of group as a whole)
   Self-chosen reward
   Teacher-chosen reward

* "Despite differences in approaches and techniques, we would propose that all behavior modification boils down to procedures utilizing systematic environmental contingencies to alter the subject's response to stimuli."

Proponents of behavior modification usually recommend definitive schedules, indicating precisely when a child should be rewarded. It must be recognized, however, that children have constantly different and shifting needs. In order to be able to reinforce desirable behavior effectively, it is therefore important to know the needs and feelings of each individual child. The child therefore should be encouraged to express his wishes, and if he is unable to verbalize them, the teacher must find out through observation to which reward or reinforcement the child will most readily respond. Premack (1959) has shown that a child will work at certain activities (such as staying in his seat, reading, and so on) in order to be able later to engage in activities he prefers (such as playing football, listening to records, and so on). If the teacher notices what a child does during his free time, either on the playground or at home, she can use these activities as reinforcers. Forness (1970, p. 359) sums it up: "The acid test of what constitutes positive reinforcement for each child is, simply, whatever works."

Everyone knows from his own experience that what to one person may be a reward may to another be punishment. (Compare the reactions of a grandmother and a teen-ager to a rock band!) The teacher must therefore be careful in planning a reward for an entire class or group of children. She might consider that going on a field trip or to a movie would be a reward to everyone, but one child may get sick on buses, another be frightened by what he sees, a third unable to sit still, and so on. A teacher working with children whose backgrounds differ from her own must be particularly wary of assuming that a reward that seems to her very desirable will appear so to the children. (Perhaps it is not amiss to remind ourselves that our rapidly changing society makes for increasing differences in expectations and value systems even among the members of a single family.)

Principles of Behavior Modification

Prescriptive teaching, a term used by O. R. Lindsley (1964), refers to the careful monitoring of four aspects of operant conditioning: stimulus, response, contingency or rate of reinforcement, and consequence (the type or kind of reinforcement). Modification of each aspect may be necessary to achieve success in a given task. This approach was first formulated while modifying the behavior of severely mentally retarded children but was later used in regular classrooms.

So far as immediate classroom behavior is concerned, the teacher's role in behavior modification* is primarily that of a technician who gives rewards for previously specified behavior as the child progresses through well-defined curricula. She also monitors and records the frequency of such behavior. The materials and directives for teaching usually include specification of the kind of reward and the frequency with which it is to be given. In most instances, the methodology is developed by research workers and clinicians trained in learning theory and/or behavioral therapy. These experts, however, may know very little about the actual curriculum. Behavioral modification does not help a teacher to determine educational goals (Macmillan and Forness, 1970, p. 292).

Homme et al. state (1970, pp. 18–19) the following basic rules concerning rewards:

1. Rewards should immediately follow the required behavior.
2. They should be earnable by small increases in quality or quantity of work.
3. The child should be able to earn them frequently.

Other principles of behavior modification state:

1. Each child needs to start at his own particular level.
2. The teacher must set up definite goals and objectives.
3. The child must be aware of these objectives.
4. The child needs to proceed in a step-by-step progression.
5. The teacher must continually monitor the child's progress, provide immediate feedback, and give rewards.
6. And, perhaps most important, the teacher must be systematic in teaching.

Recently a seventh principle has been added to the list of characteristics that a good behavior-modification program is supposed to have, namely, individualization (Martin, 1972).

These principles of operant conditioning are basic to good teaching, even if the teacher's main orientation to the educational task stems from some quite different philosophy.

---

* Most authors (see review by Krasner, 1971) use the terms *behavior modification* and *operant conditioning* interchangeably.

Appraising Behavior

Before a teacher can modify learning behavior, she must know the child's level of achievement and be aware of his abilities and general level of intelligence. What multiplication facts does he know? Can he spell from dictation three-letter words containing a short vowel? What letters can he write legibly, and so on. She must make a careful inventory of his skills. The teacher must also be aware of the behavior that she wants to elicit or eliminate. Objectives, too, must be stated in specific terms.

Conservative and orthodox behaviorists state that all they need to know to affect the child's behavior is the goal to be achieved, the steps (program) that need to be followed, and the optimum schedule of rewarding the child (e.g., Bijou and Baer, 1961). This point of view is not shared by other behavior therapists. Some agree with the authors that intervention is more effective when it is based on an understanding of the causes of a child's behavior. The following is an example of an incident illustrating the latter viewpoint. A group of children were told that they could bring objects from home only on certain days and that they were to leave them with the teacher until "sharing time." But one child, new to the school, brought an object on other days and refused to yield it to the teacher. The teacher considered offering him a reward for each hour he parted with his object, but after carefully observing the child and talking to him, she concluded that his behavior was the result of acute anxiety in the school situation. Instead of depriving him of his comforting symbol of home, she decided to let him keep the object until he no longer felt the need for it. After a few days, when the child felt more at home in the classroom, he observed the rules without further discussion. (As a general rule, accepted classroom methods should be used until the child's behavior indicates that new or supplementary procedures are necessary.)

If a teacher understands the reasons for behavior, she will not make the error of seeking to alter it only because it is disturbing to herself—an abuse of behavior modification that occurs all too frequently. Sometimes disturbing behavior may be very important to a child's learning.

For example, one teacher was made very nervous by a child who incessantly scribbled on pieces of paper and sometimes on his schoolwork. She noticed, however, that he was a hyperactive child, who seemed to be in continual motion, and realized that his scribbling channeled some of the hyperactivity. She therefore did not forbid the scribbling, but instead provided him with a "scribble pad" on which he could mark as much as he liked. At the same time, the child was admonished not to deface his desk, his books, or his workpapers. Like many hyperactive children when their hyperactivity is channeled, he became less anxious, and his hyperactivity diminished.

Importance of Definite Objectives

In the various applications of behavior modification, detailed instructional procedures are suggested to enhance academic progress.

The teacher needs to outline immediate and concrete objectives. Some of these might include such goals as not turning around for five minutes, tracing precisely on top of ten vertical lines five inches in length,* forming twenty letters of equal height, reciting without any mistakes the eight times multiplication table, and so on.

The child must understand precisely what is expected of him. Such awareness helps him to pay attention to the relevant stimuli and to compare his own responses with an agreed-upon criterion. He thus learns to discriminate and to monitor his own performance.

To enable a child to progress smoothly and easily toward the outlined goals, the teacher must work out the successive steps by which the child should proceed. These steps should be designed in such a way that easy associations can be formed with what has already been learned. Progression is systematic and carefully designed.**

Continuous observation of the correctness of each response is necessary to ascertain progress, as well as to ensure that a change of procedure can be initiated at once should the child fail.

Hewett (1967) gives a task hierarchy, with suggested teacher intervention if a child fails at any level of the hierarchy. The task may be simplified; the amount and type of reward changed; or the degree of structure altered. For example, if the child cannot sustain attention (the first level), he may be put on a one-to-one tutoring relationship with the teacher's aide, or his reward for appropriate behavior may be changed, or the number of rewards may be increased.

Steps can be so small that much learning becomes nearly automatic. But the child needs to comprehend how major steps are related to each other. Whenever a major step is to be taken, he is helped if he understands how the new task is similar to, and differs from, whatever

* Of course, the teacher need not measure each line. But she must have the standards of performance clear in her mind and communicate them to the child.

** Two major types of programs are those employing linear progression (step-by-step from entering to the goal) and those employing branching (presentation of same material in different form whenever difficulties occur).

preceded it. For example, the teacher may say, "Yesterday you learned how to add two numbers. You remember these numbers had only units, no tens. You wrote one above the other, and then found their sum. Today you will again write your numbers vertically just as you did yesterday, one above the other, but the top number will have two digits. There will be both units and tens in it. Be careful to write the answer so that the units are under the units and the tens to the left."

Monitoring the Child's Progress

Every completed task should immediately be evaluated and recorded. Measurement of the child's accomplishment should be continuous, and if possible, quantitative. A few of the methods of measurement that may be used are discussed below. (See also, for example, Haring, 1968, and Schaefer and Martin, 1969.)

The number of examples correctly executed in a certain unit of time may be recorded; for example, the number of problems involving addition of two-digit numbers without carrying that were correctly solved in three minutes,* or the number of words or sentences read correctly, or fractions reduced in a certain length of time, and so on. By keeping careful records, the teacher can estimate when to introduce the next step, and can also graphically demonstrate to the child his progress. (Graphs of various kinds are excellent for this purpose and can be used with children from first grade on.)

Other quantitative measures include recording the percentage of correct responses, or the number of definite steps (frames) covered by the child while working with programmed material.

The quality of the work also needs to be measured (Patterson, 1965). Such aspects might be assessed, for example, as whether written words have been fitted into a given space or whether a figure has been colored so that the color is solid, with the crayon marks remaining within the boundary, and so on.

Changes in classroom behavior can also be measured. Data can be kept, for example, on the number of minutes a child works without being distracted, or the number of times he leaves his seat in a given period, and so on.

The child should be made a partner in assessing his own progress.**

* The child may use an egg timer, but most children prefer a stop watch.
** Patterson (1965) had a hyeractive child chart the maladaptive behaviors of other children. As Forness (1970, p. 360) comments, "An advantage of both methods [self-charting and student's charting of each other] is that the child, in labeling the behaviors, is forced to an awareness of misbehavior and in effect thinks twice before acting."

A child who is young or has severe learning problems must be helped with the quantitative measures and graphic presentation, but the older child can generally assess his behavior himself. The teacher may provide a notebook in which the child can graph aspects of his own behavior. He may also prepare his own report card with the teacher's help, including aspects that cannot be presented graphically.

The teacher's function is to ensure that the child's progress is monitored consistently, because consistency is the most important factor in modifying behavior. The teacher therefore must consistently monitor her own behavior also; she must discover from the child's behavior whether her teaching materials and methods are helpful to the child and keep her own records.

Limitations of Quantification

It is essential to realize that not all a child's responses can or should be quantified. Eleanor Gibson (1968, p. 148) states that learning cannot be measured, if by learning we mean something more profound than acquiring a skill or learning facts. Such aspects of learning as the number of words a child knows how to spell can of course be measured, but it is impossible to calculate the amount of understanding, meaningful connections, incentive to explore, ability to arrive at solutions, ability to form human relationships, and appreciation of beauty that a child has achieved. The authors are of the opinion that a teacher must always beware of concentrating upon quantifiable behavior to such a degree that a narrowing of objectives occurs. Children need to explore, discover, create, and develop their powers of self-expression. These objectives must on no account be neglected because they involve behavior that cannot be quantified.

Immediate Feedback

It is essential to inform children immediately concerning the correctness of their responses. If a mistake is not immediately corrected, it may be retained in memory and learned.

If the teacher of a large class finds it impossible to correct immediately graphic (written) responses herself, she might adopt one of the following procedures:

1. Give the correct answer to the children verbally, so that they can correct their own papers.
2. Have the children correct each other's papers.
3. Present the tasks in such a way that the responses are given in

the form of letters or numbers that each child can write on his paper in a large size. The children can then hold up their papers, so that the teacher can see if the answers are correct.

4. The children may be given self-correcting materials—a program to be used with a computer console or a teaching machine, for example.

The way in which children are grouped in the classroom can also facilitate correction of responses. It is easier and less time-consuming for the teacher to visit three or four small groups, if each group is seated around its own table, than to go from one individual to another.

Additional material should always be at hand for any child who has completed his work, to ensure that he is never idle. If individual free time is used as reinforcement, adequate activities should be available, so that the child may be engaged in a way that gives him pleasure, without disrupting the rest of the class.

Individualization

In the section below on contingency contracting, a method of individualizing behavior modification is discussed. In the article "Behavior Modification: The Current Scene" (Lovitt, 1970, p. 87), the author states, "Certainly, a major unifying feature of those committed to behavior modification is the individualized nature of their work."

The same opinion has been voiced by other educators. Individualization has become increasingly characteristic of behavior modification. The range of behavior for which behavior modification is used has been enlarged; the evaluation procedures have broadened; and diagnosis and treatment have become adapted to individual needs. It is important that the teacher should keep these facts in mind, and not assume that the value of behavior modification results only from the effect of a reward.

The following examples illustrate the importance of altering a well-prepared plan in response to a child's interests or because progress is faster or slower than expected:

1. George learned about the topography of the Soviet Union and about the climate and vegetation of various Soviet regions. He had recently read that a mammoth's tooth had been found in the frozen tundra of Siberia, and he concluded that there must have been a climatic change, because otherwise a mammoth could not have found enough food on the tundra. The teacher heeded his request for books from

which to learn about the theories concerning climatic changes. George shared his knowledge with the class, and all the children gained from George's creative insight and the teacher's willingness to modify her program.

2. Esther had kept up with reading in a second-grade book without deviating much from the teacher's expectations for second-grade children. A week before Christmas, Esther was given a set of books as consolation for being sick. Having little else to do, she began to read. She felt very proud of reading a book consisting of only one long story, instead of the short stories she had read in the books in school, and she continued to read a great deal during the Christmas vacation. When she read in school after vacation, her teacher became aware of Esther's spurt in performance. The teacher helped Esther select books from the library that were at her level, and excused her from reading with the regular reading group.

    The teacher knew that children show sudden spurts, and was guided by the child's actual—now superior—level of response. She did not impose the preselected curriculum on the child, and avoided giving her work that was not challenging to her.

3. During a workshop for teachers, one of the participants said, "I don't know what to do with John, one of the children in my class. He seems unable to do anything. One morning, when we had gym, the other children walked along the balance beam, but he fell off. Then we had reading, and he missed every other word, even though he had read the same book twice before. When we had addition in math, he couldn't even count without making mistakes. Then we had arts and crafts and when he wanted to cut out the figure of a girl with his scissors, he cut her head off instead. Then we had lunch, and that's when he was really good."

    During the discussion that followed, another teacher pointed out that John might walk on a cord on the floor or hold another child's hand while walking on the beam, if the teacher did not want to exclude him from the exercise. She also pointed out that John should do other simple balance exercises, such as stepping from one block to another.

    Another teacher inquired about John's specific reading mistakes. The answers led to the conclusion that John had a severe disability in auditory perception and no understanding of grapheme-phoneme correspondence. The teacher suggested training in auditory perception and a matching method for beginning reading until John could learn by a speedier method (e.g., a kinesthetic method) or had improved in auditory-perceptual skills.

    The teachers further suggested that in arithmetic John should work with three-dimensional materials—counting, seriating, classifying, and exploring number relations by joining and separating sets. Counting could be practiced by a method that would slow down his own counting. For instance, he could count rods, grasping each one as he did so, or he could count jumps while jumping, or count objects while transferring them from the left to the right side of a ruler placed vertically on his desk. Such practice would help him avoid mistakes.

Eye-movement and eye-hand coordination exercises were also suggested. In regard to cutting with scissors, a teacher suggested that John should try cutting out simple curves; if this did not work, he should further retrace a step and cut straight lines; and if this task was too difficult, he should backtrack further and practice cutting off the edges of a paper; and, if he still had trouble, he should cut fringes (cut into the paper instead of cutting it off) and to strengthen his fingers, he should do exercises with clothespins.

Contingency Contracting

All forms of behavior modification use contingency management; that is, the giving of a reward is dependent (contingent) upon a particular response being made whenever a particular stimulus is present. The phrase *contingency management* usually refers in education, however, to situations where a child contracts with a teacher to perform a certain amount of work, at a specified level of accuracy, perhaps in a given amount of time, in order to obtain an agreed-upon reward.

Contingency contracting permits an individual approach, because the contract between teacher and student can be highly individualized. This is the reason why it is discussed here at some length.

In contingency contracting, the student earns a mutually agreed-upon reward provided he meets conditions explicitly stated by the teacher. This is a *positive* contingency contract. Negative contingency contracts will not be discussed here as the authors do not believe their use to be appropriate. If a child's response is undesirable, it is more effective to reinforce compatible behavior. For example, it is better to reward a child for doing his arithmetic than to punish him for doodling.

Homme et al. (1970, pp. 19–21) give several conditions for forming the contract:

1. The contract must be fair; the child must be able to earn the reward.
2. The conditions must be clearly stated; the child must understand them. "The child must always know *how much* performance is expected of him and *what he can expect as a payoff*." (Homme et al., 1970, p. 20).
3. The promise of the reward must be kept. (The contract must be honest.)

4. The payment must be made consistently each time the child earns it.

Both the statement of the task and the difficulties that the child experiences should be carefully and specifically recorded. An assignment such as "practice reading" is relatively meaningless. "Read Paragraph 2 (200 words) and answer the questions below it; write down how long it took you to complete this task" would be a specific assignment. The diagnosis must also be equally specific: "He has difficulty with long vowels" would be nonspecific. "John missed the long i in words ending with two consonants (*mind*, and the like)" would be adequately specific. Of course, the reward must also be specific.

In contingency contracting the child is given a card that specifies what the task is. When he has completed the task, he is given a progress check, and he may receive a reward that he chooses from a list. If the child fails to perform the task in the specified time, an easier task is substituted. He gains the reward when he succeeds.

Before contingency contracting is used in the classroom, the procedure must be explained. The children must be told that they will be given assignments and tests, and that they will be permitted to choose rewards for tasks that are completed with 90 percent accuracy.

Contingency contracting necessitates much preparation on the part of the teacher. The task cards have to be prepared and sorted before the children enter the classroom, and the list of reinforcing events (rewards) must be prepared, and the availability of them—whether activities or gifts—ensured.

As the student progresses he can become "self-contracting"; that is, he himself specifies the task, the reward, or both. More advanced students are able to manage *"macro contracts,"* which are "package deals" composed of several contracts. An example of a macro contract would be the promise to a student of a trip, provided he fulfills all his daily contracts for a week.

All other methods are the same in contingency contracting as in other forms of behavior modification. Homme et al. (1970) mentions the following preconditions for correct contingency contracting:

The teacher must know what to teach; must set clear goals; must break down the goals into daily objectives; and choose daily tasks (task units) to reach these objectives. For this purpose she must collect materials and assign the appropriate materials for each daily task. Tests (progress checks) must be prepared and given daily to check on the performance of the daily task unit. (These conditions apply to all good teaching, not only to behavior modification.)

Contingency contracting, as well as other forms of behavior modification, is often of help in motivating a child to put forth greater effort.

However, we agree with Broden et al. (1970) who state that although contingency contracting may be of help in changing behavior temporarily, often other methods of classroom management may be more appropriate.

Classic (Pavlovian) Conditioning

In this country, operant conditioning (also termed instrumental conditioning) is the major form of conditioning currently used in most classrooms. It has given rise to the technology of behavior modification discussed in this chapter. In the Soviet Union, conditioning has also resulted in a technology of behavior modification, based on Pavlov's work. While Skinnerian conditioning is effected through a reward following an elicited response, Pavlovian conditioning is effected by the simultaneous presentation of an unconditioned and a conditioned stimulus. An example of an unconditioned stimulus is food. The animal reacts to food through a reflex action with an unconditioned response, salivation. When another initially neutral stimulus—such as the ringing of a bell—is continuously and simultaneously paired with the presentation of food, the animal will learn (be conditioned) to salivate when he hears the bell. The conditioned stimulus (the tone of the bell) now elicits the same reflex as the food.

One finding of Pavlovian (classical or respondent) conditioning that is important for education is that repetition of the conditioned stimulus without its being paired occasionally with the unconditioned stimulus, leads to extinction of the reflex; the response is lost. We can infer that overlearning is necessary, but it has to be diversified and meaningful.

Watson in this country was one of the pioneers in classical conditioning (Watson and Rayner, 1920). Later, Guthrie (1935) developed a theory on the basis of Pavlovian conditioning. A stimulus-response pattern is learned when a stimulus is immediately followed by a movement.

Learning therefore results if two or more stimuli occur together and the subject reacts to them. Such learning can be observed in the classroom. A child may be told, for example, "The red hook is for your coat," while he hangs his coat on the hook. The simultaneous experience of the sight of the hook, the sound of the words, and his own actions should help him to remember next day on which hook to hang his coat. In Russia, verbal directions (auditory stimuli) and pictures (visual stimuli) are presented while the child follows the directions of the speaker or the visually presented direction on the picture. The child may also repeat the instruction himself during the action he is learning. Such methods are used with many variations with very young children, and are reported to be of special benefit for mentally retarded children and children with learning problems.

Soviet educators emphasize verbalization on the part of the child for facilitation of learning. The child says what he is doing while he is doing it: "I hang my coat on this red hook." Accompanying actions with verbalization is highly beneficial for children with learning difficulties. (See the later chapter on language training.)

Summary

The behavioristic point of view advocates systematic teaching, stress on associative learning (presenting material that the child can connect with what he already knows), careful monitoring of the child's behavior, immediate feedback, and step-by-step progression.

The goals of teaching are stated in terms of detailed performance objectives for each child, and the child is informed of at least the limited daily objectives.

All these procedures seem helpful in teaching children with learning difficulties, provided that the teacher encourages independent learning as much as possible and helps the child to become increasingly self-directive.

The emphasis on extraneous rewards that also characterizes the behaviorist approach seems appropriate for children who are so discouraged or alienated that they will not learn otherwise; it might give such a child sufficient incentive to achieve success, an experience that subsequently becomes motivating by itself.

The street-corner research of the Schwitzgebels (1964) has demonstrated how a progression from extrinsic to intrinsic motivation can take place. The youngsters involved in the street-corner research were at first only willing to work for money, but gradually the relationship with the experimenters, the pleasure in learning and mastering new skills, and the stimulation inherent in working together in a group played an increasing role.

WORKS CITED

Axelrod, S. Token reinforcement programs in special classes. *Exceptional Children*, 1971, 37(5), 371–379.

Bijou, S. W., & Baer, D. M. *Child development*. Vol. 1. New York: Appleton-Crofts, 1961.

Broden, M., et al. Effects of teacher attention and a token reinforcement system in junior high school special education class. *Exceptional Children*, 1970, 36(5), 341–349.

Forness, S. R. Behavioristic approach to classroom management and motivation. *Psychology in the Schools*, 1970, 7(4), 356–363.

Forness, S. R., & Macmillan, D. L. The origins of behavior modification with exceptional children. *Exceptional Children*, 1970, 37, 93–100.

Gassholt, M. Precision techniques in the management of teacher and child behaviors. *Exceptional Children*, 1970, 37, 129–135.

Gibson, E. In R. M. Gagne & W. J. Gephart (Eds.), *Learning research and school subjects*. Itasca, Ill.: Peacock Publishing Co., 1968.

Guthrie, E. R. *The psychology of learning*. New York: Harper, 1935.

Haring, N. G. *Attending and responding*. San Rafael, Calif.: Dimensions Publishing Co., 1968.

Haring, N. G., & Phillips, E. L. *Educating emotionally disturbed children*. New York: McGraw-Hill, 1962.

Hewett, F. M. Educational engineering with emotionally disturbed children. *Exceptional Children*, 1967, 33(7), 459–467.

Hewett, J. H. *The emotionally disturbed child in the classroom*. Boston: Allyn & Bacon, 1968.

Homme, L., Csany, A. P., Gonzales, M. A., & Rechs, J. R. *How to use contingency contracting in the classroom*. Champaign, Ill.: Research Press, 1970.

Krasner, L. Behavior therapy. In P. H. Mussen & M. R. Rozenzweig (Eds.), *Annual review of psychology*. Vol. 22. Palo Alto, Calif.: Annual Reviews, 1971.

Lindsley, O. R. Direct measurement and prothesis of retarded behavior. *Journal of Education*, 1964, 147, 62–81.

Lovitt, T. Behavior modification: The current scene. *Exceptional Children*, 1970, 37, 85–92.

Macmillan, D. L., & Forness, S. R. Behavior modification: Limitations and liabilities. *Exceptional Children*, 1970, 37(4), 291–297.

Martin, E. W. Individualism and behaviorism as future trends in educating handicapped children. *Exceptional Children*, 1972, 38(7), 517–525.

O'Leary, K. D., & Becker, W. C. Behavioral modification of an adjustment class: A token reinforcement program. *Exceptional Children*, 1967, 33, 637–642.

O'Leary, K. D., & Drabman, R. Token reinforcement programs in the classroom: A review. *Psychological Bulletin*, 1971, 75(6), 379–398.

Patterson, G. An application of conditioning techniques to the control of a hyperactive child. *Behavior Research and Therapy*, 1965, 2, 217–226.

Premack, D. Toward empirical behavior laws: I. Positive reinforcement. *Psychological Review*, 1959, 66, 219–233.

Risley, T., & Hart, B. Developing correspondence between non-verbal and verbal behavior of preschool children. *Journal of Applied Behavioral Analysis*, 1968, 4, 267–281.

Schaefer, P., & Martin, P. (Eds.). *Behavior therapy*. New York: McGraw-Hill, 1969.

Schwitzgebel, R. *Streetcorner research: An experimental approach to the juvenile delinquent*. Cambridge, Mass.: Harvard University Press, 1964.

Skinner, B. F. Are theories of learning necessary? *Psychological Review*, 1950, 57, 193–216.

Skinner, B. F. Operant behavior. *American Psychologist*, 1963, 18, 503–515.

Ullman, L. P., & Krasner, L. *Case studies in behavior modification*. New York: Holt, 1965.

Watson, J., & Rayner, R. Conditioned emotional reactions. *Journal of Experimental Psychology*, 1920, 3, 1–14.

6
THE HUMANISTIC
POINT OF VIEW

Various humanistic goals of education have been formulated by psychologists, educators, and philosophers. According to Maslow (1969), a humanistic psychologist, education needs above all to demonstrate and foster a concern for the human race in general and for the individual in particular. He states that the educator should strive to produce what he terms "the good person," one who is concerned not only with his own life but also with his influence upon others. Charlotte Bühler (1969) and other humanistic and existential psychologists see the goal of education as "self-realization." Bühler emphasizes self-fulfillment through creativity. Piaget (1970), Erikson (1963), and others formulate the goal of education as the production of mature persons, who can keep far-reaching goals in mind and pursue them, while maintaining an interest in, and concern for, the lives of others. Buscaglia (1971) emphasizes the ability to love. One problem that humanists face in attempting to define their goals is that they are concerned with feelings and values, whereas language can be used with far greater ease and precision in exploring rational concepts. Of course, the question then arises as to whether such topics as feelings and values are scientific.

Importance of Human Values

One of the central concepts of science is that of causality. Scientists search for invariant sequences of events, so that prediction of certain future events can safely be made on the basis of knowing what has already happened. The idea that everything that happens is part of a chain of causes and effects has led many workers in the behavioral sciences to believe that all mental processes are ultimately reducible to physiological processes, and that psychologists should only explore directly observable behavior. Feelings and values, they believe, cannot be scientifically examined.

But scientists have an obligation to explore feelings and values, and even more, do educators, who must be concerned with all aspects of human life. In our time, feelings of anxiety and hatred have taken hold of vast numbers of people, and vituperative criticism and disapproval are expressed far more frequently than friendly acceptance. The problems that bar peaceful living together and cooperative endeavor seem so overwhelming that our response is often a defeated retreat into apathy (Rollo May, 1969). When the future of mankind seems to be at stake, it is imperative to examine feelings and values. Values properly conceived suggest the directions for social change; feelings positively channeled provide the motive power to achieve it.

The need for change is evident, and various schools of thought try to promote it in various ways. The behaviorist Skinner (1971), for example, advocates employing rewards in such a way that the behavior of every member of society is shaped to the end of preserving his culture. ("Culture" is apparently defined as a more agreeable status quo.) Skinner believes that if children were educated ("shaped") in this way during their formative years, they would learn to *want* to do whatever their society demands. There would be no conflict between individual desires and the collective will.

The humanist, on the other hand, considers the dignity of the individual to be paramount. According to the humanist, education should help the child to reconcile his personal freedom with social responsibility by developing a deep feeling of connectedness with the world around him. Humanist education nurtures the child's ability to identify with the feelings and value systems of other human beings; it also encourages his identification with the wider environment. The position of a child educated in the humanist tradition in regard to pollution, for example, will stem not only from rational considerations, but from his feelings for the beauty and oneness of the world, which is mirrored in himself and in all life. The humanist is inevitably involved in social evaluation and criticism because he perceives himself as a social being, as a part of humanity. He is deeply shocked by dehumanized attitudes in social relationships and dehumanizing forces in social institutions, in which category unfortunately we must often include the schools.

Humanistic Educational Goals

Present-day education in public and private schools has not been effective in reaching the goals staked out by humanism. The rise in crimes of violence, the pervasive promotion and acceptance of materialistic values, which is reflected in the destruction of the environment, the prominence of war, hunger, and poverty, and the desperation and anger of suppressed minorities, all suggest that the school has not contributed to the development of a mature, concerned, and harmonious society. Of course, the school is not the only institution that has failed, but it must bear at least partial responsibility for the disorders in our society. The evidence is the low classroom achievement of broad classes of young people, the high incidence of drop-outs from high school, and the anger expressed by many college students at the inadequacy of the educational practices to which they must submit. We have not only failed to foster the values and attitudes that lead to a more just, happy, and fulfilled society; we have also failed in the fulfillment of the personal needs of our children and young people.

Lavaroni (1970) doubts that society can survive if education does not change and emphasize humanistic values, instead of materialistic values and competition. He states (p. 5): "More and more emphasis must be placed upon cooperation. More and more emphasis will have to be placed upon the development of the individual to achieve his full potential. More and more emphasis will have to be placed upon helping each human being to become more open and more aware of his responsibilities to society. Greater emphasis will have to be placed upon intrinsic rewards, concern for others and respect for differences."

Education in general has not emphasized these goals sufficiently. But what can an individual teacher do in the small universe of her classroom?

A humanistic teacher will be tolerant if a child does not reach the practical goals she has staked out for him. She will not push, pressure, punish, or threaten, because the negative results of feelings of shame and anger in the individual and disharmony in the classroom will in her view far outweigh any short-term gains in conforming behavior or immediate learning. She will be committed to her work, but will neither work to exhaustion herself, nor exhaust the child. She will try instead to give the child feelings of satisfaction in whatever he is doing, fostering equally his perception of himself as an important member of his social group, the classroom, and his academic learning. She will respect the child as a human being whom it is her privilege to assist in unfolding his abilities. At the same time, she will foster in the child the understanding that the responsibility for the way he lives his life is his own.

The concept of *becoming* (Allport, 1955; Maslow, 1962; Tillich, 1952) is one of the central concepts of humanism, and this may be the most important concept for the teacher. She will realize that she has responsibility for helping the child develop *in his totality*. She not only has to set tasks, provide stimulation, and guide the child's physical, mental and emotional development, including a system of values based on empathy with and respect for others, but she also has to be very clearly aware of those aspects of his life that could hinder his development. She will therefore not only concentrate on the child's achievements, but be continually sensitive to his feelings. Only when he feels free and happy can he develop fully.

Erich Fromm, in *Escape from Freedom* (1941), states that to be a human being in the deepest sense is far from easy. One has to struggle all one's life to be human, which means to be loving, compassionate, and understanding. The humanistic teacher, committed to helping children become more self-fulfilled and giving persons, is confronted daily—even minute by minute—with situations in which she must test her own belief that all human beings are worthy of respect and she must transmit that belief to her students.

The following example in which the claims of nationalism and humanism were in conflict, may serve as an illustration. A fourth-grade class was reading its nationally circulated weekly current-events newspaper, which contained a statement that President Nixon and the Chinese leaders had decided on an open door policy. One youngster questioned, "That really means you can close it again. Why was it closed up to now?" A classmate replied, "The Chinese were bad." "Yes," said a third, "The Chinese are Communists, and Communism is bad." The first child, puzzled, asked, "Well, they're still Communists. Why aren't they bad now?"

The teacher attempted to explain how different systems of government evolve as the result of many years of history, and originally take their shape in a people's striving to get enough food and gain some personal security and dignity. She explained that different nations have different beliefs and develop different institutions based on their historical experience and present needs. But the teacher realized that abstract verbal explanations are not very useful; they are not absorbed (assimilated) by children who have not experienced any of the things she was talking about. Her class having never experienced real hunger or oppression, could barely understand the origins of the Russian Revolution; never having experienced homelessness or life in a concentration camp, they were limited in understanding the founding and development of Israel; never having been exploited tenant-farmers, they could not truly identify with the conditions that brought about the revolution in modern China. Nor, on the other hand, could they identify with the despair caused by a revolution, such as the feelings of a member of the government who is in danger of his life, or a farmer whose land is taken from him.

Although factual knowledge provides a base, compassion and understanding can best be gained through personal experience. The teacher therefore initiated an approach based on that of Bruner (1966) in teaching about early man, and had the children immerse themselves in different roles in order to gain understanding.

A humanistic teacher will not need situations related to subject matter to promote compassionate understanding. The experiences of each member of the class are different, and can be the subject of class discussion and dramatization. That is one reason why the presence in any classroom of children with different ethnic backgrounds is desirable. Moreover, the teacher's demonstration of her own respect for each child and his individual differences provides a model for the children.

Specific Suggestions

Specific suggestions to the teacher drawn from the humanistic point of view include the following:

1. The teacher needs to keep in mind that self-confidence and self-respect are not inborn characteristics but are developed as a result of the individual's experiences. In this sense, they are learned, and the teacher's actions and attitudes can either promote or retard their development. Punishment, whether in the form of a bad grade, a trip to the principal's office, scolding, and so forth, lowers a child's self-respect. It is much more constructive to accentuate instead whatever is positive, and a great number of measures can be instituted in a classroom to help a child feel worthwhile. The teacher may point out to the class what each child has done well and in what unique way he has contributed to the group. Examples of the children's work might be displayed on bulletin boards. Children may be asked to demonstrate to the class whatever they do well. The teacher's public acknowledgment of every child's unique contribution will also help the children to more appreciate each other's individuality. This will be further fostered if the teacher shows each child that she knows how he feels.

2. A student's physiological needs have to be met, as well as his intellectual needs. His living conditions should be such that he can remain healthy. He should have enough to eat, a clean and quiet room in which to learn, to rest and to play, and the opportunity to make friends. The teacher should know if a child's home environment does not meet these requirements. If the home conditions cannot be ameliorated, she must endeavor to meet them at school as far as possible by such measures as the

provision of a snack, an additional rest period, and a quiet place in which to study.

Humanistic philosophy advocates an open classroom structure, in which the child can behave according to his own physiological rhythm. Physical and intellectual activities should alternate. If there are indications that the children are tired, bored, restless or overstimulated, a change of acitivity is indicated.

3. The child can learn responsibility for his actions and become self-directing in the classroom, but he will need help. The teacher needs always to ask herself, "Can the child perform this task by himself?" "Should I prepare this material for him?" "Will I need to demonstrate this method to him?" Whenever the child can do something by himself he should attempt it. Besides doing independent work, he can learn to prepare materials, keep the class-room orderly, and monitor his own progress.

4. The child can also learn to show consideration for others and take responsibility for giving help. He should be encouraged and rewarded for assisting others and promoting in any way the classroom's optimum functioning.

5. When the teacher stimulates curiosity, she develops an intrinsic pleasure in learning. Much learning can be experienced as play.

When asked by his parents what he did in school one day, a second grader replied: "We just played." When his parents inquired at the school, they found that he had actually engaged in a multitude of educational activities. Among others, he and another child had taken various measurements of their bodies and compared them, marking paper strips which they then aligned against a yardstick. They recorded the measurements, and these were subsequently used to construct a graph of the measurements of the whole class. When the mother remarked that all this was work, the child said, "No, it was fun." Many other activities such as class meetings, "dress-ups," dramatic presentations, and arts and crafts may be regarded as play by the child when in reality they provide much learning.

6. It is necessary to carefully plan a child's activities in order to reach various carefully formulated goals, and the child's progress toward these goals must be carefully monitored. It is therefore necessary for the teacher to be well organized, to make careful preparation for each lesson, and to keep detailed notes of each child's progress and behavior.

7. Since the children take part in every aspect of classroom activity, they are also involved in preplanning and the on-going evalua-

tion. They should discuss the goals, the material required, the methods to be used in their work, and the help they will need. The teacher should ask the students to predict how the activities will turn out, and will later heighten their awareness of the activity, and of their progress, by having them compare the outcome with their initial plans.

8. Humanistically based education is not restricted to narrow achievement, but attempts to acquaint the child in as great depth as possible with many aspects of human life and enterprise. It is to be hoped that the old-style curriculum, which formerly made the child acquainted in a stereotyped way with the supermarket, the mailman, and the fire station, is gone forever. Jerome Bruner (1966) has discussed how stultifying and banal such a curriculum is. Instead, the teacher can use the mailman as a starting point for learning about geography, history, transportation, and the duties of the people whose services are needed to maintain the mail service—truck drivers, mail sorters, a stamp designer, and so on.

Adults can be invited to tell about their job experiences. In this way the children can learn at first-hand what a banker, a physician, a tax collector, a street cleaner, an electrician, a pilot, a scientist, or a paper boy does. The children also tell about their own experiences and projects. Communication in the classroom should always be a two-way process.

9. The teacher tries to understand and respect the individuality of each student. She also tries to individualize the program, letting each child keep his own pace. She helps the child to find alternative means of learning, if he encounters difficulties. For example, if he has difficulty in learning by methods that involve visual abilities, the teacher introduces methods that involve auditory abilities, and vice versa.

The student will progress much faster if he is permitted to help in making the decisions concerning materials, methods of study, and goals. The child can write down his lesson plans for the day and as far as possible evaluate his own performance as he proceeds, getting help whenever necessary.

Individualization does not mean that every child has to be doing something different. Nor does a situation in which every child is doing something different necessarily mean that the instruction is individualized. Individualization occurs only when the meaning of the work is directly related to the needs of the child. Individualization, of course, cannot occur unless a great variety of materials are available to meet each child's different needs.

Teacher-Child Relationship

Humanistic philosophy has contributed much to the education of children with learning and adjustment problems.

According to Buscaglia (1971), the most powerful agent in enriching the lives of more children, helping them to learn, and changing their behavior when necessary, is the teacher's love.

Children with learning difficulties feel both rejected and dejected. Perceiving this, the humanistically oriented teacher will aim to help the child to develop a sense of his own worth, which is not something that is dependent on his academic prowess in comparison with others.

When children begin to believe in their own wholeness and worth, they may progress at a fast pace, despite their former difficulties. The humanistic point of view encourages self-discipline, and the willing and eager acceptance of responsibility by both the teacher and the child. The child with learning problems, in particular, needs to feel that he is able to take responsibility and be self-directive.

Because individualization is emphasized, the child with learning difficulties will be protected from attempting to learn by a method that is inappropriate for him.

Finally, the emphasis on emotional and social values assists the child to become an adult who experiences life as deeply satisfying because he will have a sense of purpose in life. In Buscaglia's words (1971, p. 13), this is "to matter, to count, to stand for something, to have it make some difference that you lived at all."

From the humanistic point of view, it is the teacher's responsibility to take into account a broad spectrum of goals with regard to both the individual and humankind. The goals of education are the integrity of the individual, his moral commitment for the good of the world, and a heightened ability to love others. The maximal learning of subject matters and skills is also an objective, but not the only one. The over-all goal of education can be summarized by Maslow's phrase: "to make the good person."

The humanistic point of view emphasizes self-fulfillment, self-realizations, interaction with others, and awareness of the needs of the other persons in the immediate environment as well as the needs and achievement of all people. Instruction in the history of other cultures is emphasized, not only that of Western culture. Understanding is valued more highly than knowledge; rote learning is therefore minimized. Skills are taught only for the procurement of the information basic to understanding. Learning is based on direct experience.

Humanistic education is not based on a science of education but on a philosophy of education. It attempts to solve questions concerning the goals of education, and does not focus primarily on teaching methodology, materials, or curriculum. Nevertheless, it influences classroom management because it substitutes a more free and open classroom with greater opportunity for individual initiative; it encourages a spirit of cooperation rather than competition. And it influences teaching methods because it requires the teacher to find the approach, the materials, and the goals suitable for each child.

WORKS CITED

Allport, G. *Becoming.* New Haven, Conn.: Yale University Press, 1955.

Bruner, J. S. *Toward a theory of instruction.* New York: Norton, 1966.

Bühler, C. Humanistic psychology as an educational program. *American Psychologist,* 1969, 24(8), 736–742.

Buscaglia, L. TACLD presents Leo Buscaglia. Texas Association for Children with Learning Disabilities, 1971.

Erikson, E. H. *Childhood and society.* 2nd ed. New York: Norton, 1963.

Fromm, E. *Escape from freedom.* New York: Rinehart, 1941.

Lavaroni, C. *Humanity.* San Rafael, Calif.: Dimensions Publishing Co., 1970.

Maslow, A. H. Toward a humanistic biology. *American Psychologist,* 1969, 24(8), 724–725.

Maslow, A. H. *Toward a psychology of being.* Princeton, N.J.: Van Nostrand, 1962.

May, R. *Love and will.* New York: Norton, 1969.

Piaget, J. *Science of education and the psychology of the child.* New York: Orion Press, 1970.

Skinner, B. F. *Beyond freedom and dignity.* New York: Knopf, 1971.

Tillich, P. *The courage to be.* New Haven, Conn.: Yale University Press, 1952.

7

PSYCHOANALYTIC THOUGHT AND ITS APPLICATION

Psychoanalysis dates from the beginning of this century. The term itself is used with a number of different connotations: it refers to a theory that explains human development and human behavior; it denotes a particular form of treatment for emotional disturbances and mental illness; and finally it refers to a particular method of research. Its practitioners differ in respect to the focus of their interest (medical, educational, sociological, and so on), in regard to their treatment methods, and in regard to their theoretical position. Different schools of psychoanalysis have developed particular aspects of the theory.

Psychoanalytic thought has influenced the way the average person in our culture views himself and others, and psychoanalytic terminology is now used by many who are quite unaware of the origin of such terms as *ego, repression, superego,* and so on. Concepts that were new during Freud's lifetime have become commonplace. Views that were unthinkable at the beginning of this century are now widely accepted; for example, that sexuality is part of the basic nature of human beings, that it is present from birth on, that it does not suddenly appear at adolescence. Psychoanalysis is a developmental psychology, and like cognitive-developmental psychology, studies the interaction between a person's constitutional makeup (determined by his heredity and reflected in the physical functioning of his body, particularly in his biochemistry and central nervous system), his maturational level, and his experiences with his physical and social environment. From such interaction arises the infinite variety and unique individualism of every human being.

Psychoanalysts consider the first developmental milestone to be birth itself, which is an event with physical and psychological dimensions. Birth requires a complete readjustment from the phase of totally dependent life in the womb to life as an independent, separately functioning organism.*

* The concept of "birth trauma" (see, e.g., Rank, 1929) as providing the prototype of anxiety in man has undergone significant changes in recent

Behavior is conceptualized as being partly dependent on the stage of the child's development. The teacher who is acquainted with the psychoanalytic stages will derive many helpful suggestions for classroom management and for curriculum.

Oral and Anal Phases

Sigmund Freud and his early followers viewed the infant in a conceptual framework somewhat similar to the early behaviorists—as an organism that has no innate ability to adapt to the demands of the environment, which it experiences as a sort of "blooming confusion." This view has been modified by later experimentation and observation. It is now generally held that from birth on, children are aware of many features of their environment and can make distinctions among them.

The infant's capacity for tolerating frustration and tension is, however, very restricted. According to Freud, the infant's behavior is governed by the pleasure principle, which states that the infant seeks to achieve a state of maximum physiological comfort and freedom from tension.

The infant's first mode of relating to his environment is through the use of his mouth (the oral stage). His need for food requires primary satisfaction; but food alone is not sufficient to relieve his tensions. Warmth, touch, and general sensory stimulation are necessary for normal growth and development (Harlow, 1970; Bowlby, 1953; Spitz, 1965).

At about the age of eighteen months, which is about the same time that most cultures begin to make at least minimal demands, the young child, now moving around on his own, becomes interested in the sensations arising from his rectum and anus. Both retention and expulsion of feces are pleasurable to the toddler. Psychoanalysts call this the *anal* stage.

Toilet training is a major milestone in development, because the child has to learn to postpone gratification (the pleasure of defecation) to meet adult demands. He learns to substitute other activities for the forbidden pleasure; in other words, he learns to sublimate. For instance, he may play with clay or finger paints, rather than smear his excrement as many babies enjoy doing.

Children of preschool age still show many characteristics of the oral and anal phases; they hoard and like to be near their most beloved

years. Psychoanalytically oriented research in infant development continues to be both diverse and intensive.

possessions and are afraid to be separated from them. They often carry their possessions around with them and may be greatly attached to a particular toy or blanket. Such behavior must be supported. It is likened by psychoanalysts to the wish of the child to retain possession of his feces, and is therefore regarded as anal behavior. But children of this age also show oral characteristics. They are highly interested in food, especially sweets. They still need a lot of physical contact. Their feeling of being loved and secure depends to a great degree on their being touched and physically supported.

Phallic Phase and Oedipus Complex*

The child enters the phallic phase at about three and a half or four years of age. This phase is characterized by the development of interest in the genitals and by daring aggressiveness, especially on the part of boys. Boys are proud of their penises, and girls may wonder why they are made differently. The first questions concerning sex are posed and must be answered. The four or five year old becomes more self-assertive; he or she is interested in such activities as climbing and bicycling, fighting and competing. He or she may be difficult to manage. An upsurge in a great variety of role-playing and fantasy can be observed, and such play helps to channel the child's behavior.

The sexual and aggressive feelings associated with the phallic phase give rise to the Oedipus complex; the resolution of this complex is usually considered by psychoanalysts as critically important to the child's development. According to psychoanalytic tenets, at about five years of age the child becomes fascinated by the parent of the opposite sex, and thereby experiences a conflict. The boy wants all his mother's attention and love, and enters into rivalry with his father for it. Eventually realizing the impossibility of his ambition, he resolves the dilemma by determining to become like his father instead. The girl's equivalent to the Oedipus complex has a more complicated course, because she gives up her first love (the mother) in favor of the father. The problem is resolved by her reidentification with her mother.

At the end of the phallic phase and the resolution of the Oedipal conflict, the child, whether boy or girl, should have a stable sex identification. The teacher can assist the process by permitting the child to

* The allegation has been made by some members of the Women's Liberation movement that psychoanalysis is biased in its emphasis on the male. The use of the word *phallic* to describe a stage common to girls as well as boys may well be a case in point.

try out various roles, to exercise initiative, and to display a reasonable amount of boisterous behavior. Active, aggressive play seems particularly necessary, at least in our culture, for male sex-role identification.

The resolution of the Oedipal conflict results in a child's identification with his parents. The child "becomes like his parents in his repudiation of his wishes" (Brenner, 1957, p. 126). The parental moral demands and prohibitions become part of the child's mental structure; they form the basis of his superego, which is very similar—though not identical—to what is commonly called conscience, and is closely allied to the child's self-concept.

Early Childhood Education

Psychoanalysts would say that the most important quality in early childhood education is to allow a child freedom to satisfy his early oral, anal, and phallic needs, and also to play, to explore, to touch others, or be alone and think and let his fantasies range as he wishes. (See, for example, Fraiberg, 1959).

Anna Freud (1965), Winnicott (1971), and others stress the importance of imaginative play. Play can be used by the teacher as a helpful way of gaining understanding of the child. The teacher can observe how the child defends himself through his play against the anxieties that are a natural part of childhood, and can infer what those anxieties may be. All children experience objective frustrations. All children also have a special need to overcome the anxieties aroused by frustration through fantasy and play, in which they can change reality and try different modes of adapting to it. Children should be given much opportunity to play. Play helps children to assimilate reality to the degree that it becomes nonthreatening and emotionally satsifying. In play children can always subjugate all enemies and emerge unharmed from all dangerous situations. In fantasy, at least, he can enjoy impossible things. It is for this reason that every child enjoys hearing about the man who put on his pants by pulling them over his head or wore shoes backwards. It is reassuring to imagine that somebody can be as tall as a mountain or change size, like Alice in *Alice in Wonderland*. The same observation has been made by behaviorists (e.g., Engelmann, 1969), who suggest that teachers use such impossible situations as examples in their teaching, because children enjoy them.

Psychoanalysts emphasize that if the preschool or school situation arouses a young child's anxiety, he should be permitted to keep by him a symbol that he feels protects him, such as a small toy or box brought from home. The anxious preschooler or kindergartener will find the separation from his home much more bearable, and the added security will enable him to handle more readily the anxieties aroused by the new environment.

A common source of anxiety in the elementary-school child is his awareness of his own performance in school in relation to the other children. He may be afraid that he will fail, and may defend himself against his anxiety by avoiding playing with other children in organized games or by refusing to learn his lessons. As a result, he may become identified as one of the failures and troublemakers, may be punished, become frustrated and angry, begin to quarrel, and get into all sorts of mischief. The teacher should be aware of the source of this unhealthy kind of defense and help the child cope with his anxiety about failure by ensuring success.

The Child in the Elementary School: Latency Phase

The child in the first or second grade has passed through the phallic phase and is said to be in the period of *latency*. According to psychoanalytic theory, the instincts and drives that caused the child to seek direct physical satisfaction in the earlier phases are now less noticeable. They remain latent until they again become active during puberty. In the latency period the child's energies are directed much more to acquiring new knowledge, new skills, new ideas, and to the development of his mental capacities. Piaget (1969) has observed how strong the child's need is to explore during this period, which he terms the "period of concrete operations."

Changes in Psychoanalytic Concepts

It was mentioned in the foregoing discussion that some concepts in psychoanalysis have changed as new observations and experiments have shown errors in earlier studies. Moreover, opinion has never been uniform in regard to all the aspects of the basic tenets of psychoanalysis, nor in their application to education.

One point on which early psychoanalysts did not agree and present-day psychoanalysts continue to differ is the question of discipline. In the beginning of psychoanalytic thought, many psychoanalysts assumed that complete freedom was necessary for the optimum development of the child. In our time a few educators (among them, A. S. Neill, 1960) have interpreted psychoanalytic tenets as implying that the child should have complete freedom of choice both in education—whether to learn or not to learn—and in behavior as long as he hurts neither himself nor others. But most people who have worked as educators and who have also been trained as psychoanalysts recognize the importance of discipline (e.g., Anna Freud, 1935; Aichhorn, 1925; Hill, 1930). By "discipline" they mean measures similar to those used by most advocates of behavior modification: encouragement and praise as a means of control rather than punishment.

In general, the development of Freudian psychoanalysis assisted our understanding of the child by pointing to the importance of ego functioning and ego development.* Human beings (and animals) have a need to act upon the environment, to master it or adapt to it, and to achieve (White, 1963; Hartmann, 1958; Kris, 1952). From the earliest days children show joy in their ability to effect changes on their environment. The ego is conceptualized as that aspect of the psyche that mediates between these functions. Sentences prefaced by "I can" refer to the ego when they denote interaction with the outside world: "I can do it," "I can perceive," "I can talk," "I can think." Ego drives are drives toward independence and creativity.

Methods of Discipline

As we have stated, most psychoanalysts and behaviorists agree that punishment should be avoided whenever possible, although their reasons differ. Psychoanalysts avoid punishment and threat of punishment because this form of discipline increases the anxiety which is a natural component of the process of growing up.

Psychoanalysts suggest gentle methods of discipline, although restrictions are necessary or the child's anxiety becomes even greater. Above all, *physical* punishment should be avoided (see James Anthony, 1969, and also Sybil Richardson, 1969). Whatever punishment has to be used should be appropriate to the child's behavior. For example, it is logical to tell a child that he can't eat in the sandbox and throw his food around, and to insist that he sit at the table and put his banana peels in the garbage can. It is less logical, and in the long run less effective, to punish him by taking his lunch away or having him write a hundred times, "I should not throw my banana peels into the sandbox."

* *Ego* as a psychoanalytic construct is that part of a person's mental structure that interacts with the environment and mediates between it and the person's internal needs.

The emphasis in psychoanalysis is on understanding the *meaning* of behavior, its relationship to the needs of the child, many of which may be unconscious. If a teacher understands the meaning of a child's behavior, she can help the child become aware of its effectiveness or ineffectiveness in coping with his needs in the face of inevitable frustrations and disappointments. For instance, the child who throws his banana peel in the sandbox may do so to express his disappointment that his mother put in a banana instead of the grapes for which he had asked. The teacher may prevent his littering, but she may also help him write a note to his mother telling her what he would like to have for lunch the next day.

It is necessary to require adherence to certain rules, even if they cannot be explained to the child. But most issues, rules, and regulations can be both explained and discussed; others can even be set up by the children themselves, and it can be of great value to initiate regular discussion groups for this purpose in the classroom (Glasser, 1969).

Psychoanalysis has shown that aggressiveness must have an outlet, or it is likely to be turned inward against the child himself, or later against those who are responsible for the child. The reduction of aggression can be achieved not by attempting merely to cut it off, but by finding a legitimate outlet for it, by redirecting it, by having the child play out his aggression in fantasies, and most of all, by providing an unthreatening environment. Anxiety, frustration, and anger engender aggressive impulses when they put too much strain on the child's ability to reconcile his emotional tensions with the demands of his environment.

Children should not be permitted to vent their aggressive impulses on other children and make them scapegoats or whipping boys. As Redl (1952) observes, when one child starts to tease another, many others in the group join in. It is important to stop such behavior. There is no reason why the classroom atmosphere should not be warm and friendly. These feelings are equally contagious and can be engendered if the teacher supports and praises those children who help each other and indicates that she strongly disapproves of unfriendliness or hurting another child's feelings.

Bettelheim (1950) believes that if children are to succeed in school, they must be motivated by the necessities of reality—the reality principle —rather than by the desire for immediate gratification. They have to be able to postpone immediate pleasure. But Bettelheim points out that children who have received insufficient gratification cannot postpone pleasure. Basic needs must be satisfied before children can work, learn, and delay gratification. Before deprived children can learn, they must experience school as pleasurable.

Pressure cannot be completely avoided in the process of education. Pressure is a part of life, a part of growing-up and a part of school, but the teacher can minimize it (Solnit, 1969). The teacher will have every psychoanalyst's backing in her effort to make learning more enjoyable.

Erikson's Concept of Developmental Stages

Erik Erikson's (cf. Erikson, 1963) work has further expanded ego psychology. He views development in terms of crises and emphasizes the solution of these crises. He describes eight phases that encompass man's life-span. The first five of these phases pertain to man's early formative years. In the terms Erikson uses to describe these five formative phases, the words "a sense" are always used: "a sense of autonomy," "a sense of industry," and so on. This phrase, "a sense," is important because it points to the fact that Erikson refers to feelings, to the individual's reactions to each developmental phase. It is the contact between the child and reality that leads to the crises.

Phase 1

The first phase begins at birth and lasts until the child is about a year and a half in age. This is the phase in which the child acquires a sense of basic trust while overcoming a sense of basic mistrust. It corresponds roughly to Freud's oral phase and to the sensory-motor phase of Piaget. The child's feeling of trust is based and depends upon a feeling of being adequately cared for. Unpredictable need satisfaction and lack of care result in a lack of trust.

Phase 2

In the second phase the child has to acquire a sense of autonomy while combating a sense of doubt and shame. This phase coincides roughly with Freud's anal phase and the first part of Piaget's preoperational phase. It begins at about eighteen months and lasts until about four years. Its main conflict is derived from the necessity of toilet training, during which the child has to give in to societal demands while at the same time developing autonomy in relation to his physical functions, directing and influencing others through language, and enlarging the sphere of his interactions with the world around him.

When the child is overcontrolled, he develops a lasting sense of doubt and shame; if he enjoys greater self-control, he acquires a sense of autonomy.

Phase 3

In this phase the child has to acquire a sense of initiative and overcome a sense of guilt. It extends from about four to about seven years of age and roughly corresponds to the Freudian phallic phase and second part of Piaget's preoperational stage. The four-year-old child often goes to school, where he must learn to conform to a new kind of discipline. He engages in creative play and becomes aware of himself as a sexual being—as a boy or a girl.

Guilt and failure may become overwhelming if a child at this stage has not achieved adequate ego development. Most often, this occurs because of severely disturbed parent-child relationships, failure to make friends, lack of success in school, an overcontrolling and critical environment, or basic abnormalities in a child's development because of some organic, constitutional cause, or some other yet unknown reason. Each or all of these factors may lead to a sense of shame and guilt, and stifle the child's initiative and his feelings of mastery and autonomy.

Phase 4

This phase lasts from the ages of seven to eleven. During these years, the child acquires a sense of industry and overcomes a sense of inferiority. This phase corresponds to Freud's latency phase and to Piaget's phase of concrete operations.

During these years, the child is very active; he tries in various ways to succeed in his tasks and to feel secure and accepted alike by adults and peers. Any failure is deeply disturbing to him. Children with developmental lags or established neurological dysfunction feel extremely threatened during this phase, because of the continuously widening demands of the environment, especially at school. Only if the teacher focuses on helping the child to establish or maintain an adequate self-concept can she hope to help him overcome any real or imagined defect or problem.

Phase 5

In this phase, the young person acquires a sense of identity while overcoming a sense of identity diffusion. Phase 5 does not concern the teacher for whom this book is written in her role of teacher, although it is of great concern for anybody working with youth. This period of prepuberty and puberty coincides with the beginning of Piaget's period of formal operations. During these years the child engages in a search for himself as a unique human being related to the world around him.

He adopts various roles with the aim of establishing a decision in relation to present and future roles. An educator speaking to the parents of junior high-school graduates said that these youngsters, thirteen to fifteen years old, know exactly and with certainty what they want to be and do when they are adults. And they change their opinion easily, having each day, hour, or week, a different opinion. The state of the preadolescent has never been more succinctly described.

Other Psychoanalytic Workers

Psychoanalytic theories of personality have also found further development by such brilliant writers and research workers as Jung (1933), Adler (1927), Fromm (1955), Horney (1937), Hartman (1958), Sullivan (1953), and others. The reason why Erikson has been singled out for more extensive discussion is that he is one of the most discussed in educational circles. It is impossible to include the discussion of the contributions of other followers of Freud in this book, but it is suggested that the reader glance through some of the references at the end of this chapter.

Implications of Psychoanalytic Thought

One important aspect of the relationship between psychoanalysis and education is the teacher's understanding of the child, particularly understanding the meaning of his behavior, and the relationship of teacher and child. Ekstein and Motto (1969)—both psychoanalysts—may be paraphrased in stating that a child, in order to learn, must first learn to love the teacher; he will therefore want to work because he wants to please the teacher; then he will begin to love the work itself. This is a point where there is disagreement between classical psychoanalysis, on the one hand, and developmental cognitive psychology and ego psychology, on the other. Piaget, Bruner, and other developmental psychologists emphasize that children are naturally curious and want to learn as a matter of course.

The authors are in only partial agreement with this view. The problem is that in addition to immediate intellectual insight, there is much learning that requires repetition, that is often not immediately gratifying to children. Rote learning is especially necessary for children who have learning difficulties and need to review certain skills again and again. Automatization of skills is especially difficult for most children with learning problems. Many a child's self-concept is shattered because he cannot remember that $6 \times 7 = 42$. Psychoanalysts emphasize the relationship of the child to the teacher as a tool through which the child is able to overcome his resistance to tedious and difficult tasks. The psychoanalyst is concerned with methods that improve the class-room climate and enhance the child's performance by developing his self-concept.

The child's self-concept must be considered the crucial factor in any child's success or failure. In remedial work the main task of the teacher may be the remediation of the self-concept. When a child is over-whelmed by anxiety about his performance, whether in school or at home, he cannot focus on a task. When a child feels that he is a worth-while human being, who respects himself and is respected by others, then his natural curiosity will enable him to concentrate on a task, and learning becomes possible.

Methods that the teacher can use to help enhance the child's self-concept are to provide him with experiences of success; to provide reassuring contacts between the teacher and the child and with the other children in the classroom; to gear tasks to the child's ability; and to show the child graphically what he has accomplished.

If emphasis is put on the psychoanalytic point of view, the classroom atmosphere will be characterized by mutual respect. The self-image hinges on the development of all psychological functions, and it is those functions that are also the concern of the educator (Frostig & Maslow, 1969). The child who feels inadequate because he cannot perform as well as other children needs to be helped to develop the required abilities, whatever they may be—memory for number facts, fine muscle control in order to hold a pencil, the visual-perceptual skills necessary for letter discrimination, or any other necessary ability. Another impor-tant way to help a child acquire a positive self-concept is to take his interests into account whenever possible in choosing subject matter.

Lili E. Peller (1969), a psychoanalyst, has summarized in the follow-ing few statements the principles of teaching that can be derived from psychoanalysis:

1. A child's intellectual and emotional development are interdepend-ent and must therefore be of equal concern to the teacher.
2. A child's relationship to his peers is of great importance to his future development.
3. A positive self-image is indispensable for normal psychological development.
4. A child needs to be active, to be an active learner. Play and work cannot be differentiated by the child, and the child is best moti-vated when work seems to him like play. The desire to explore,

the wish to achieve mastery and to be as good as another child, are important motivating factors. The child should always be aware of his progress.

The writer concludes (p. 268): "A school that leaves choices of many kinds to the student makes learning more efficient. I plead for such a school, not only for efficiency, but because the experience of commitment to serious work is more significant than any learning of content."

References

Adler, A. *The practice and theory of individual psychology.* New York: Harcourt, 1927.

Aichhorn, A. *Wayward youth.* Zurich: International Psychoanalytic Publishers, 1925.

Anthony, J., In R. Ekstein and L. Motto (Eds.) *From learning for love to love of learning: Essays on psychoanalysis and education.* New York: Brunner/Mazel, 1969.

Bettelheim, B. *Love is not enough.* Glencoe, Ill.: Free Press, 1950.

Bowlby, J. *Child care and the growth of love.* London: Penguin Books, 1953.

Brenner, C. *An elementary textbook of psychoanalysis.* Garden City, N.Y.: Doubleday Anchor, 1957.

Ekstein, R., & Motto, L. (Eds.). *From Learning for love to love of learning: Essays on psychoanalysis and education.* New York: Brunner/Mazel, 1969.

Engelmann, S. *Preventing failure in the primary grades.* New York: Simon & Schuster, 1969.

Erikson, E. H., *Childhood and society.* 2nd ed. New York: Norton, 1963.

Fraiberg, S. *The magic years: Understanding and handling the problems of early childhood.* New York: Scribner's, 1959.

Freud, A. *Psychoanalysis for teachers and parents.* Boston: Beacon Press, 1935.

Freud, A. *The ego and mechanisms of defense* (3rd ed.). New York: International Universities Press, 1946.

Freud, A. *Normality and pathology in childhood.* New York: International Universities Press, 1965.

Fromm, E. *The sane society.* New York: Rinehart, 1955.

Frostig, M., & Maslow, P. Treatment methods and their evaluation in educational therapy. In J. Hellmuth (Ed.), *Educational therapy,* Vol. 2. Seattle, Wash.: Special Child Publications, 1969.

Glasser, W. *Schools without failure*. New York: Harper, 1969.

Harlow, H. H., & Soumi, S. J. Nature of love—simplified. *American Psychologist*, 1970, 25(2), 161–168.

Hartmann, H. *Ego psychology and the problem of adaptation*. New York: International Universities Press, 1958.

Hill, J. A. A case of retarded development associated with restricted movements in infancy. *British Journal of Medical Psychology*, 1930, 3:68.

Horney, K. *Neurotic personality of our times*. New York: Norton, 1937.

Jung, C. G. *Modern man in search of a soul*. New York: Harcourt, 1933.

Kris, E. The psychology of caricature. *Psychoanalytic explorations in art*. New York: International Universities Press, 1952, pp. 173–188.

Neill, A. S. *Summerhill*. New York: Hart Publishing Co., 1960.

Peller, L. In R. Ekstein and L. Motto (Eds.) *From learning for love to love of learning: Essays on psychoanalysis and education*. New York: Brunner/Mazel, 1969.

Piaget, J., & Inhelder, B. *The psychology of the child*. New York: Basic Books, 1969.

Rank, O. *The trauma of birth*. New York: Harcourt, 1929.

Redl, F., & Wineman, D. *Controls from within*. New York: Free Press, 1952.

Richardson, S. In R. Ekstein and L. Motto (Eds.) *From learning for love to love of learning: Essays on psychoanalysis and education*. New York: Brunner/Mazel, 1969.

Solnit, A. J. In R. Ekstein and L. Motto (Eds.) *From learning to love to love of learning: Essays on psychoanalysis and education*. New York: Brunner/Mazel, 1969.

Spitz, R. *The first years of life*. New York: International Universities Press, 1965.

Sullivan, H. S. *The interpersonal theory of psychiatry*. New York: Norton, 1953.

White, R. W. Ego and reality in psychoanalytic theory. *Psychoanalytic Issues*, 1963, 3(3, Whole No. 11).

Winnicott, D. W. *Playing and reality*. New York: Basic Books, 1971.

8

COGNITIVE DEVELOPMENTAL CONCEPTS

We hear so much about psychology, and our daily lives are so influenced by psychological considerations—in our art forms, school teaching, industrial management, and so on—that it is sometimes difficult to realize that psychology is really a very new science. Even what we know today about child development is very new.

The first European student to systematize findings in the various aspects of child development, so that a developmental scale could be developed, is Charlotte Bühler, who preceded Gesell in this country. Both Bühler and Gessell were interested in the total development of the young child, whereas Heinz Werner, a follower of the Gestalt school of psychology, and Karl Bühler (Charlotte Bühler's husband) were mainly concerned with the cognitive aspects.

Werner has had a considerable impact on the education of the child with learning problems. His book, *Comparative Psychology of Mental Development* (1957), includes observations that are invaluable to anyone interested in the field. It constitutes a summary and revision of many of his previous studies, among them being his exploration of the perceptual processes of normal children, of children with learning difficulties, and of retarded children. Werner brought about a new understanding of the role of perception and the treatment of perceptual disturbances. In a long series of experiments, he and his colleagues demonstrated the interdependence of movement, emotion, and perception in human development. He also showed that children who were unable to perceive accurately or remember a visual sequence, could be helped to do so if they were taught by a method that involved movement. He investigated figure-ground perception and various kinds of perceptual constancies, employing such devices as the marble board and tests of embedded figures, which are still widely used.

Two Main Principles of Development

Heinz Werner, who, like most of the early developmentalists, was
greatly influenced by Gestalt psychology, has formulated the two main
principles of development—differentiation and hierarchization. *Differentiation* means that global characteristics are split into more specific
subgroups. For instance, whereas the infant only exhibits affective
states of rage, fear, and satisfaction, the adult undergoes innumerable
emotions—delight, surprise, excitement, elation, remorse, despair, disappointment, and so on. *Hierarchization* means that characteristics can be
grouped in subordinate, coordinate, and superordinate categories and
that the emergence of some categories depends upon others.

Both principles are applicable to teaching practices. The principle of
differentiation is applied, for example, when a teacher helps a child
apply his skill to throwing a ball in a number of different ways—overhand, underhand, while running or dodging, forcibly or gently, with a
football or baseball, and so on. Such diversified practice helps the
child not only to improve his throwing skill in general, but also to
apply it appropriately.

Hierarchization requires an order in the mastery of certain skills. A
child, for example, must be able to maintain his balance while standing
or walking erect before he can learn to stand on one foot, stand on a
narrow beam, balance on a hand and a foot, balance his body while
walking on tiptoes, and so on. Similarly he must know how to count
before he can learn to add, subtract, multiply, or divide.

Both differentiation and hierarchization are tacitly recognized by the
teacher who first teaches the primary colors, then orange and purple,
and finally shades like magenta, ocher, and siena.

The Contributions of Piaget

Any discussion of the cognitive-developmental point of view must
focus on its major contemporary proponent, Piaget. He is the undisputed leader in the study of the development of cognitive functions, if
not in the entire discipline of child psychology. His influence on education has steadily grown although he himself has developed no educational methods.

While the early students of child development showed particular
interest in various delineated aspects of development, Piaget and his
students attempted to develop a coherent picture of the total cognitive
development of the child, of how the child "constructs reality." (See,

for example, Piaget, 1954.) The development of the child's intelligence begins with sensation and movement (sensory-motor intelligence), and the child learns that the world around him has permanence. Piaget describes the child's expanding understanding of events and of change, and how the child learns to bring about change himself.

There are four concepts that are basic to understanding Piaget's view: decentration, assimilation, accommodation, and equilibration. Underlying all of them is the belief that the child's mind itself is an active agent; even the mind of the infant does not merely register stimuli or react habitually. The mind has certain ways of responding to stimuli. These basic ways of "grasping" events and of reacting to them are called structures, or schemas. They determine the interaction with the environment. (See Chapter 16, p. 240–241.)

When the child's attention is focused on an external event, he first attempts to incorporate it, to assimilate it into his pre-existing structures. That is to say, he tries to understand it and adapt to it in the light of his existing repertoire of mental structures (the understandings and actions he has learned to apply automatically). When, for example, a baby feels an object touch his lips, he immediately sucks; he expects the object to be assimilated into his schema of sucking. But objects have different qualities—not all give milk. The infant *accommodates* (changes, generalizes) his schema of sucking according to the object. He learns to discriminate between his bottle, his thumb, and his rattle, as evidenced by differences in the rate and strength of sucking. Later he coordinates several schemas into a more complex one; for instance, he may combine the schema of bottle sucking with the schema of watching his mother's face and listening to her voice. His experiences become integrated.

Assimilation and accommodation are processes that continue throughout life. At each developmental level the modes of the processes change —from the sensory-motor level of the infant to the perceptual processes of the child at the age at which he begins school, to the beginnings of abstract logical thought in the pre-adolescent.

According to Piaget, all behavior entails *assimilation* (perceiving, knowing, and understanding) of reality, which always occurs in relation to prior schemata; simultaneously all behavior is an *accommodation* (application and adjustment) of these schemata to the actual situation.

When assimilation and accommodation are in balance, an equilibrium is achieved. All behavior tends toward assuring an equilibrium. This balance is not achieved once and for all, however, but is the result of a continuous interaction of assimilation and accommodation. It is a dynamic life process.

The terms *assimilation, accommodation,* and *equilibrium* are taken from biology; and the concept of equilibrium is a biological one refer-ring to a balance between internal and external factors. A certain amount of food, of fluid, of rest, of movement, is necessary to assure the body's physiological equilibrium. When Piaget (1967) speaks of an equilibrium in relation to mental phenomena, he refers to the balance and continuous interaction between assimilating experiences into the cognitive schemas (perception, knowledge, understanding, are roughly equivalent to cognitive schemas) and accommodating (roughly, adapt-ing to a new situation).

For Piaget, the striving toward equilibrium is the dynamic force behind all learning and all development. We long to understand; we need to adapt and use reality. This driving process, termed *equilibra-tion*, propels change. Thus, in Piaget's theory of development, motiva-tion is intrinsic—it is the biologic nature of the child to strive for equilibrium, therefore to achieve greater balance in knowing and act-ing. As the child matures, he generally becomes increasingly better able to meet the demands of his environment. The child only achieves a more or less permanent equilibrium at or close to puberty.

How can the teacher further this progress toward equilibrium? It can be enhanced by bringing the child face to face with his errors in the interpretation of reality and by helping him to integrate new experi-ences and learning with previous ones.

One of Piaget's most fruitful concepts in relation to education is *decentration*. Decentration is the antithesis of centering. Centering refers to the focusing of attention on a specific part or attribute of a situation to the exclusion of other parts. The child, for instance, may focus on the length of a Plasticine object and not on its thickness; therefore he may well believe that when "the snake" he rolls out be-comes longer he has more Plasticine. Perceiving the relationship between attributes requires decentration, the ability to shift from sub-ordinate to coordinate to superordinate categories in classifying objects. For example, a child needs to be able to decenter to understand that a frog and a salamander are both amphibians, that amphibians are a branch of the reptiles, and that the reptiles are a branch of the verte-brates. Decentration is required in shifting the basis of classification; e.g., when a child first sorts blocks according to form and then sorts the same blocks according to color. Decentration is also required for multi-ple classification; it is involved, for example, in sorting blocks varying in size, color, and shape according to all three attributes (e.g., the large blue circles, the small yellow triangles, and so on). Perceiving the reversibility of processes also requires decentration. A child may know that $2 + 4 = 6$. To understand that therefore $6 - 4 = 2$ requires adopt-ing another point of view in examining the same number relationship.

The concept of decentration has wide-reaching implications for social life as well as for cognition. A person who cannot decentrate is bound to one rigid view; he cannot mentally shift his position and see the same situation from another's viewpoint. He can only understand and accept those having outlooks coincident with his own. He may get in trouble with most of his classmates because he hurts their feelings, or even hurts them bodily, because he can only perceive that they interfere with what he wants to do and does not see how he affects them and interferes with their activities.

Not only decentration, but all the concepts discussed above, are based on the child's own actions in his encounters with his physical and social environment. Piaget states that only through his own activity can the child understand and adapt to reality. The implications of this for educational practice are far-reaching and profound.

Representative Functions

Piaget defines representation as follows (1962, p. 67): "In its broader sense representation is identical with thought, i.e., with all intelligence which is based on a system of concepts, on mental schemas, and not merely a perception of actions." He continues: "With words, thoughts, and images, gestures and movements, a human being can represent (express) what he knows and feels about himself and the world around him." In its narrower sense, representation is restricted to the mental or memory image, i.e., the symbolic evocation* of absent realities; the child remembers aspects of the world that are not present to the senses at the time the image is retrieved.

The child first begins to imitate movements of others during the second half year of life. He plays pat-a-cake, waves good-bye, repeats sounds. A six-month-old infant, however, does so only if a model is presented. But from these imitations of immediately perceived actions, the child learns to form mental images. When his actions show (at twelve to eighteen months) that he "remembers" an object not present to his senses (acquisition of the schema of the permanent object), he has acquired the first form of representation—the mental image. At about the same time his play begins to imitate past actions—movements no longer present. He reenacts what happens when Daddy drives the car or Mommy bakes a cake. This is another form of representation— deferred imagery.

During this period also, the child's language functions develop apace.

* Literally "calling up" in the mind, voluntarily forming mental pictures.

Imagery and imaginative play (deferred imitation) are representations that are private and unique to the child; they can be formed in isolation. In contrast to imagery, language can only be acquired through social interaction.

Soviet psychologists, particularly Vygotsky (1962) and Luria (1961), have explored the ways in which language controls or determines actions and its relationship to thought. Like Piaget, Vygotsky believes that thought is based on action, and that sensory-motor schemas are the first forms of intelligence. The early use of language remains apart from thought; language is used only to communicate basic feelings or needs. But as the persons in the child's environment use language to direct his attention to relevant stimuli and to guide his actions, the child increasingly interiorizes the language and uses it to guide his own thinking. Vygotsky has pointed out the way young children frequently carry on a monologue with themselves as they go about their work or play. We have all smiled at the child who puts his hand in the cookie jar while saying, "No, bad boy. Mommy says 'don't do that.'" Such speech, at the age of four or five, has become *inner speech* (thought).

Piaget acknowledges the role of language in social communication and its usefulness for memory functions, as well as its contribution to thought. He insists, however, that thought is separate from language and develops prior to it.

Piaget's studies of imagery illustrate how thought processes (operations) determine the ways in which representation (imitation, imagery, and language) can be used. During the preoperative stage (from approximately eighteen months to seven years), the child's images appear to be more or less complete reconstructions of events or objects in the outside world. But they are static reconstructions—that is, they are like snapshots. As the child learns to decenter his perceptual encounters— that is, to scan the entire figure and to analyze its parts—his images become more complete "copies" of the original. Not until the child is seven or eight years old, however, when he has entered the stage of concrete operations and his mental operations are reversible (he can go back to the starting point after a mental or physical process or action), can he imagine movement and change in his images (kinetic and anticipatory imagery). For instance, Piaget and Inhelder (1971), showed children two squares, one on top of the other (in A, below), and asked them to choose from a set of three pictures (B) the one that showed the upper square displaced to the right. Many children between the ages of four and seven were unable to choose the correct one. Young children were also unable to imagine the sequence and results of a series of movements (Piaget and Inhelder, 1971).

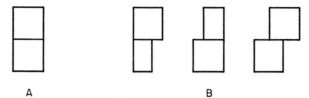

A   B

All major theories concerned with imagery stress the development of imagery from movement. Because movement integrates temporal and spatial relations, the image is a powerful form of representation. Piaget (Piaget and Inhelder, 1971, p. 390) calls it an "indispensable auxiliary in the functioning of the very dynamism of thought." Not only Piaget, but Hebb (1968), employing neurophysiological constructs, and Zaporozhets (1965), a Russian exploring movement and language, stress that imagery is internalized imitation. Planning and problem-solving depend on the use of images that can be (mentally) changed and transformed.

Cognitive Development Theory in the Classroom

The central role of the child's own actions in developing intellectual structures is the recurring theme in the work of the cognitive-developmental psychologists, particularly Piaget.

In the young child, physical activity is essential, because he has to learn both to perceive and to check the correctness of his own perceptions through handling objects and through body movement. Language is essential because it assists thought, although it is not the origin of thought.

This point of view makes a particular kind of school environment necessary—a classroom structure that promotes and fosters activity of all kinds: exploration, object manipulation, and self-direction. Opportunities for social interaction are also essential, because experiences can be thereby compared and pooled. The use of oral and written language for communication and the recording and discussion of observations make certain that the use of language in a variety of forms assists the optimum development of thought.

The cognitive-developmental point of view emphasizes the teaching of a curriculum that is adapted to the child's changing level of abilities during the formative years, as well as teaching methods that are in accord with the child's natural mode of interacting with the world around him. Body movement is essential for all learning during the sensory-motor phase (infancy to about one and a half or two years of age). During the period of maximum language development (from one and a half to about three years of age), the child needs to listen to verbal interpretation of what he experiences. For instance, his mother may say, "Johnny, here is the pudding you like. It tastes sweet and cool and creamy, doesn't it?" Language becomes increasingly more effective in guiding his actions. When Johnny reaches for his mother's spoon, he may stop if his mother says, "No, that is my spoon. You use your spoon." Physical action remains, however, one of the most important tools of learning.

The next phase (from three and a half to about seven and a half years of age) is the phase of maximum perceptual development. Ideally, language, action, and perception will all assist the child in learning. The child needs to continue to be active and explore at the same time that the teacher promotes language in every possible way, helping the child to perfect the use of this relatively new tool for symbolic expression. As pictorial representation becomes increasingly meaningful, he will be able to understand simple maps, graphs, and so on.

At all levels, new learning should be taught by methods that recapitulate the sequence from active movement to abstract symbols. The child should first manipulate, then only perceive, and finally represent with symbols what he is studying. He should experiment with and manipulate objects, then look at pictures or listen to explanations, and then use symbols to encode (write down), graph, or illustrate what he has learned. The teacher does not give a verbal abstract rule* but guides the child's manipulative activities to help him experience it for himself. For instance, in order to understand that the number of objects in a set is not changed by their spatial arrangement (conservation of numbers)** the child should be helped to perceive many different sets of objects of a given amount in many different patterns, and he should manipulate the objects in these sets. The teacher can help him to count the objects and record what he has experienced.

Cognitive-developmental theory states that the curriculum must be adjusted to the child's developmental level. No learning will take place if the task is too easy or too difficult. Vygotsky (1962), in agreement

---

* Piaget states that before the age of about eleven or twelve, children are unable to apply general rules consistently. For example, a child of seven or eight may be able to recite the spelling rule, "I before E except after C," but be unable to apply it during a spelling test.

** Conservation of numbers refers to the ability to perceive numbers as independent of the kind of objects counted and of their spatial or temporal arrangement. For example, this set o o o o and this set o o o o o o are equal in number.

with Piaget, states that instruction must somewhat precede development.

A teacher who successfully applies Piaget's principles in the classroom ensures that the child has a variety of experiences to illustrate a common principle. As discussed earlier, the principle of diversified practice is important from a neurophysiological point of view. The cognitive developmentalist also points to the importance of diversified practice. He sees it as being necessary for the wider application of basic maturational achievements. For instance, number concepts must be applied to many objects and many situations before they can be used effectively when needed.

Piaget uses the term *horizontal decalage* to refer to the fact that children do not automatically apply learned principles to new materials and situations. They must be exposed to many experiences to achieve transfer, and the common elements in each situation must be pointed out to them.

Piaget's position that motivation is intrinsic (see above, p. 90) implies that the teacher's role is to help the child satisfy his curiosity and make learning meaningful. Meaning always derives from the perception of relationships. It is achieved by referring past learning and past experiences to current experiences and future goals. The presentation of subject matter has therefore to be so structured that each successive experience can be related to and built upon what the child already learned or is currently learning.

The meaning of what has been learned is also enhanced through reference to the child's wider environment. The child needs to understand what he is learning in relation to his culture, his values, his daily experiences. This does not mean that his learning need be trite. For example, a discussion about a visit to the supermarket can be made meaningful if the child learns about the services connected with food distribution or the way people get food in other climates or what would happen if there were no grocery stores. All learning should be a window toward a wider world, and all learning should open up further avenues for thought.

WORKS CITED

Bühler, C., & Hetzer, H. *Kleinkinder tests* (3rd ed.). Munich: Joh. Barth, 1961. (First published 1927). See also Bühler, C. *The first year of life.* New York: Day, 1930.

Bühler, K. *Die geistige Entwichlung des kindes.* Jena: G. Fischer, 1927.

Hebb, D. O. Concerning imagery. *Psychological Review*, 1968, 75, 466–477.

Luria, A. R. *The role of speech in the regulation of normal and abnormal behavior*. London: Pergamon, 1961.

Piaget, J. *The construction of reality in the child*. New York: Basic Books, 1954.

Piaget, J. *Play, dreams and imitation in childhood*. New York: Norton, 1962.

Piaget, J. *Six psychological studies*. New York: Random House, 1967.

Piaget, J., & Inhelder, B. *Mental imagery in the child*. New York: Basic Books, 1971.

Vygotsky, L. S. *Thought and language*. Cambridge, Mass.: Massachusetts Institute of Technology Press, 1962.

Werner, H. *Comparative psychology of mental development* (Rev. ed.). New York: International Universities Press, 1957.

Zaporozhets, A. V. The development of perception in the preschool child. In P. Mussen (Ed.), European research in cognitive development. *Monographs of the Society for Research in Child Development*, 1965, 30(2, Serial No. 100).

TABLE 1

Comparison of Implications of Behavior
Modification, Humanistic Psychology, Psychoanalysis,
and Cognitive-Developmental Psychology for Education.

	Individualization	Motivation
Behavior Modification	Individualization of task assignment taking the child's level of functioning into account. Individualization of rewards and of discipline.	The child's interests and needs are not accepted as a "given"; they are to be changed and manipulated, whenever this seems of advantage. A reward system motivates the child. Motivation is extrinsic. Rewards may be material, social, or fulfill other needs. In contrast to psychoanalysis and humanism, satisfaction of needs is the consequence and not the precondition of learning.
Humanistic Psychology	Individualization of total approach according to needs and individuality of child, on an intuitive basis as a consequence of shared experience.	Satisfaction of needs is necessary for optimum learning ability. The child's need for experience, his wish to be helpful and to communicate with others—in short, social motives and need for experience —are emphasized. Motivation is mainly intrinsic.
Psychoanalysis	Individualization in relation to differences of needs and maturational level, task assignments, personal relationships, and total approach.	Satisfaction of needs regarded as the prime source of motivation ("the pleasure principle"). Needs for love, security, and mastery and emotional and social needs must be satisfied before energy and interests are available for learning. Motivation is both extrinsic and intrinsic.
Cognitive-Developmental Psychology	Adaptation of tasks to child's developmental stage and previous experiences.	Interests are the expression of a "drive" toward equilibrium. Knowing is a motive in itself. Motivation is intrinsic. The need for equilibrium is as compelling as physiological needs.

TABLE 1 (Continued)

	Degree of Systematization	Methodology
Behavior Modification	Very specific methods of classroom management and teaching are prescribed. Systematization is emphasized. Programmed material is suggested.	Extensive and detailed methods and sequences to develop skills and specific knowledge are advocated. Use of computer and other machine technology to assist teacher.
Humanistic Psychology	A balanced curriculum and balance between freedom and discipline is advocated. Recognition of developmental progression is only one of the factors to be taken into account in adjusting to the child's needs. The teacher must be attuned to the child's intellectual, emotional, and social needs.	Emphasis on integrated project approach, with particular stress on social studies.
Psychoanalysis	Systematization is not especially stressed; the classroom environment must be stable but flexible. Teaching takes developmental level of child into account. Curriculum usually shows progressive steps, except in the type of school like Summerhill.	No special developments or innovations, except in the type of school like Summerhill where total freedom prevails.
Congitive- Developmental Psychology	Progress in teaching is systematic, but classroom environment free enough for exploration and discovery. Theory of cognitive development results in definite teaching approaches suitable for the child's developmental level.	Materials and curricula to develop basic cognitive skills, such as classification, seriation, conservation, imagery, and problem-solving have been developed, as well as specific curricula in science, math, and social studies.

TABLE 1 (Continued)

	Curricular Objectives	Form of Classroom Management
Behavior Modification	Focus on academic knowledge and skills and on socially defined personal and social behavior characteristics.	Teacher-centered. The teacher prescribes curriculum and classroom procedures. Social relationships are not emphasized as goals but utilized as means.
Humanistic Psychology	Focus on social development, communication skills, and sensitivity to beauty and other humanistic values. The child's sensitivity to group needs as well as to individual needs is to be enhanced. Social influences are more emphasized than biological ones. The goal is optimum interrelationship with the environment, not adjustment.	Child-centered. The teacher assists child but does not direct him in his learning. The classroom structure permits freedom of choice for the child and fosters creativity and exploration. The importance of human relationships is recognized. The classroom situation permits and should foster social learning.
Psychoanalysis	Focus on emotional development, communication skills, and social institutions. Social interaction is used as a tool to further emotional growth. Academic knowledge and skills are tools to achieve the main objectives of later mature adjustment.	Opinions among this group vary. In certain schools it is partly child-centered, with the roles of teacher and child specified in relation to each other. The teacher's role includes her influence on character formation and adjustment of the child. In others, a Summerhill-like atmosphere prevails, and the school is totally child-centered. The value of peer relationships is emphasized.
Cognitive-Developmental Psychology	Focus on total development: sensory-motor, language, and cognitive. Social interaction serves as a tool to develop decentration, intelligence, and logical thought.	Child-centered. The teacher assists the child and guides him in his learning, explorations, and discovery. The classroom structure permits and fosters self-direction.

TABLE 1 (Continued)

	Making Teaching Meaningful	Active Participation
Behavior Modification	Emphasis is usually not on integration of topics but rather on a linear progression in teaching content and skills. Behaviorists are not concerned with "meaning" except as meaning is derived from understanding previous steps. Mastery is emphasized in behavioristic terms of specific mastery of subject matter or adjustment to classroom demands. Mastery or attainment of extraneous rewards makes learning meaningful.	Behaviorists are little concerned with activity, except if the activity is the behavior to be elicited. The child may be a rather passive recipient of knowledge, and should follow directions. The behavior is shaped, not guided.
Humanistic Psychology	As in psychoanalytically influenced teaching, meaning derives from integration of topics and relating the content to child's personal needs. Additional emphasis is put on human needs in general, on creativity and involvement, and on developing the child's feeling of "being in the world" and awareness of the world around him.	Experience requires action. The child needs to relate himself actively to the environment and to share with others in common activities. Also, the child's need for play and activity has to be satisfied.

TABLE 1 (Continued)

	Making Teaching Meaningful	Active Participation
Psychoanalysis	Meaningfulness of material taught is achieved through integration of topics, and by relating topics to satisfaction of the child's past experiences, present needs, and future goals. In certain schools, the child chooses the topic he wants to study and even whether or not he wants to learn.	Activity is deemed necessary, first, because it is the mode in which younger children can best express thoughts and feelings. Activity, including play, also helps the child to understand and to adjust to the environment. Finally, the physiologic need for movement has to be satisfied.
Cognitive-Developmental Psychology	Integration of knowledge is emphasized. Integration is not merely achieved by associations between thoughts or between contents of curricula or by addition of new knowledge. The hierarchical order of concepts and skills must be grasped to make meaningful what has been learned. Concepts are related to other coordinated, supraordinated, and subordinated concepts.	Activity is regarded as the basis of all mental development. The child learns by exploring and experimenting. In new learning, he proceeds from activity (enactive learning) to perceptual learning (iconic) and then to symbolic learning. To make symbolic learning possible, he must learn to read, write, make graphs, use mathematical language, etc.

TABLE 1 (Continued)

	Use of Early Symbolic Abilities (not including language)	Language Instruction
Behavior Modification	The topic of symbolic play and imagery has not been discussed by behaviorists, as these are activities which are not at all or only partly overt. Repetition, modified repetition, and imitating a model are methods used extensively in teaching.	The approach to language teaching is structured. Syntax, vocabulary, and articulation are taught specifically. Imitation is used in the teaching of language, as well as modified imitation and the learning of rules. Correct use of language is the goal of language instruction, and includes oral and written language.
Humanistic Psychology	Experience involves imagery. Empathy requires imagery and is developed by imagining playing another person's role. Imagery is basic to all understanding and must be developed; one method is symbolic (dramatic) play.	Language is developed through use of creative language, poems, story-writing, and dramatic play. Expressions of feelings and ideas are furthered. Language includes body language, gestures, and creative expression.
Psychoanalysis	Imagery and role-taking are forms of learning. Imaginative and symbolic play assist the child in adjusting to reality and in his emotional growth. Imitation helps the child to learn behavior patterns.	Language is enhanced through social contacts and small group learning. Little formal teaching of language. Reading and writing are introduced late. The child is taught to substitute language for "acting out" in achieving need satisfaction.
Cognitive-Developmental Psychology	Imitation, symbolic play, and imagery are basic to symbolic behavior. Imitation and symbolic play are therefore utilized in instruction. Development of images (kinetic and anticipatory) must occur prior to logical thought and can be developed through planning and self-direction.	Language and thought cannot be separated in instruction. Language is the most important form of symbolic expression. Language needs to be used to describe and explain action. Written language is taught very early, together with beginning reading.

TABLE 1 (Continued)

	Rote versus Insight Learning	Goals
Behavior Modification	Rote learning and associational learning in small steps are emphasized. Skills are greatly emphasized.	A person able to fill a job well or to continue with his education because he has mastered skills and knowledge taught on a lower level. Competence is the goal of education.
Humanistic Psychology	Emphasis is on insight learning and understanding, in contrast to mere acquisition of knowledge.	A loving, creative human being with a strong social conscience, aware of the needs of others, feeling fulfilled, and helping others to feel fulfilled. Self-fulfillment and understanding are the goals of education.
Psychoanalysis	Emphasis is on insight learning and understanding. The importance of understanding current behavior in light of the child's previous experiences is also stressed.	A person free of neuroticism and not suppressed by cultural demands who is socially aware and responsive, cherishes human values, is self-assured, and feels enriched by his culture, to which he adjusts and attempts to contribute. Adjustment and interaction with society are both goals of education.
Cognitive-Developmental Psychology	Emphasis is on insight learning and understanding.	A person who has optimally developed his cognitive functions and who is innovative and flexible in his thought processes. Most important, he is a person who can decentrate, especially by taking into account the points of view of others as well as all possible outcomes in making decisions and carrying out actions. Intelligence used equally well in decisions pertaining both to oneself and to others is the goal of education.

PART III

9

CHILD
DEVELOPMENT
AND EDUCATION

It is self-evident that during his formative years a child changes so much that every aspect of education—the *how*, *why*, and *what* of the subject matter to be taught—depends at any given moment on the child's developmental level. The teacher and auxiliary school personnel must, therefore, repeatedly evaluate the child in order to adjust their educational efforts to his changing interests, capabilities, and learning style. Throughout this discussion, the authors have preferred to use the term *programming* rather than curriculum because *curriculum* usually refers to the set selection of subject matter that is to be taught at a particular age or grade level, as when we refer to "the science curriculum for the third grade," for example; the curriculum in this sense is usually specified by local authorities or state decree, and therefore any discussion of it is outside the sphere of this book. The term *programming*, however, refers to the individualization of the curriculum—its adjustment to a student's individual differences, capabilities, needs, and preferred style of learning. It does not refer to a preconceived step-by-step progression or to prepackaged materials.

The phrase *developmental level* refers, of course, to the ongoing changes in all aspects of a child's growth and behavior—his movements, perceptual abilities, language, thought processes, feelings, and social adjustment. In discussing a child's development, the authors have placed their emphasis on the relation of the child's communicative and cognitive development to school learning.

Cognitive development can be understood as a continuous progression in which various changes of magnitude and complexity take place (Burt, 1954; Isaacs, 1930). But in recent decades it has become increasingly accepted that cognitive development is not a continuous process but occurs in identifiable stages.

The Developmental Sequence

The characteristics that a child acquires during the first stage of his development are integrated with the abilities that evolve during the next stage, and each later phase continues in this pattern, with the most recent stage modifying and changing, and being modified and changed by, what has been acquired during earlier phases.

Observations of the course of development of the so-called normal child has led both to the formulation of principles valid for all children and to the recognition that there are also innumerable individual differences. A multitude of measurements and other evaluative procedures have been needed in order to distinguish both the universal characteristics of development, and the ways in which one individual differs from another.

The study of the development of the healthy child has been further complemented by the study of pathological deviations from, or slow development in, the orderly evolution of psychological functions. Such deviations and lags may occur after trauma or illness, or may be due to genetic factors. The study of abnormalities has shown that a global measurement, such as the I.Q., is insufficient for evaluating a child's ability to master his environment. Children with difficulties in learning and adjustment are often found to be superior in certain psychological functions, although deficient in others. This unevenness in development applies to a lesser degree to all children, and need not be regarded as pathological, but if the unevenness is exaggerated, it can have ill effects. If a child with slightly lagging abilities cannot achieve according to expectations in any of his tasks, he may feel himself to be inadequate and inferior and his entire subsequent course of development may be distorted. Such occurrences will become increasingly frequent if the present trend toward beginning to teach academic subjects at an ever earlier age continues. Early diagnosis of mental lags is therefore important.

The major groups of psychological abilities need to be evaluated both individually and in relation to each other for all children, not only those with learning difficulties. Detailed observation will provide the educator with the knowledge on which to base the optimum individualized program. She needs to know a child's strengths so that she can capitalize on them; she also must know what the child's weaknesses are—his lags or deficits—so that she can try to ameliorate them.

Knowledge of child development also helps the educator to develop a curriculum. At some stages of development it may be impossible (or possible only after great difficulty) for a child to learn concepts that could later be easily mastered. On the other hand, it may prove more difficult to ameliorate deficits in each group of abilities after the peak period of development has passed. Thus a curriculum based on knowledge of the developmental sequence may well concentrate more on language and perceptual skills at the preschool and beginning-school level, on content learning and learning academic skills during the elementary-school years, and on theories and logic in the secondary-school years. Knowledge of the developmental sequence will also influence classroom management.

Four Developmental Phases

Most modern theorists of child development distinguish definite stages, and specialists and laymen alike have no difficulty in agreeing on these major divisions. Everyone is aware of four major temporal divisions during a person's formative years: infancy; the preschool period; the period roughly corresponding to the time a child attends elementary school; and finally pubescence and adolescence.

Four broad areas of human abilities also have their periods of maximum development at fairly predictable ages. These four areas are the sensory-motor functions, language, perception, and higher cognitive processes. All four of them also contribute to cognition—to knowing and understanding the self and the environment.

The Sensory-Motor Phase

The first group of functions to develop are the sensory-motor functions, which develop maximally between birth and about two years of age.

The phrase *sensory-motor functions* denotes the child's method of exploring himself and his world, using all the senses and movement simultaneously. He explores an object by handling it, licking it, biting it, sucking it, throwing it, or trying to bang it, hide it, retrieve it, change its location, make sounds with it, and so on. Through these simultaneous activities, the child develops four distinct groups of sensory-motor skills. The first two groups emphasize awareness—awareness of the self and awareness of the environment. As a baby becomes aware of the outside world and learns to recognize many features of his environment, he also becomes aware of himself as distinct from his environment. The two other groups pertain to movement—the ability to move in space and the ability to move objects. The child's ability to move in space involves learning to shift his body position—from lying to sitting, for example, or from standing to kneeling—and to change his location, by crawling, walking, running, and so on. The final group of skills involves the child's ability to change the form and placement of objects. The child learns to grasp, hold, release, squeeze, pull, tear, and manipulate objects in various ways. The mastery of these sensory-motor skills constitutes the child's first steps toward independence and future learning.

The sensory-motor functions, which develop during the first twelve to eighteen months, are a necessary basis for the child's ability to discriminate sights and sounds and to focus attention. During this phase, the child learns to grasp spatial location and time sequences and sequential order through the acquisition of movement patterns and expectations concerning the results of his own actions.* Such learning is a prerequisite for the acquisition of language because the development of language (oral, written, printed) is sequential.**

Phase of Maximum Language Development

All normal children, regardless of culture or social class, acquire some form of language. Moreover, certain categories or features of language are acquired in the same invariant order. Children usually utter their first words when they are from ten to fourteen months old, combine words from eighteen to twenty-four months, and use and understand almost all the grammatical structures of their native language when they are from forty to fifty months. Maximum growth in the development of both receptive and expressive language occurs between the ages of twelve to eighteen months and three to four years.

The child's language development is fostered by, and even to a degree dependent upon, experiences and perceptions shared with adults, and the more empathetic adults are with the child's thoughts and feelings, the greater will be the child's interest and verbal ability.

By the time a normal child is approximately five years old, he is able to understand and use a few thousand words and almost all the syntactical forms of his language. By this age, also, the child is able to use "inner speech," or internalized language, as a guide to action (Luria, 1961). This is also the age at which many children first go to school.

---

* In Piaget's terms, he develops a sense of time and sequential order based on sensory-motor schemata.

** Language also involves reordering parts (words) or "subassemblies" into new combinations for a definite purpose. For example, "The boy bit the dog" and "The dog bit the boy" use the same words; the very different meaning is conveyed by the changed order. Bruner's research (1972) indicates that the human infant, unlike other primate infants, is able to recombine sensory-motor schemata, or "subassemblies," in a flexible goal-oriented way.

The course of early language development depends upon the inter-action of biological, social, cognitive, and affective influences. If any one of these deviates from the norm, language development will tend to be affected—either retarded or accelerated. Remediation or amelio-ration of language deficits must therefore take these factors into account.

Phase of Maximum Perceptual Development

Perceptual functions develop maximally during the period from approx-imately three and a half or four to seven or seven and a half years of age. From birth on, the child has at least a limited ability to dis-criminate and recognize stimuli present in the environment; during infancy he learns to understand and adapt to his world through the simultaneous use of his own senses and movements. Now looking and listening (the use of the distance receptors, the eyes and ears) become the main channels for understanding the environment.

Visual Perception

Although infants can distinguish between circles and other geometric forms cut out of wood or other material, perception of two-dimensional space does not develop until much later. Piaget and Inhelder (1956), for example, found that young preschool children could accurately dis-tinguish two-dimensional figures only on the basis of whether they were closed or open; i.e., according to the topology of the figure. Differen-tiation of two-dimensional Euclidian geometrical figures, such as the square, rectangle, and parallelogram, that requires comparison of lengths of sides, width of angles, and so on, is not achieved until children are four years old or older.

A child may be able to perceive some feature of an object and yet ignore it because it has no meaning for him; that is, it helps him neither to adjust to his environment nor to master some aspect of it. Young children can discriminate between two objects that have different spatial orientations (i.e., are turned different ways), but spatial orien-tation has no personal meaning in most of their experiences. It is more adaptive and meaningful for a child to be able to recognize his mother whether she is glimpsed from the front or the back, the left or the right; to recognize a car as a car whether it is seen approaching or going away; and a dog as a dog (that can bite) whether viewed from the head or the tail. Learning to read might therefore be said to involve the violation of naturally adaptive perceptual achievement, because the child has to distinguish between the letters of the alphabet, such as *b* and *d*, *p* and *q*, and has to pay attention to the spatial orientation of each letter (Bryant, 1971, citing evidence from Gibson, 1969).

The recognition of the role played by lagging visual-perceptual development in learning difficulties has led to attempts to screen children's visual-perceptual abilities by having them draw geometrical figures. According to the Stanford-Binet norms, a three year old should be able to draw a circle; a four year old, a square; a five year old, a triangle; and a seven year old, a diamond. But visual-perceptual maturity cannot be equated with the ability to *draw* a geometrical figure. Drawing is a sensory-motor and not a visual-perceptual task; a child may be able to match geometrical figures correctly and still be unable to draw them. This is one of the reasons that the authors developed a test that differentiates between visual-perceptual and perceptual-motor tasks. (See chapter on evaluation.)

Between the ages of seven and eight and a half, visual-perceptual development tapers off; in fact, all visual-perceptual abilities needed for successful school learning are in the repertoire of the six- to eight-year-old child who has developed normally.

Auditory Perception

Auditory perception has not been studied extensively apart from language development. The ability to be aware of and attend to sounds is innate in newborn infants or soon develops. Discrimination between sounds also begins early; Siqueland and Lipsett (1966), for example, found that newborn infants can differentiate between tones.

As with visual-perceptual abilities, the more complex auditory-perceptual abilities (see Chapter 14), such as auditory figure-ground perception and recognition and discrimination of auditory sequences, seem to develop maximally at about the time the child first attends preschool or kindergarten.

Development of Higher Cognitive Abilities

Integrative and Associative Abilities

A baby rapidly learns to associate perception with movement (the sight of a bottle is often followed by reaching and sucking movements). Later he learns to recognize an object or person regardless of the sense organ through which it is presented. (The mother's face or the sound of her voice or her footsteps will all indicate "mother.")

Birch and Lefford (1967) found that the child's ability to judge whether the perceptions received from different sense modalities were or were not identical improves with age, the greatest growth in accuracy occuring between the ages of five and eight. An eight year old, for instance, can usually choose from a variety of visual patterns whichever one is the equivalent of a given rhythm; that is, he hears

and selects from such alternatives as

$$\left(\bullet \ \bullet \ \bullet \bullet \bullet \right) \left(\bullet \bullet \bullet \quad \bullet \right) \left(\bullet \bullet \quad \bullet \bullet \right)$$

The maximum development of integrative and associative functions thus also occurs at the time that the child begins to attend school, and disturbances of these functions frequently lead to learning difficulties (see below, p. 311).

Imagery

Whereas language represents the environment through the use of verbal symbols (words), imagery represents the environment through remembered auditory, kinesthetic, and visual images.

The ability to visualize is necessary for imaginative play. It is also necessary later for understanding what is read, since statements (written or spoken) must evoke visual images. (See Chapters 8, 16, and 18.) As pointed out earlier, imagery is indispensable for thought processes.

Rohwer and his coworkers (1970) have shown how important visualization is in helping the child to form associations. Younger children do not always use images to help form associations, but can do so if the teacher reminds them. Older children with learning disabilities need to be reminded to use imagery as a learning tool, because deficits in imagery are frequent and very handicapping in these children. For instance, the child may remember that the freezing point of water is 32 degrees by visualizing a huge thermometer reading 32 beside an ice cube or a frozen lake.

Auditory imagery is also an important tool in learning. Certain people use auditory imagery more than visualization—they spell words, for example, by remembering the sequence of sounds rather than by visually perceiving the letters. Auditory imagery can be developed by such classroom activities as music instruction, auditory spelling, oral arithmetic, and so on.

Operational Thinking

During infancy and the preschool years—the periods of maximum development of language and perception—the child's adaptation to the world is generally bound to his own particular experiences, but from six to seven and a half years of age, the child enters what Piaget (1970) calls the stage of concrete operations.

At this stage the child is usually curious, active, eager to explore. He is able to compare his immediate perceptions with his memories of previous ones. He seems interested in identifying relationships, such as those that concern quantity, length, breadth, distance, time, speed, and so on.

The teacher can capitalize on the child's drive to learn more about the world around him by providing materials, integrating the teaching of academic skills (reading, writing, math, and so on) with information that satisfies the child's interests, and encouraging him to discuss and record his experiences.

The child enlarges his sphere of interests, which is no longer restricted to the world he can perceive directly. The development of imagery permits him to substitute inner processes for outer reality. He becomes increasingly able to separate (distance) himself from the actual, immediate, concrete world in space and time (Sigel, 1968). The child represents (visualizes, draws, verbalizes, or writes about) sequences of events that may be distant in time and space, so that he can use them for future planning and for drawing inferences about what has happened in the past (White, 1965) or may happen in the future.

Emotional Development

Emotion is defined by most modern writers as an inner feeling, or reaction, to some outer situation. For instance, Fraisse (1968), writing in the cognitive-developmental tradition, and Pribram (1971), writing from a neurophysiological point of view, both regard emotion as a form of adaptation.

There are no clearcut phases in a child's emotional development. It changes in accordance with the main tasks a child faces in life and his ability to master them.

The stages of psychosexual development posited by psychoanalytic theory are not the same as the stages in emotional development. They are based on hypothesized changes in the direction of the child's energies, which in turn are based on his biological maturation. The early stages—oral, anal, phallic, and latency—have already been briefly discussed.

These definitions do not give sufficient guidelines as to how to deal with the affective states of the child. Probably the most important signposts in regard to every aspect of the educative process are the child's directly observable emotional reactions. Very slight anxiety may be conducive to learning and to mastering a task; greater anxiety may be totally disruptive. Love for the teacher may be a spur to greater effort; jealousy and anger may make learning impossible. By and large, the teacher needs to prevent and avoid the occurrence of negative and highly emotional states and emotional upheaval. She needs to tread a fine line between providing firmness and exerting too much pressure, and only the child's emotional reactions can indicate how she should adjust her demands. She can be certain, however, that success and approval are indispensable for the child's emotional health.

Social Development and Adjustment

Social adjustment can be defined as the ability to interact with other human beings in such a way that no individual is injured and common goals are achieved.

Erikson's tasks (discussed earlier in Chapter 7 on psychoanalysis) may be viewed from the standpoint of socialization—learning to trust the caretaker (usually the mother), learning to adjust to the demands of others while acknowledging the needs of the self, learning how to play and to work with peers, to contribute to society, to care for a new generation, and to improve the conditions of life for all.

Social development and adjustment may also be viewed from the point of view of a study of child-rearing practices (e.g., Caldwell, 1964; Sears, 1957), of psychopathology (e.g., Bowlby, 1952; Spitz, 1958; Winnicott, 1957), and of the development of moral judgments (Piaget, 1932; Kohlberg, 1964). The latter approach vividly illustrates the central role of cognitive processes in the social behavior of the child. As the child learns to understand the point of view of others, and to separate himself from what he himself immediately experiences, he is able to progress from judging the morality of his own and others' actions solely on the basis of physical consequences (rewards and punishments) to judging in terms of community welfare. He will be concerned whether his actions are in accord with his own value system.

Social adjustment, which includes the formation of a value system,* is learned from life experiences. The school structures and guides enough of the young child's experiences to make a critical difference in the child's concern for others and for his community.

Several years ago the senior author visited an English school. A group of eleven-year-olds were working together on a project concerning gasoline. One child was studying how oil is formed in the earth; another was drawing maps; another was making a diagram of the refining process; another was calculating the costs of running a car; and another was constructing notebooks, carefully lettering the covers. One of the children looked up, noticed the observer watching the notebook maker, and remarked that they were glad Charlie was making such attractive notebooks for all of them—it was a big help. The headmistress later commented that Charlie had suffered a head injury and had difficulty with eye-motor coordination. The other children had helped him spontaneously, not only by their complete acceptance and their tact, but also by assigning him jobs within the group that helped him overcome his handicap.

The incident illustrates the high degree of mutual concern and interpersonal responsibility in working toward shared goals that children can achieve. The children in this school had been guided in their social development by methods that have a wide application.

First, the children were given opportunities to work together and to share activities. Problems that arose during a project were treated as group problems. The teacher was a resource, not a dispenser of packaged wisdom.

Second, the children frequently acted out roles, put on plays, and discussed what a character in a story or picture might be thinking and feeling and why. In this way they were helped to understand the emotions of others and to recognize their own feelings more clearly.

Third, a great deal of creative writing was encouraged, so that the children learned to express their emotions. In sharing their writing, they learned about common feelings and problems.

Fourth, the teachers provided models. They never shamed a child. They praised cooperative behavior.

Fifth, the curriculum included many projects dealing with community problems ranging from local traffic to national defense. The children

* The value system can also be thought of as a system of motivations; that is, what the person wants and strives for. A person may verbalize his concern for his family, but express his true values by spending all his time and energy striving for money or prestige. The dichotomy may lead to a sense of alienation and meaninglessness in life.

became aware at an early age that they lived in a larger society, the various members of which were interdependent as the children themselves were interdependent in their classroom. The teachers fostered a belief that most faults in this society could be corrected. For example, while working on the gasoline project, the children learned that wastes from refineries were often dumped into rivers or oceans. The teacher encouraged children to discuss how they could help enforce existing laws, frame new ones, invent antipollution devices, turn the wastes into saleable products, and so on.

These children were happy and productive. They liked themselves, and they liked each other. They were aware of their feelings; they recognized the emotions of others; and they had learned ways to channel these emotions constructively. The reason for this success was that their social, emotional and cognitive development had been considered as a whole, and their program planned accordingly.

Summary

Table 2 summarizes most of the foregoing discussion. The broken lines indicate the ages when development of a particular function takes place and the solid lines indicate the ages at which maximum development occurs.

The division of the various aspects of development is, as has already been stated many times, artificial and is used only to make it easier to focus on important considerations. All abilities influence each other. The child's whole development must always be kept in mind.

The invariant sequence of at least certain aspects of the child's developmental phases must not lead the teacher to conclude that the child must reach a certain level of proficiency in an earlier stage before beginning training appropriate to a later stage. A paralyzed child (if he has eye movements or can move his head) can learn to perceive; a child with visual-perceptual difficulties can learn to read; and so on. Abilities that develop later may help to bolster abilities that have developed earlier. The teacher is reminded that she can help the child to acquire age-expected skills by using methods that utilize the child's strengths—at the same time that training is given to ameliorate his deficits.

TABLE 2

Basic Psychological Characteristics and Developmental Functions

Control, Arousal-Inhibition, Alertness, and Attention	Social, Emotional, and Conative° Adjustment and Development		Sensory Motor
(understood as temperamental characteristics) Relatively stable Can be influenced by environment Neurophysiological factors are the main determinants	Freud's psychosexual-developmental stages: a) oral phase b) anal phase c) phallic phase d) oedipal phase e) latency	Erikson's model combines social, emotional, and conative factors. The teacher must consider each stage separately: a) trust vs. mistrust b) autonomy vs. shame c) initiative vs. guilt d) industry vs. inferiority e) identity vs. role diffusion f) intimacy vs. isolation (young adult) g) generativity vs. stagnation (adulthood) h) ego integrity vs. despair (mature age)	Awareness of self Awareness of environment Motility (attributes of movement): strength flexibility balance coordination agility endurance speed Mastery of environment through movement (manipulation)

Age	(a) (b) (c) (d) (e)	(a) (b) (c) (d) (e) (f)	
0–5 mos.			
6–12 mos.			
12–18 mos.		11 to 16 yrs.	
18–24 mos.		young adults	
2–3 yrs.			
4			
5			
6			
7			
8			
9			
10			

11 yrs.　　　　11 yrs.

* The desire or will to act; the motivating force.

118

nguage	Visual Perception	Auditory Perception	Intersensory Integration	Visualization	Thought Processes
ceptive ssociative xpressive	Eye-motor coordination Figure ground Form constancy Position in space Spatial relationships Visual decoding of complex stimuli	Discrimination Figure ground Recognition Decoding	Integration of inputs from two or more channels simultaneously, e.g., visual-auditory in reading	(includes mental manipulation)	Categories of intellectual operations (Guilford, 1967): Memory, e.g., cognitive sequential memory Cognition, e.g., recognition, comprehension or understanding Convergent, e.g., arriving at necessary conclusions based upon objective information Divergent, e.g., originality, flexibility, fluency Evaluation, e.g., comparing and relating two or more attributes simultaneously

AGE

0–5 mos

6–12 mos

12–18 mos

18–24 mos

2–3 yrs

4 yrs

5 yrs

6 yrs

7 yrs

8 yrs

9 yrs

10 yrs

119

WORKS CITED

Birch, H. G., & Lefford, A. Intersensory development in children. *Monographs of the Society for Research in Child Development,* 1967, 32(2, Serial No. 110).

Bowlby, J. *Maternal care and mental health.* Geneva: World Health Organization, 1952.

Bruner, J. S. Competence in infancy. Unpublished address, March 13, 1972. Colloquia on Behavioral Sciences, University of California at Los Angeles.

Bryant, P. E. Cognitive development. *British Medical Bulletin,* 1971, 27(3), 200–205.

Burt, C. The differentiation of intellectual ability. *British Journal of Educational Psychology,* 1954, 24, 76–90.

Caldwell, B. M. The effects of infant care. In M. L. Hoffman, & L. W. Hoffman (Eds.), *Review of child development research.* Vol. 1. New York: Russell Sage Foundation, 1964.

Fraisse, P., & Piaget, J. *Experimental psychology: Its scope and method.* Vol. 5. *Motivation, emotion and personality.* New York: Basic Books, 1968.

Guilford, J. P. *The nature of human intelligence.* New York: McGraw-Hill, 1967.

Isaacs, S. *Intellectual growth in young children.* New York: Humanities Press, 1930.

Kohlberg, L. Development of moral character and moral ideology. In M. L. Hoffman and L. W. Hoffman (Eds.), *Review of Child Development Research,* Vol. 1, New York: Russell Sage Foundation, 1964, 383–432.

Luria, A. R. *The role of speech in the regulation of normal and abnormal behavior.* New York: Liveright, 1961.

Piaget, J., & Inhelder, B. *The child's concept of space.* New York: Humanities Press, 1956.

Piaget, J. *The moral judgment of the child.* New York: Harcourt, 1932.

Piaget, J. *Science of education and the psychology of the child.* New York: Orion Press, 1970.

Pribram, K. *Language of the brain.* Englewood Cliffs, N.J.: Prentice-Hall, 1971.

Rohwer, W. D., Jr. Mental elaboration and proficient learning. In J. P. Hill (Ed.), *Minnesota symposia on child psychology.* Vol. LV. Minneapolis: University of Minnesota Press, 1970.

Sears, R., Maccoby, E., & Levin, H. *Patterns in child rearing.* New York: Row, Peterson, 1957.

Sigel, I. The distancing hypothesis: A hypothesis crucial to the development of representational competence. Paper presented at the Annual Meeting of the American Psychological Association, San Francisco, Calif., 1968.

Siqueland, E. R., & Lipsitt, L. P. Conditioned head turning in human newborns. *Journal for Experimental Child Psychology*, 1966, 3(4), 356–376.

Spitz, R. On the genesis of superego components. In *The psychoanalytic study of the child*. Vol. 13. New York: International Universities Press, 1958.

White, S. H. Evidence for a hierarchical arrangement of learning processes. In L. P. Lipsitt & C. C. Spiker (Eds.), *Advances in child development and behavior*. Vol. 2. New York: Academic Press, 1965.

Winnicott, D. *The child and the outside world*. London: Tavistock Publications, 1957.

10
EVALUATION

The teacher is the key figure in any evaluation. Evaluation of a child's level of functioning means evaluating each aspect of his developmental level in relation to the performance normally expected at his age level. The teacher needs to know the child's level of functioning, his abilities, and his previous learning, in order to be able to adapt the curriculum and classroom management to the child and make optimum learning possible. A comparison with the expected performance at the child's age level will indicate his strengths and deficits. This comparison in terms of psychometric norms can be made both by using psychological tests and by observational methods.

Standardized tests alone can never evaluate a child's functioning. Evaluation is an ongoing process. When the child reads from a book, the teacher must be aware of what and how much the child has really grasped. She must know if he has learned the multiplication facts to which he has recently been introduced, or if he can keep a thought in mind long enough to write it down, or if he has learned to differentiate between a trapezoid and a parallelogram. It is necessary for her to be able to assess the child's current learning in order to be able to plan each successive step.

Evaluation by the teacher is also indispensable because behavior is subject to more or less temporary deviations, and testing may therefore produce incorrect results.

No single test or observation, nor even any battery of standardized tests, can be considered as anything more than a sample of behavior at a given time. A child's scores may be low because he is hungry, tired, or feverish, or because he is afraid of the testing situation itself.

The information assembled by the interdisciplinary team or the school psychologist must be made accessible to the teacher so that she can utilize the information to gain knowledge of the child's whole life situation and current developmental status, and if need be, adjust classroom management. For example, a child with poor visual acuity may need to sit where he can watch the blackboard from close range; or a child with a severe emotional problem may need frequent reassurrance either verbally or by touch. The classroom teacher remains primarily responsible not only for teaching the child appropriate skills and providing appropriate information, but also for helping him to develop his maximum potential in all psychological functions.

The standardized tests described in detail in this chapter are the ones used at the Frostig Center, and in many school districts and clinics throughout the country, as a basis for planning educational programs for children with learning difficulties.

Evaluating Sensory-Motor Abilities

Four different aspects of the curriculum are concerned with the improvement of sensory-motor abilities: visuo-motor and fine motor coordination (arts and crafts, use of three-dimensional objects, etc.); oculo-motor training (including specific exercises to improve eye-hand coordination and eye tracking); the education of movement skills; and the development of sensitivity and awareness, which includes body awareness, awareness of space and time, awareness of objects, and especially, awareness of other human beings.

Most commonly used sensory-motor tests and screening devices [such as the Purdue Perceptual-Motor Survey (Roach and Kephart, 1966), the Lincoln-Oseretsky Test (Sloan, 1955), the Kraus-Weber Test (1963), the Cureton Motor Fitness Test (1942), and the Cratty battery (1969)] evaluate a combination of motor skills only. The Frostig Movement Skills Test Battery (Orpet, 1972)* evaluates six of the seven attributes of movement (motor skills) identified by factor analytic studies,** thus providing a basis for a more focused and individualized training program. The teacher's own observations, if done systematically, can substitute for formal testing and provide needed additional information. The Move-Grow-Learn Movement Skills Survey (Orpet and Heustis, 1971), can facilitate such observations.

Most checklists, including the Orpet and Heustis, do not include a detailed evaluation of fine motor skills. Their use must be supplemented by comparing the child's performance with those of his classmates in tasks requiring fine muscle coordination and eye-motor coordination, such as tracing lines, coloring and pasting, stringing beads, and transferring objects from one hand to the other.

The child's knowledge of direction and of the parts of the body have also to be checked independently of the use of a motor scale.

* A super-8 film demonstrating this test is available from the Frostig Center.
** These attributes are defined on pages 163–164.

Evaluating Auditory Perception

The evaluation of auditory perception is discussed in detail in Chapter 14.

The Wepman Test (1958), a standardized test most frequently used to assess discrimination of speech sounds, is used as part of the Frostig Center's basic test battery. It requires a child to indicate whether words read to him in pairs sound the same or different; obviously, it therefore cannot be used unless the child understands the meaning of *same* and *different*.

The Wepman Test should be considered as a screening instrument, to be supplemented by having the child repeat digits, words, phrases, and sentences, and by having him recognize certain sounds in the context of words in initial, final, and medial positions. If a child seems to have difficulty in discrimination of speech sounds, he should be referred for auditory-acuity testing and given some more thorough evaluation of his auditory abilities, such as those discussed later in this book and those recommended by Myklebust (1954).

Visual Perception

Tests of visual-perceptual ability include the Bender Visual Motor Gestalt Test (Clawson, 1962; Koppitz, 1964), the Benton Revised Visual Retention Test (Benton, 1955), the Goodenough Draw-a-Man Test (Goodenough, 1962), and others. These perceptual-motor tests have the disadvantage, however, of requiring the child to reproduce figures and patterns, and therefore involve other abilities than perception alone. This has been shown by Abercrombie (1964), among others. She demonstrated that children who were unable to copy a diamond freehand were able to do so when permitted to use a ruler. The children matched the slant of the ruler with the oblique lines of the diamond and were then able to reproduce the figure. In other words, they were unable to copy a figure unaided that they perceived perfectly. Similarly perceptual-motor tests do not differentiate between various perceptual abilities.

The visual perceptual test used in the basic test battery, the Frostig Developmental Test of Visual Perception (Frostig et al., 1964), is designed to measure five visual-perceptual functions and permit comparison between a child's performance and the norms for his age. The five visual-perceptual functions evaluated are eye-motor coordination, figure-ground perception, perception of constancy (of shape), perception of position in space, and perception of spatial relationships.

Visual-motor coordination is the ability to coordinate vision with movements of the body or parts of the body.

Figure-ground perception is the ability to attend to one aspect of the visual field while perceiving it in relation to the rest of the field.

Perception of constancy refers to the fact that an object is perceived as possessing invariant properties, such as shape, position, size, and so on, in spite of the variability of the impression on the sensory surface.

Perception of position in space is perception of the position of an object in relation to the observer (that is, perception of the direction in which it is turned).

Perception of spatial relationships is defined as the ability to perceive the position of two or more objects in relation to each other.

Table 3 illustrates some items from the subtests and suggests related activities.

Worksheet exercises from *Pictures and Patterns* (Frostig, Miller, and Horne, 1972), or other similar material, may be used to screen the child's visual-perceptual ability by comparing an individual child's performance with that of his classmates. The child's difficulties in academic tasks may also indicate visual-perceptual difficulties.

Evaluating Psycholinguistic Functions

The clinical test most frequently used to assess language functions is the Illinois Test of Psycholinguistic Abilities (revised edition, 1968). As part of the basic test battery administered at the Frostig Center, its results, together with scores on the other tests, serve as the basis for initial programming. The ITPA, as it is generally called, was devised by Samuel Kirk, James McCarthy, and Winifred Kirk, with preliminary work reported in Dorothy Sievers' doctoral dissertation (1955) laying a basis for its construction. The purpose of the test is the detection of specific abilities and disabilities in communication, thus providing a basis for instituting an effective educational program in psycholinguistic functions.

The ITPA consists of twelve subtests, which involve not only language functions in the usual sense of the phrase but also perceptual-motor tasks, memory, thought processes, and other psychological functions.

The subtests of the ITPA are based on a model of the communication process posited by Osgood (1957). The present version of the

TABLE 3

Frostig Developmental Test of Visual Perception (Brief Summary)

Subtest Name	Example	Some Functions Covered	Some Suggested Training Procedures
Eye-motor coordination	Draw straight lines horizontally. Stop and start on target.	Eye-hand coordination. Necessary for handwriting, drawing, arts and crafts, manipulatory and self-help activities.	Eye-movement training. Arts and crafts. Manipulatory exercises. Handwriting exercises. Physical education program.
Figure-ground	Find a hidden figure. Find one of two or several intersecting figures.	Ability to focus visually on relevant aspects of visual field and disregard irrelevant background.	"Finding" games; e.g., hidden figures included in many children's activity books. Sorting exercises. Unscrambling intersecting words such as
Form constancy	Find all the squares on a page regardless of color, background, tilt, size.	Ability to see sameness of essential form despite changes of image on retina. Has implication for learning to identify letters presented in various printing styles.	Identifying objects or drawings at different distances or angles. Drawing diagrams of three-dimensional patterns. Finding all objects of a certain shape in the room.

126

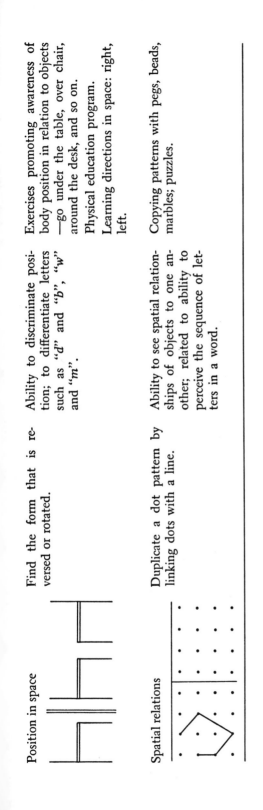

Position in space	Find the form that is reversed or rotated.	Ability to discriminate position; to differentiate letters such as "*d*" and "*b*", "*w*" and "*m*".	Exercises promoting awareness of body position in relation to objects —go under the table, over chair, around the desk, and so on. Physical education program. Learning directions in space: right, left.
Spatial relations	Duplicate a dot pattern by linking dots with a line.	Ability to see spatial relationships of objects to one another; related to ability to perceive the sequence of letters in a word.	Copying patterns with pegs, beads, marbles; puzzles.

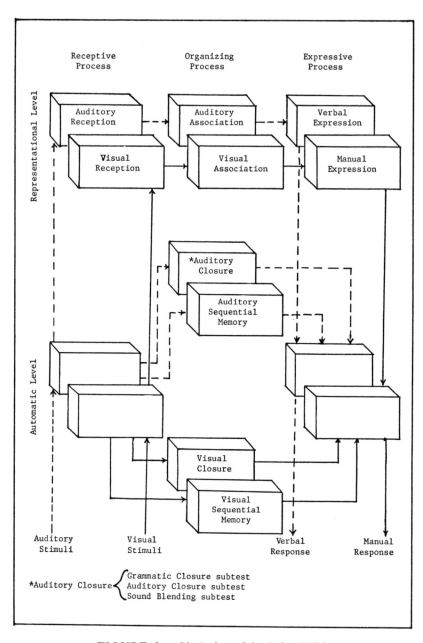

FIGURE 1.   Clinical model of the ITPA.

128

ITPA is represented by a clinical model (see Figure 1, reproduced from Kirk and Kirk, 1971, p. 20) which illustrates the interrelationships among the dimensions that form the basis of the ITPA subtests. In fact, the ITPA may be considered a structured intelligence test based on communicative abilities.

The first dimension concerns the channel, or modality, through which the child receives stimuli from his environment. The ITPA explores only visual and auditory input; it has no subtest requiring the child to respond to or discriminate between stimuli impinging on the other senses, although kinesthetic and tactile stimuli are important in learning.

The second dimension classifies the content of the required task into two levels: (1) automatic and perceptual, and (2) symbolic and conceptual. Kirk and Kirk (1971, p. 22) define this dimension as "the degree to which communication behavior is organized within the individual." A task at the higher level (called "representational" by the ITPA model) requires the use of meaningful symbols. The "automatic" level includes behavior that is often below the level of awareness (such as articulation and even grammar) but that is nevertheless highly organized. (The normal adult is able to count automatically, although counting is actually a highly organized skill.) The ITPA also puts memory for visual and auditory sequences on the automatic level.

The third dimension involves three main processes involved in acquiring and using language: (1) the receptive process, or decoding, which is the recognition and understanding of what is seen or heard; (2) the organizing process, or association, which is the formation of connections and relationships between and among stimuli and responses: modes of input (auditory, visual, kinesthetic, and so on), modes of response (verbal, motor), and modes between input and response (auditory-vocal, visual-motor, and so on); (3) the expressive process, or encoding, which is the expression of ideas, either verbally or by movement.

This third dimension, comprised of receptive, associative, and expressive functions, may be particularly useful to the teacher in providing a framework within which to plan and evaluate language activities in the curriculum. Table 4 lists the individual subtests of the ITPA and corresponding observations which can be used for evaluation in the classroom.

According to Bateman (1968), "One of the greatest contributions of the ITPA is that it has provided a frame of reference which makes it easier to know which behavior to observe, facilitates the observation, and provides guidelines for planning the modification of those behaviors through remediation."

TABLE 4

ITPA Subtests

	Test Description*	Examples of Classroom Observations
Auditory reception	The child indicates "yes" or "no" to such questions as "Do babies drink?" "Do barometers congratulate?"	Does the child understand what is said? Can he follow written directions but not verbal ones? Can he take down dictated sentences? Can he identify common animal sounds? musical instruments? classroom noises?
Visual reception	The child must select from a group of pictures the one of an object that is used in a same or similar way as a stimulus picture.	Can the child get specific requested information from pictures or films? Does he have a wide acquaintance with everyday objects, such as tools?
Manual expression	The child must show through gesture how an object (e.g., a phone, a toothbrush) is used.	Can the child express action through movement? Can the child play charades? Is he hesitant and awkward when the class does creative movement?
Verbal expression	The child is asked to describe a familiar object, such as a ball.	How well does the child express himself? How many different concepts does he use? Is he creative and imaginative?
Auditory association	The child is required to make analogies in completing sentences: e.g., "Cotton is soft; stones are (hard)."	Does the child understand the concepts of "same" and "different?" Can he understand math relationships? Does he have difficulty in classifying?
Visual association	The child must associate pictures on the basis of relationships such as functional usage (sock and shoe) and conceptual categories (horse and cow, both animals; bread and cheese, both foods).	How large is the child's store of concepts? Does he make logical connections between ideas? Does he understand that the same object can be classified in different ways?

TABLE 4 (Continued)

Grammatic closure	The child is asked to complete sentences using the correct inflection: e.g., "Here is a dog; here are two (dogs)." "The man is painting. He is a (painter)."	Does the child speak correctly?
Auditory sequential memory	The child is requested to repeat a series of digits presented rapidly.	Can the child, after hearing a spoken sentence or number fact or a word spelled orally, repeat the information?
Visual sequential memory	The child is shown a sequence of geometric forms; it is removed, and the child is asked to reproduce the sequence by placing chips in proper order.	Can the child focus his attention? Can he discriminate among similar geometric forms? Can he copy a pattern? Can he reproduce it from memory?
Visual closure	The child is asked to identify all the partially obscured pictures of common objects against a distracting background; he must do so in 30 seconds.	Does he scan pictures? Can he work rapidly? Is he easily distracted? Can he locate specific information on a printed page? Does he have special difficulty in reading hyphenated words or blurry ditto copies?
Auditory closure (optional)	The child is asked to repeat words or phrases in which certain sounds have been omitted: e.g., "Ea ter unny" (Easter bunny).	Does the child understand a speaker with a different accent? Does he understand phone conversations? Can he understand speech in a noisy room? Does he leave off word endings?
Sound blending (optional)	Sounds are spoken at half-second intervals, and the child must blend them into a word: e.g., "f-oo-t, f-u-n, wh-e-n."	Can the child decode unfamiliar words in reading if he can associate the sound with the individual letter? Can he blend sounds into words, as in the test?

Evaluating Integrative Functions

Integrative functions are evaluated to a certain degree by all tests, because such functions are a prerequisite for all purposeful behavior. But the child's performance should be observed in a variety of tasks, as well as in the standardized tests. The following are examples of integrative tasks:

1. Following verbal directions with a movement sequence. (Auditory-motor integration)
2. Following a direction given in print or with the help of a picture. (Visual-motor integration)
3. Pairing a visual pattern of dots and dashes with an auditory rhythmic pattern; e.g., the child hears a certain rhythm and must select the corresponding visual pattern (such as "0 − − 0 − − 0") from among several similar patterns (cf. Birch and Lefford, 1967; Birch and Belmont, 1965; Muehl and Kremenak, 1966); or choosing the correct picture from among several pictures following a verbal description or reading. (Auditory-visual integration)

Evaluating Higher Cognitive Functions

The Wechsler Intelligence Scale for Children (1949)—known as the WISC—is, like the Binet, widely used. It is a test of higher cognitive functions which is part of the basic test battery used at the Frostig Center. The advantage of the Wechsler Scale is that it is made up of ten or eleven subtests that may suggest the areas of training that need to be emphasized.* Other tests and scales may be used in addition to, and as a replacement for, the WISC. Children younger than about seven years of age should be tested with the Wechsler Preschool and Primary Scale of Intelligence (WPPSI) instead.

The WISC subtests were not designed to assess a single ability; most involve a number of integrated functions. For example, in performing the object-assembly subtest, it is necessary to keep an idea in mind while perceiving other stimuli; to analyze and synthesize a pattern; to perceive figural relationships; and to plan a sequence. Conversely, several other subtests may reflect the same ability. For example, the

---

* The WISC is presently in the process of being revised. One new subtest has been added, viz., "Visual Motor Memory" that involves immediate visual-sequential memory.

subtests for similarities, comprehension, vocabulary, and picture completion all involve concept formation.

Table 5 describes briefly the WISC subtests and suggests observations that may be used by the teacher instead of the standardized test.

TABLE 5
WISC Subtests

	Test Description*	Examples of Classroom Observations
Verbal		
Information	Questions to assess general knowledge acquired through everyday activities (e.g., How many eyes do you have? How many dimes make a dollar?).	Does the child contribute relevant material in classroom discussions? Is he generally aware of and interested in what is going on around him?
Comprehension	Questions requiring common-sense judgment about social and "moral" behavior (e.g., Why do we need shoes? What do you do when you see a big piece of metal on the street?).	Is he able to give reasons for classroom or playground rules? Can he draw inferences from the material he has read?
Arithmetic	Word problems to be solved without paper and pencil (e.g., Susie had two pieces of candy, and her sister gave her three more. How many pieces of candy did Susie have altogether?).	Can he solve oral arithmetic problems?
Similarities	Questions regarding ways in which two things are alike (e.g. In what ways are a carrot and a potato alike?).	Can he place objects, pictures, or symbols into categories? Can he reorganize the same material according to a different concept (e.g., first by color, then by shape?). Can he recognize similarities that are not obvious? (e.g., In what way are a rose and a toad alike?—They both live.)

TABLE 5 (Continued)

Vocabulary	Child defines words.	Does the child use a varied vocabulary? Can he understand the new terms in his reader?
Digit Span	Child repeats a series of digits forward and another series of digits backward. Digits are presented at one-second intervals within a series (slower than in the ITPA).	Can the child immediately repeat what he has heard? Note whether or not he remembers his phone number, zip code, tables of measurement, multiplication facts, etc. Does he remember such facts for a short period after he has supposedly learned them or does he retain them in his memory?

Performance

Picture Completion	The child is shown a picture with one part missing and asked to name or point to the missing part (e.g., a picture of a chair with no seat).	Can the child remember what an object looks like (visualize)? Can he interpret a picture in which parts are hidden (e.g., a boy whose legs are hidden by a bush), or in which parts are left out (e.g., a baseball hitter with no bat)?
Picture Arrangement	The child is asked to arrange a series of pictures in correct order to tell a story or establish a time sequence. (Timed Test.)	Can he read stories presented in comic-strip form? Can he recognize when a picture in a comic strip is in the wrong order?
Block Diagram	The child is asked to reproduce a pictorial pattern with blocks. (Timed Test.)	Can the child follow a pattern in stringing beads or placing pegs, marbles, blocks, etc.? Can he reproduce a model?
Object Assembly	The child is asked to assemble four jigsaw puzzles of familiar objects within timed limits.	Can the child complete a puzzle in which the pieces are cut according to logical parts (e.g., a face, the separate parts of which are eyes, nose, etc.)?

TABLE 5 (Continued)

Coding	The child is asked to mark visual symbols according to a given code, and to match symbols with numbers. (Timed Test.)	Does the child have difficulty in discriminating between letters and numerals? Can he use such math symbols as $> < - + = $? Can he read and understand a map, a graph, a rebus, etc.?
Mazes	Pencil-and-paper mazes.	How does the child compare with his age-mates in solving a maze from a children's activity book?

* The questions used as examples are not those actually used in the WISC.

Basic* Test Results

The WISC, Frostig, Wepman, and ITPA furnish a rough measure of the cognitive functions** that educators need to explore: visual perception (Frostig), auditory perception (Wepman), higher cognitive processes (WISC), and language functions (ITPA). The tests do not reflect a clearcut division between these functions, however. The ITPA, for example, taps thought processes, such as concept formation and memory functions, as well as perceptual and language functions.

The pattern that emerges from comparing the results of several tests provides more useful information than the results from any one individual test. Such a pattern permits informed decisions to be made about the child's educational program, including his preferred sense modality of learning; his ability to visualize, to remember, to form concepts, and so on. Test results, however, never reveal such factors as what the child finds rewarding, his approach (impulsive, passive, and the like) to problem-solving, his worries and interests, and so on, which may be of equal or even greater importance in instituting an individualized educational program.

* The term "basic" is used in relation to tests used as a basis for the child's educational program.
** A survey of the four tests seems to indicate that Guilford's factors of the intellect at the six-year-old level, studied by Orpet and Meyers (1965), are well represented by the subtests.

Social Adjustment and Emotional Development

It is not possible to evaluate the child's social and emotional development in quantitative terms, and this is why evaluation of social and emotional development is often considered unscientific. Opinions of what can and should be measured range from that of orthodox behaviorists who hold that nothing should be explored or studied which cannot be objectively measured to such investigators as Eleanor Gibson who state that nothing worthwhile in learning can be measured.

Projective tests*—such as the Rorschach (1942) and Children's Apperception Test (Bellak and Bellak, 1949–61)—are used by clinical psychologists and psychiatrists to gain insight into the child's self-concept, motivations, and ways of relating to others. These tests are more difficult to administer and interpret than other forms of testing, and may be available only rarely; but interviews with, and observation of, a child will reveal his feelings, attitudes, wishes, complexities, and his own individual way of handling the struggle involved in every child's growing-up. In fact, the teacher has the advantage of being able to observe the child over an extended period of time in what Caldwell (1969) terms his "ecological" (i.e., his natural) environment.

Those who work with children are usually attuned to the many tiny clues to inner states that behavior reveals. The sensitive observer knows that a child's temper tantrum may indicate pent-up emotion unrelated to the immediate situation, or constitute a dramatic display intended to attract the adult's attention to the child's state of despair or helpless frustration. She will also understand that nervous scribbling on a piece of paper during a lesson is not necessarily an act of defiance directed at the teacher, but may indicate hyperactivity caused by brain dysfunction or an attempt to master restlessness originating in worry and gnawing uncertainty.

A child's behavior—his verbal and his active expressions—mirrors his feelings and attitudes, and permits the teacher to choose from her repertoire of teaching procedures and methods of classroom management those with which he will be comfortable.

The theme of a child's "make-believe" play or composition, for example, often expresses his central concerns. The major character may reflect his view on his relationships with adult authorities, with his siblings, and with his peers, and indicate whether the child feels able

---

* These tests are called "projective" because they are designed to encourage the person to "project" his attitudes and feelings upon the neutral or ambiguous stimuli given by the test and to interpret them accordingly.

to cope with his situation or feels helpless. The child's drawings and compositions will also reveal his wishes, feelings, interests, and worries. Often the provision of opportunities for self-expression permits the child to recognize and master many of his problems.

Information that the teacher learns from the child may serve as a guide for action.* Knowledge that Johnny's parents are in the process of getting a divorce, for instance, may suggest to the teacher that Johnny may need to keep one of his toys in his desk to give him reassurance that he still has the security of his home. His sense of achievement may need even more bolstering than usual; he may need explicit verbalization that separation does not mean personal rejection. The teacher's knowledge of Johnny, of herself, and of the total situation may suggest to her many other measures.

The ability to draw conclusions in regard to a child's feelings by observing his behavior diminishes if the adult feels frustrated by the child's behavior. In such circumstances the adult perceives the child as manipulating, without understanding why. If a child throws a spitball, what is the cause and who is the real target? The difficulty in the teacher-child relationship sharply increases when the teacher regards herself as the target. It may be neither the teacher nor another child who was the cause of the anger, but a customer on the child's paper route who did not want to pay his bill. It is often possible to open channels of communication by maintaining an attitude of open friendliness, and to lessen the child's anger by listening to his story, results certainly not achieved by summarily punishing the child.

Among the most difficult tasks for the teacher of children with learning difficulties are observing them with understanding, reacting to their emotional upheavals in a restrained, warm, and helpful manner, and remaining loving when feeling hurt and angered.

Group behavior

In order to understand how her class interacts as a group, the teacher is encouraged to make simple sociograms—diagrams that symbolize social interaction in a group.** She might ask the children, for example, to indicate which children in the class they would most like to sit by. Using circles for girls and triangles for boys (or any other

* A child may inadvertently give confidential information. This information, of course, should not be shared with others, except with a psychiatrist or psychologist called in for evaluation or consultation.
** A brief description of the technique is given by Lister (1969, pp. 199–202).

figural code), she can diagram with arrows the preferences expressed. Sociograms can also be formed on the basis of the choices made when teams are formed on the playground, or discussion groups for current events, partners for a science experiment, or any other situation in which the children naturally express their preferences.

No teacher needs a sociogram to identify hostile exhibitionist children; but many teachers who use the sociogram are surprised, for example, to find that the quiet student who earns such good grades is really isolated by his peers, that the class president is neither the classroom nor the playground leader, that several relatively rigid cliques appear to exist, or that she has structured the classroom so that nearly all interaction is teacher-directed. Again, such findings should serve as a basis for choosing activities to promote satisfying social relationships. Children who are relatively isolated can be paired with popular children for an occasional activity, for example. If another child chooses the isolate, the teacher can encourage the association in future assignments.

Evaluating Learning Tasks

The foregoing discussion has been primarily concerned with evaluating the abilities the child brings to the learning task. The task itself can also be used as a diagnostic tool, as advocated by Luria (1966), Dale Bryant (1970), and Chalfant and Foster (in press). All these approaches involve analyzing the child's performance* under different conditions, and require an attitude of inquiry on the part of the teacher. The teacher analyzes the child's responses (the product), the steps used by the child in performing a given task (the process), the conditions before, during, and after the learning experience (the situation), and the task outlined by the teacher (procedure) (Chalfant and Foster, in press). The teacher may find, for example, that a child's responses are accurate when he does a page of arithmetic problems all involving the same process, but that he becomes confused if some problems require addition and others subtraction. She might then present a mixed page with the plus and minus symbols written in different colors. If the child is still unsuccessful, she might tell the child to verbalize, "Plus means addition; I must add these numbers. . . . Minus means subtraction; I must subtract . . .," before attempting to solve a problem. In short, once the learning problem is clearly defined, a method for overcoming the difficulty can then be attempted.

* The child's performance on standardized tests may be analyzed in a similar way.

Recording

Systematic, accurate notes on the child's behavior are indispensable. Recording, or educational-data collection, must be concerned with three kinds of responses—motor, vocal, and graphic. Too often the child's written work is used as the sole means of evaluating his progress. Motor and vocal behavior are equally important for understanding the processes by which the child learns and assessing his general social and emotional status.

The response may be recorded as timed samples (all behavior occurring in one minute, for example), as frequency counts (e.g., the number of times the child leaves his seat in ten minutes), as tape recordings (a story told or read aloud), or in other ways.

All records serve the purpose of helping the teacher to discern a pattern of behavior, which she may then decide to attempt to alter or support.

Ongoing Educational Evaluation

The four main means by which educational data today are collected are standardized achievement tests, observational notes, progress charts, and mastery tests.

Standardized achievement tests evaluate the child's progress toward the objectives that are to be achieved by a certain grade level. For instance, if the third-grade curriculum includes cursive writing, then a standardized test of third-grade achievement can discover if the child knows the cursive alphabet. To state it differently, standardized achievement tests compare a child's skills with the skills of other children in the same school grade.

Standardized achievement tests have great disadvantages for the child with learning problems. They do not accurately measure either the child's learning deficits or progress. Moreover, performance on these tests may be disrupted because of feelings of pressure and anxiety and a long history of failure. Standardized tests may, however, have to be used with the problem learner; either because other methods of evaluation, such as progress charts, mastery tests, and so on, are not used extensively and precisely in the classroom, or because the child's achievement has to be compared with that of other children for purposes of placement or prognosis. Standardized tests unquestionably permit a quick and global appraisal. Bloom (1968) is among the educators who believe that standardized tests are the best available diagnostic tool and should be used with all children; others, such as Glass (1968), Scriven (1967), and Cronbach (1963), disagree.

Observational notes are needed to supply data concerning the child's temperament, learning style, relationships, moods, and so on, as well as temporary changes in these characteristics.

Progress charts inform both the teacher and the child how the child is progressing. Objective visible proof of change in any area is a powerful incentive to success. The child can use his progress chart to monitor his own behavior (Lindsley, 1971).

A *mastery test* is a test given to see if the child has reached a clearly defined objective. A mastery test, for example, might be designed to see if a child can recognize a short vowel in the context of a word when the printed word is shown to him. It would take the form of checking on the child's ability to read correctly a certain number of words in which the consonants remain the same but the vowel changes:

sip   sap
hip   hop
tip   tap
bed   bud

And so on. If mastery has not been achieved, training in the skill must continue.

WORKS CITED

Abercrombie, M. *Perceptual visuomotor disorders in cerebral palsy.* The Spastics Society Medical Education and Information Unit, London: Heineman, 1964.

Bateman, B. D. *Interpretation of the 1961 Illinois test of psycholinguistic abilities.* Seattle: Special Child Publications, 1968.

Bellak, L., & Bellak, S. *Children's apperception test.* Washington, D. C.: Center for Psychological Service, 1949–61.

Benton, A. *The Benton revised visual retention test.* New York: Psychological Corp., 1965.

Birch, H. G., & Belmont, L. Auditory-visual integration, intelligence and reading ability in school children. *Perceptual and Motor Skills,* 1965, 20, 295–305.

Birch, H. G., & Lefford, A. Visual differentiation, intersensory integration, and voluntary motor control. *Monographs of the Society for Research in Child Development.* 1967, 32 (2, Serial No. 110).

Bloom, B. S. Toward a theory of testing which includes measurement—evaluation—assessment. Occasional Report No. 11, Los Angeles: University of California, Center for the Study of Evaluation of Instructional Programs, 1968.

Bryant, N. D. Trial remediation. Presented at the First Critical Practicum on Advanced Techniques in the Management and Remediation of Learning Disabilities and Associated Behavioral Disorders, sponsored by the *Journal of Learning Disabilities*, 1970.

Caldwell, B. M. A new approach to behavioral ecology. In J. P. Hill (Ed.), *Minnesota symposia on child psychology*, Vol. 2. Minneapolis, Minn.: University of Minnesota Press, 1969. Pp 74–109.

Chalfant, J. C., & Foster, G. E. *Analytic teaching: an approach to individualized instruction*. In press.

Clawson, A. *The Bender visual motor gestalt test for children*. Los Angeles: Western Psychological Services, 1962.

Cratty, B. J., and Martin, M. M. *Perceptual-motor efficiency in children; the measurement and improvement of movement attributes*. Philadelphia: Lea & Febiger, 1969.

Cronbach, L. J. "Course improvement" through evaluation. *Teachers College Record*, 1963, 64, 675–83.

Cureton, T. *18-item motor fitness test, Physical fitness workbook*. Champaign: University of Illinois Press, 1952.

Frostig, M., Miller, A., and Horne, D. *Pictures and patterns* and *Teacher's guides to Pictures and patterns*. (Rev. ed.) Chicago: Follett Educational Corp., 1972.

Frostig, M., Lefever, D. W., and Whittlesey, J. R. B. *The Marianne Frostig developmental test of visual perception*. Palo Alto, Calif: Consulting Psychologists Press, 1964.

Glass, G. V. Comments on Professor Bloom's paper entitled "Toward a theory of testing which includes measurement-evaluation-assessment." Occasional Report No. 11. Los Angeles: University of California, Center for the Study of Evaluation of Instructional Programs, 1968.

Goodenough, F. *Draw-a-man test. The measurement of intelligence by drawings*. Yonkers-on-Hudson: World Book Co., 1962.

Kirk, S. A., and Kirk, W. D. *Psycholinguistic learning disabilities: Diagnosis and remediation*. Urbana, Illinois: University of Illinois Press, 1971.

Kirk, S. A., McCarthy, J. J., and Kirk, W. D. *The Illinois test of psycholinguistic abilities*. (Rev. ed.) Urbana: University of Illinois Press, 1968.

Koppitz, E. M. *The Bender gestalt test for young children*. New York: Grune & Stratton, 1964.

Kraus, H. *Kraus-Weber test for minimum muscular fitness. Therapeutic exercises*. Springfield, Ill.: Charles C Thomas, 1963.

Lindsley, O. Speech before the ACLD–CANHC Western Regional Conference, January 29–30, 1971, San Diego, California.

Lister, J. L. Personal-emotional-social skills. In R. M. Smith (Ed.), *Teacher diagnosis of educational difficulties*. Columbus, Ohio: Charles E. Merrill, 1969.

Luria, A. R. *Human brain and psychological processes*. New York: Harper & Row, 1966.

Muehl, S., & Kremensk, S. Ability to match information within and between auditory and visual sense modalities and subsequent reading achievement. *Journal of Educational Psychology*, 1966, 57, 230–238.

Myklebust, H. R. *Auditory disorders in children*. New York: Grune & Stratton, 1954.

Orpet, R. *Frostig movement skills test battery*. (Exp. ed.) Palo Alto: Consulting Psychologists Press, 1972.

Orpet, R., & Heustis, T. L. *Move-grow-learn movement skills survey*. Chicago: Follett Educational Corp., 1971.

Orpet, R., & Meyers, C. A study of eight structure-of-intellect hypotheses in six year old children. Draft Report NIMH Grant No. MH 08666–01, June 9, 1965.

Osgood, C. E. A behavioristic analysis of perception and language as cognitive phenomena. In J. Bruner (Ed.), *Contemporary approaches to cognition*. Cambridge, Mass.: Harvard University Press, 1957.

Riessmann, K. F. *The culturally deprived child*. New York: Harper & Row, 1962.

Roach, E. G., & Kephart, N. C. *The Purdue perceptual-motor survey*. Columbus, Ohio: Charles E. Merrill, 1966.

Rorschach, H. *Psychodiagnostics* (trans. P. Lemkau & B. Kronenberg). Bern: Hans Huber, 1942.

Scriven, M. The methodology of evaluation. Perspectives of curriculum evaluation. AERA Monograph Series on Curriculum Evaluation, No. 1. Chicago: Rand McNally, 1967.

Sievers, D. J. Development and standardization of a test of psycholinguistic growth in preschool children. Unpublished Doctoral dissertation, University of Illinois, 1955.

Sloan, W. *The Lincoln-Oseretsky motor development scale*. Chicago: C. H. Stoelting Co., 1955.

Wechsler, D. *Wechsler intelligence scale for children*. New York: The Psychological Corp., 1949.

Wepman, J. *Wepman test of auditory discrimination*. Chicago: Language Research Associates, 1958.

11
PROGRAMMING

The term *programming* is used in this book to differentiate the planning of *individualized* education procedures from the planning of a curriculum for a whole group. Curricula are commonly designed on the basis of age levels, community needs, tradition, or the supposed or real needs of special groups of children (e.g., retarded, blind, and so on). Traditionally curricula have not been designed to cater to the child's individual differences and needs. Evaluation of the learner was therefore unnecessary in designing the traditional group curriculum. Testing was usually used only to estimate how much of the curriculum the learner would probably be able to assimilate or how much he had mastered.

We must also differentiate the term *programming* as used in this book from its use with reference to nonindividualized programmed textbooks and other teaching aids. The word *program* is used in the latter context when the material to be learned is presented in a step-by-step fashion. Individualizing in that context consists of the provision of self-correcting materials that permit variation in the amount of material learned in a given period of time—some children may progress faster; some, slower. The use of prepackaged programmed textbooks, or teaching machines with which programmed teaching materials are used, is not the topic of discussion in this chapter. To reiterate, the term *programming* is used here to denote the planning of a learning sequence based on a careful evaluation of the learner's individual abilities and disabilities.

The purpose of programming is to effect a match between the abilities of the individual child and what and how he is to learn.

Let us illustrate what is meant by the word *match* with an example from the teaching of reading. Whenever the results obtained from the use of various materials and methods have been compared, no clear-cut superiority of one method over another has been evident. In each classroom there are children who will learn by any method, but there are also others who can progress only when the emphasis is on a particular approach, such as phonics, or the whole-word method, or linguistics, or a kinesthetic or tactile method, and so on. To help such a child, it is necessary to establish which specific method will be most helpful, what materials are preferable, whether group or individual work is indicated, and so on, before optimum progress in reading can be expected.

In schools where thorough testing is possible, results from the four "basic" tests mentioned in the previous chapter, combined with classroom observation, provide a good initial foundation with which to design a program. An understanding of these tests is of value, however, even when the tests themselves cannot be used—after all, the test items are designed to elicit samples of the child's abilities which are necessary for adequate life adjustment, including learning in the classroom. When testing is not available, the equivalent can still be observed in the classroom—provided the teacher knows what to observe. She, therefore, has to understand the underlying rationale of the test and know what behavior it is designed to evaluate. One ultimate goal is to help the child develop the functions tapped by the tests.

Constructing an Individualized Program

Classroom organization, the teacher, the peer group, the curriculum, and the methods and materials used are all relevant to the child's progress and can be adapted to his needs.

The principles of teaching remain, of course, the same in any kind of instruction, but they need to be particularly heeded and emphasized in educating the child with learning difficulties. Nevertheless, in this as in other chapters, the methods, techniques, and materials that are discussed are important for all children and not only for the child with learning deficits.

As has been stated, an individualized program is always based on the results of the evaluation of the child, but the evaluation is only one factor in programming effectively. The second is the resources the teacher has at her disposal. They have already been enumerated: the teacher, the classroom structure, the peer group, the curriculum, the methods, the materials, and community resources.

The child who is healthy, whose needs are satisfied, often adjusts to the various types of classroom management found in private and public schools with little outward manifestation of inner unrest. But this adjustment may only be superficial—many children do not like school. This sad state is brought about by the fact that the classroom routine often does not take the child's needs into account, at least not to any significant degree. In fact, many administrators and teachers seem not to be well informed as to what these needs are.

Observing children at play reveals as much about their needs as the treatises of scholars. Children need to move, to explore, to translate their ideas into action, and to communicate with other children. They should not be expected to sit still for hours at a time, to be interested when told routinely what to do, or to listen passively to the teacher's voice.

It was stated earlier that the public-school system rarely satisfies the needs of the culturally different or economically deprived child. This statement also holds true for all children with learning difficulties. In fact, many school routines are likely to stultify some abilities in most of their students—the ability to move skillfully, to communicate verbally, to generate ideas, to appreciate beauty, and to relate to others in a friendly and trusting way. Although schools tend to fail all children in some ways, the failures are most apparent in children who have difficulty in adjusting to the school environment, particularly culturally different, economically deprived, emotionally disturbed, or brain-damaged children. The violent reaction of these children, their anger, their crying and complaining, their disorganization, impulsivity, hyperactivity, or withdrawal, their inability to pay attention or to follow through a plan or complete their assigned tasks, are warning signs to both the teacher and the school authorities that some adjustment must be made. Often machinery is set in motion and diagnostic procedures are introduced, but limited therapeutic measures follow. On the other hand, the quiet, compliant, well-behaved child remains unnoticed, if he passively submits to the routine, though he may dislike it intensely and perform far below his potential.

In our time of anxiety and unrest, of noise and overcrowding in the cities, and abysmal poverty in some rural areas, children need a therapeutic classroom environment because all of them *may have* problems, although not all of them *are* problems to the teacher and school authorities.

The classroom routine should be adjusted to the physical, emotional, and cognitive needs of each individual child, rather than providing a rigid structure to which the child must conform. We have already called such a classroom the open classroom.

The open classroom permits the individualizing of both classroom management and curriculum. Its structure supports the child's development and does not stultify it. Although it would be ill-advised to change the structure of a traditional classroom suddenly and completely, certain measures that are of specific importance for the child with learning difficulties can be introduced without difficulty.

Task Cards

One example of a teaching aid that permits individualization and also provides the necessary guidance for the child is the task card. These can be routinely prepared by the teacher.* The task card for a child who needs a more structured program, as do most children with learning problems, may spell out his tasks in great detail, including where he should work, what materials he should use, what he is to accomplish, and in what period of time. The child who needs less structure may be permitted to choose those cards that require him to solve the problem or express his ideas in the areas that interest him most. The teacher may use color coding (blue, green, or yellow cards, and so on) to indicate different levels of difficulty. Telling the child to choose cards of a certain color narrows his choice.

The three examples of task cards described below all give practice in drawing bar graphs, but each requires a different degree of structure. Card I would be given to those children who need very careful structure; Card III to children who have the greatest skills in self-direction; and Card II to those of intermediate ability in working self-directedly. When using task cards, two or three children can work together. Group work helps the children to cooperate and learn how to divide tasks in solving a common problem. This provides excellent experience in planning.

Task Card I**
The principal of a school ordered chairs of different sizes: 4 chairs with a seat 12 inches from the ground, 6 chairs at 14 inches, 8 chairs at 16 inches, and 2 chairs at 18 inches. Now get a sheet of paper from the box with the green label on the top shelf. Draw a bar graph showing how many chairs of each height the principal has ordered, then color the bar graph.

Task Card II
In your room there are 3 round tables and one rectangular table. The chairs around them are supposed to be arranged so that there are 4 smaller chairs with seats 14 inches from the ground, and 2 bigger chairs with seats 16 inches from the ground around each of the round tables. There should be 2 chairs with seats 18 inches from the ground at the rectangular table. How many chairs of each size should there be in the

---

* Task cards for certain subjects are also commercially available. An example is "Let's Discover Mathematics Workshop 1," printed in Great Britain by Robert Cunningham & Sons, Ltd.
** A child who might have difficulty reading the card can have another child assigned to help him.

room? When the other children are doing their free reading on the carpet, take a tape measure and check to see if the chairs are correctly arranged. Write a note to the teacher if all the chairs are not correctly arranged. Make a bar graph showing the number of chairs of each size in the room. You may choose another child to work with you.

Task Card III
The principal of our school needs to make an inventory of the available chairs. Take a tape measure and measure the height of the seats of the chairs in this room and the height of the chair seats in Mrs. Black's room. Find out the number of chairs of different heights. Draw a bar graph for each room separately, and one for both rooms together, showing the number of chairs at each height. Don't forget to ask Mrs. Black when it would be convenient for you to measure the chairs. Choose a child to help you.

Task cards and the flexible classroom organization that results from the use of task cards can be of help in integrating the child with learning and behavior problems into the classroom, because the following measures become possible:

1. Scaling down tasks for the child with learning difficulties without singling him out as one who can't do what the other children are doing.
2. Remediating learning difficulties by means of specifically designed task cards.
3. Pairing the child with an advanced and more controlled child who can give guidance to the slow learner and help him with his task. This practice is of benefit to both children.
4. Including the restless child in a small group. Group pressure will often eliminate disturbing behavior.
5. Permitting children to move and change body positions for a purpose (as measuring the chairs). The child's body movements are then channeled into necessary behavior, helping the restless child to avoid disruptive behavior and enabling him to adjust to the classroom routine with greater ease.

Classroom Grouping

Not all aspects of classroom management need to be individualized. The teacher can assist the child in his emotional and social growth through a wise choice of the group size in which the child works and the number of children with whom he interacts during any activity. For example, John may work by himself doing an arithmetic exercise; Don, Edward, May, Mary, and Leo may act in a play in a corner of the room, following an outline they prepared the preceding day; Max,

Alphonse, and Susan may work at the research table, finding information in various books on how to take care of tropical fish and compiling
a report for the class; Thomas, Marian, and Bill may have chosen a
task card telling them to measure each other's height, both standing
and sitting, to measure across the shoulders and around the waist, to
note down the measurements, and then make a proportional drawing
of the three of them, using two inches for each foot of their real size.

On the other hand, the teacher may prefer to have most of the
children engage in the same activity with just one small group working
on another task. But provision should always be made to have everyone
work together on some activities during the school day. Activities that
permit a great deal of self-expression, such as painting or working with
clay, need not be individualized, although at times certain children
may have to be excused because they may have problems in handling a
given task or situation.

The following is an example of an activity that was shared by all
the children in a high first-grade class. It is described because of its
multiple values for the children, and because, although a group activity, it permitted individual self-expression.

The teacher* explained to the children the meaning of flags. She
cited as her first example the stars and stripes on the American flag.
She said, "We have the stars and stripes on our flag because they show
something that is important to us. There are fifty stars because there are
fifty states. Initially there were only thirteen states, so there are thirteen stripes in our flag to remind us of the beginnings of our big
country." She continued to explain the meaning of the designs on various flags, then asked the children, "Now would you please each draw
your own flag. Put on your flag what is important for you."

Sam drew two skis because skiing was the most important thing in
his life. Max decided to draw symbols of nine different things (among
them his family and a plate of cookies) because all of them were
important to him, while Jane drew the apple tree in her garden. Each
child then described in writing what he had drawn.

This example shows how a gifted teacher can choose activities that
take into account the children's emotional and social as well as cognitive development. She gave the children new information, helped
them to understand the meaning of the salute to the flag, clarified a
concept (flag), assisted them in developing skills (drawing, writing),
and provided the opportunity for creative expression. Above all, she

* Susan Brown, teacher in an open classroom in a public school in Hart-
ford, Connecticut.

helped in the development of self-awareness and a positive self-image that is of such crucial importance for all young children, especially for those with learning and behavior difficulties.

Structuring the Curriculum

A few sentences need to be said about structuring the curriculum for the child with learning difficulties. As a rule the teacher does not have much freedom in designing the over-all curriculum. It is usually prescribed. But the teacher can usually make significant adjustments adapting the standard curriculum to the needs of the child. What has been unrelated to the child's needs—abstract, foreign, or too technical —can become interesting, meaningful, and even fascinating if the teacher relates it to the child's own experiences.

Decimals, for example, are often not understood, but may become self-evident and most important when they are presented in money problems involving the purchase of candy, car models, a minibike, or a racing car—depending on the age level of the learner (and the income of the parents!).

Bruner (1971) describes in his book *The Relevance of Education* how rough and rowdy leather-jacketed teen-agers became involved in the subject of Julius Caesar's conquests; the last ruler-general of the Roman republic became their hero, and they detested Pompey. Learning Roman history or any other subject matter, problem-solving, using written language, reading books, and above all, understanding another person's point of view (decentrating) can become rewarding activities, even for the child with learning and behavior problems.

New curriculum materials continually appear on the market, and the teacher must keep up with them in the same way that a librarian must keep up with the new books. Curriculum-materials centers can be of great help.*

The teacher's choice of materials, methods, and tasks obviously depends upon the child's developmental levels. The authors use the plural form of the word *level* to emphasize that each of a child's various psychological functions may be at a different developmental level;

---

* The Special Education IMC/RMC network is administered by the United States Office of Education—Bureau of Education for the Handicapped. Regional centers, such as the Instructional Materials Center for Special Education, University of Southern California, can supply information concerning methods and materials resources related to special education to schools in surrounding states.

children with learning problems usually show marked discrepancies, as evidenced by their test scores. The materials used for any given child must therefore be at varying levels of difficulty. A youngster in third grade may work at the first-grade level in reading and at the fourth-grade level in arithmetic. He may have to struggle to accomplish visual-perceptual tasks that usually pose no difficulties to first graders, while showing excellent ability to judge and reason and infer.

In spite of the variety of materials on the market, the teacher faces two taxing problems in deciding on an individual program. The first is the problem of using the materials prescribed for a particular grade level when the child is not yet ready for the activity. Some of these materials are often too difficult for some of the children; sometimes they are too difficult for most of the children. Much preparation on the part of the teacher may be needed to help the child understand the new concepts presented in regular textbooks. Sometimes easier materials can be substituted for those prescribed. When this is not possible, the child has to be guided step by step. And as the example of teaching the significance of the flag illustrates, highly abstract concepts can be made meaningful if they are tied into personal experiences.

The second problem with which the teacher is faced is choosing the teaching materials most suitable for ameliorating the child's deficits. It is important to have materials ready that match the child's specific disability patterns. A series of task cards, for example, might be prepared to provide practice in each ability tested or observed.

Principles of Teaching

Many principles that characterize good teaching and are necessary in the education of a child with learning or behavioral disabilities have already been discussed (e.g., immediate feedback and reinforcement, step-by-step progression, providing for self-direction, enhancing the child's self-concept, and so on). A few principles need further discussion.

One well-known rule is that tasks need to be so structured that they progress from the simple to the complex. If a task seems too difficult for a child, the teacher should analyze it to pinpoint the aspect that has given difficulty and ascertain the reason. It may be the result of any of a number of disabilities. For example, if a child makes spelling mistakes because he spells phonetically (e.g., "korekt" for "correct" and "mite" for "might"), the reason may be that he has visual-perceptual difficulties. If he spells "correct" as "cracked" and "might" as "mind" he probably has auditory-perceptual difficulties, or difficulties in auditory-visual association.

Equally important, the teacher must analyze the component steps in the task with which the child is faced. Task analysis is basic to the choice of methods in reading, math, and writing.

Often aspects of a task have to be solved before the task can be taught as a whole. For instance, the child may have to practice making straight and curved strokes before he can form a written letter, and each letter before he can write a word.

Motivation

The problem of motivating children also deserves additional discussion. While the term *ability* denotes what a person can do or could do under optimum circumstances, *motivation* denotes what a person will do or want to do. It is often difficult to separate the two, and in no situation can one better observe the interaction between ability and motivation than in teaching children with learning problems. Their low abilities cause them to have a sense of failure and therefore low motivation; and their low motivation prevents them from exerting themselves and being successful in their work. If motivation does not improve, it often seems that the ability to learn progressively diminishes as time goes by; but if motivation to learn increases, the ability to learn increases also, with a concomitant change in test scores.

In an article, "The Teacher and Motivation," Walter B. Waetjen (1970) states that motivating the child is the teacher's responsibility. He mentions stimulation through animated speech, the use of films, and interesting diagrams. It it true that such teaching materials and instructional procedures can arouse interest, but the teacher should be aware that children with learning difficulties are often aroused only for short periods of time and their interest swiftly diminishes. Waetjen's suggestions are important, but it is equally important to provide frequent changes of tempo to avoid fatigue and boredom.

A survey of the literature discloses numerous suggestions for increasing motivation by specific teaching methods, but important as these may be, such measures are bound to fail with some children.

Frymier (1970, p. 31) refers to a more general factor, the teacher's "style," as playing an important part in motivation. He points out that every teacher interacts with her students hundreds of times each day; she "bounces off" the children in her class. By "bounces off" Frymier refers to feedback, and to the teacher's reactions in general. Some teachers have a positive "bouncing" style (cf. Engelmann, 1969); they react to the various children with frequent encouragement. Remarks such as "That's good," "Fine," "Keep it up," "How about repeating it to show your group exactly how you did it?" help to focus the child's attention and build his self-concept. Frymier states (p. 32): "Feedback is the stuff out of which self-concept and values are built. Teachers must be aware of the kinds of feedback they provide for their students to perceive."

Children with learning difficulties often need an inordinate amount of approval and continuous reassurance that they are doing well. Their exaggerated demands for attention complicate the situation for the teacher, who may become annoyed and react negatively. (Teachers are, after all, human.) It is therefore very important that children become as "self-reinforcing" as possible, that they observe their own progress and note down what they accomplish. For instance, if the child or the teacher keeps adequate records, the child can see for himself that he forms letters better, writes longer sentences, solves more complicated arithmetic examples, controls his movements better, interrupts less often, and so on, and his anxiety will be assuaged even when progress is slow.

Children are helped most by a teacher who attempts to motivate them by using all the tricks in the book, who provides much encouragement, but who also uses the most effective methods to improve the abilities that are necessary for learning, and is aware of the conditions that promote or hinder progress.

Proactive and Retroactive Inhibition

Two kinds of inhibition in learning may occur. They are termed *proactive* and *retroactive* inhibition. Both are caused by incorrect sequencing and articulation of what is taught. Proactive inhibition refers to the interference that past learning may have on present learning. For example, if a child is taught manuscript writing for too long, it may be difficult for him to learn cursive writing, especially if it is presented as something totally new rather than as an extension and modification of a form of skill already learned. Proactive inhibition can be avoided if the child perceives the connection between what he is doing and learning and some later objective or goal. He must understand that he is to learn something more complicated later on that will be easier because of what he is learning now.

Retroactive inhibition means that new learning interferes with previous learning. While learning something new, the child seemingly forgets what he has learned before. If the teacher makes connections between the sequence of items learned, and if one task is developed as a natural extension and amplification of another, neither proactive nor retroactive inhibition will occur. The similarities and differences between various tasks and skills, and the relationships among facts and processes, have to be pointed out to all children, but especially to those with learning problems who have difficulty in perceiving similarities and differences and making connections among their experiences.

Proactive and retroactive inhibitions are also called negative transfer.

Transfer

Possibly the most important topic discussed in this section on instructional methodology is *positive transfer*. This, in its widest sense, forms the whole criterion of instruction. The choice of subject matter and methods is determined on the basis of whether or not the curriculum will help the child adjust to life's demands; or, in other words, whether he will be able to *transfer* what he has learned to other places, times, and situations.

Not very much is known about the transfer of skills and content learned in the classroom. According to Wittrock (1968), a definition of transfer of training is that it is "the effect of *prior* learning upon *subsequent* learning." But transfer may also have a positive effect on *prior* learning. Subsequent learning may help to generalize, keep in memory, and associate what has been learned before.

Positive transfer is of enormous importance in learning. A student who has learned a skill should be able to use the skill in many different situations. To give a simple example, a student who has learned that $4 + 0 = 4$ and $6 + 0 = 6$ generalizes that adding 0 to a number does not change the number (he learns that zero is the identity factor in addition). This is an example of stimulus generalization. Transfer also enables the student to learn more difficult subject matter because of what he has learned previously. This involves differentiation, as well as generalization. For example, it is far easier for a child to distinguish between a pentagon and a square after he has learned to distinguish between a triangle and a square.

Transfer can also be expressed in terms of *response* generalization and differentiation. Learning to tie a bow on a ribbon leads to learning how to tie one's shoes. This example demonstrates how both perception of similarities and discrimination of differences may be necessary for transfer. In tying a bow on a ribbon, the movements differ somewhat from tying shoe laces, because the loops of the bow on the ribbon will be looser to allow for passage of the wider material, and the bow needs to be spread out and made symmetrical for esthetic effect.

The teacher who understands transfer as resulting from generalization and differentiation will point out both the common elements and the differences between responses that have been learned earlier or will be learned later. When different stimuli require different responses, the emphasis is on the differentiation of stimuli. When different stimuli require the same response, the emphasis is on perception of communalities.

Language plays an important role in transfer. Ellis and Muller (1964) found that training in discrimination by itself does not result in transfer, but that labeling does. Labeling points to the similarities and differences in stimuli. The importance of verbalization for transfer has been studied intensively by Osgood (1961). The crucial importance of using language for the transfer of perceptual skills will be discussed later.

One important condition for transfer is the child's attention. It is difficult, if not impossible, to differentiate and generalize without paying attention to the various dimensions of the stimuli.

Two concepts are basic to the understanding of the value of transfer in education. The first is that of the *learning set*. Harlow (1949) found that skill in discrimination can be acquired, and that animal or human subjects who have learned to discriminate between certain stimuli may subsequently discriminate *at the first attempt* between stimuli they have never before encountered. This refers to the formation of a learning set, not to transfer. In addition to presenting novel stimuli, the task involved in a learning set is not essentially the same as one in which the child had previously been involved. What has been acquired are discrimination skills which can be applied to new tasks directly and immediately. The formation of a learning set has important implications for education. Montessori's sense training constitutes early training in discriminating stimuli. Montessori's (1965) method is intended to prepare a child to solve different discrimination tasks. For instance, a child who has learned to discriminate between geometrical shapes is supposed to be able to discriminate more easily between letters later on. This is an example of forming a learning set.

Learning to learn, which has also been called discrimination learning, is another form of transfer. Learning to learn is a far broader form of transfer. It does not necessarily involve solving a subsequent problem on the first trial, but it involves solving quite different problems with greater ease. The mechanisms in learning to learn are not yet fully understood, but it has most important implications for the classroom.

The transfer of learning to new tasks depends on the degree of learning in the prior task. Overlearning therefore enhances transfer, and in the case of children with learning difficulties, overlearning is indispensable in achieving transfer.

Gagné (1962) defines the conditions of transfer broadly. He relates learning to the student's abilities, general intelligence, and store of knowledge. His theory states that learning consists of building learning sets that are hierarchically related. The acquisition of subordinate learning sets facilitates the subsequent learning of higher learning sets. In practical terms, the teacher needs to help the child develop more complicated skills after he has acquired mastery of easier skills. She has to ask herself what skills the child needs to solve a task and whether he has these skills.

Behavioristic methodology suggests careful task analysis to build learning hierarchies. Gagné's conceptualization of the role of transfer in learning is certainly of great help to those who teach more complicated processes than can be acquired through stimulus or response generalization.

Another facilitator of transfer can be the teacher's guidance through verbal instruction. This guidance can take the form of drawing the child's attention to relevant factors, assisting him to recall relevant learning sets (previous learning), and directing his thinking so that he grasps learning sets of a higher order. For example, a student who has learned to conclude that lowering temperature has an effect (positive or negative) on the growth of plants, and that the amount of watering also influences growth, may conclude that air, its amount, movement, water content, and so on, will also have an effect. He may then combine various previously learned measurements in order to understand the relationships between these factors.

Programming for Training Specific Psychological Abilities

Tables 4 and 5 of Chapter 10 juxtapose explanation and description of the subtests of the ITPA and the WISC with observation in the classroom. They show how an individualized program can be based upon an analysis of each child's assets and difficulties. For instance, if a teacher observes that a child cannot organize materials according to different concepts and scores low on the similarities subtest of the WISC, she can use commercial programs or self-made task cards and activities to help the child develop perception of similarities and differences, enlarge his store of concepts, and categorize.

Specific programs which develop basic underlying abilities are discussed in Section IV.

WORKS CITED

Ellis, H. G., & Muller, D. G. Transfer in perceptual learning following stimulus predifferentiation. *Journal of Experimental Psychology*, 1964, 68, 388–395.

Engelmann, S. *Preventing failure in the primary grades.* Chicago: Science Research Associates, 1969.

Frymier, J. R. Motivation: The mainspring and gyroscope of learning. *Theory into Practice*, 1970, 9, 23–32.

Gagné, R. M. The acquisition of knowledge. *Psychological Review*, 1962, 69, 357–358.

Harlow, H. F. The formation of learning sets. *Psychological Review*, 1949, 56, 51–65.

Montessori, M. *Dr. Montessori's own handbook.* New York: Schocken Books, 1965.

Osgood, C. E. Comments on Professor Bousfield's paper. In C. N. Cofer (Ed.), *Verbal learning and verbal behavior.* New York: McGraw-Hill, 1961. Pp. 90–106.

Waetjen, W. B. The teacher and motivation. *Theory into Practice*, 1970, 9, 10–15.

Wittrock, M. Three conceptual approaches to research on transfer of training. In R. M. Gagné & W. J. Gephart (Eds.), *Learning research and school subjects.* Itasca, Ill.: Peacock Publishers, 1968. Pp. 150–210.

PART IV

The training of psychological skills advocated in this book and discussed in Chapters 12-16 is a relatively new idea in education, but more and more volumes discussing certain aspects of this training are now available.

Training of sensory-motor functions has been discussed by Kephart (Godfrey and Kephart, 1969), Barsch (1965), and Frostig (1970), among others; of auditory-perceptual training, by Semel (1970), Berry (1969), and others; of visual-perceptual training by Frostig (Frostig and Horne, 1972), Dubnoff (1968), Fairbanks and Robinson (1967), Fitzhugh (1966), and others; of language functions based on the psycholinguistic model, by Bush and Giles (1969), Hart (1963), Kirk and Kirk (1971), Minskoff, Wiseman, and Minskoff (in press), and others; of higher cognitive functions, by Aurelia Levi (1966), Bruner (1960), Gagné (1965), and others.

The authors have tried to describe in detail those methods that have received less attention in the available literature. Particular emphasis has been given to the training of psycholinguistic functions and the development of the higher cognitive functions in the context of the regular curriculum. In regard to sensory-motor functions and visual perception, frequent reference has been made to existing publications.

It may be important to stress at this point that *remedial* training of psychological functions needs to be individualized, focusing on the particular areas of disability, while *preventive* ability training is synonymous with a systematic and broadly conceived program to be used by all children. Such training should be directed toward the optimum development of all psychological functions.

The authors also want to reemphasize that careful observation and recording can and must supplement test results in both preventive and remedial training. A child's needs change, and without a careful recording of the child's daily performance, these shifting needs may well be insufficiently considered. Whenever a teacher notices a difficulty, she should examine her teaching methods, the tempo of presentation, and the content of the subject matter presented.

12
MOVEMENT
EDUCATION
AND ITS IMPORTANCE

According to Piaget, as the reader will remember, intelligence develops from early sensory-motor functions. With their help the infant learns about objects and actions; space, time, and causality. Through moving his hand or body in one direction and then back, the child experiences the reversibility of processes. Through the changes his actions bring about in the environment, he experiences the fact that events are linked.

The development of sensory-motor functions during infancy influences the development of all mental processes later on because, as already stated, each developmental stage influences the next, and the functions that develop in each stage become fused with those that evolve later.

Thus sensory-motor intelligence does not lose its significance when language and thought become tools for understanding, decision-making, and mastery.

It has also been discussed previously that the optimum functioning of any ability is not possible without education. The optimum development of the child's total functions is, after all, to a great extent the whole concern of education. The training of the sensory-motor functions must therefore be included in the educational process.

The way in which the sensory-motor functions can be trained through movement education follows in part from an understanding of the functions that develop during the sensory-motor period. The reader is reminded that they are body movement, manipulation,* awareness of the self—including the body—and awareness of the outside world.

All these abilities are of significance for the child's total well-being, and much assistance may be needed to assure their optimum development.

* Manipulation refers to the ability to change the form and placement of an object; it involves visuo-motor and fine motor coordination. Arts and crafts, self-help skills, using Montessori materials—all are examples of manipulation.

Movement education is of importance in the over-all development of every child, but it is crucial in the development of the majority of children living in an urban environment. Imagine children playing in the country. For them, the landscape comprises, in effect, the equivalent of a beautifully equipped gymnasium. There are trees to climb, a slope to roll down, a lawn to run on, a fallen tree for balancing, a ditch to jump over, a branch to swing on, and a rock to throw. Contrast this picture with a city schoolroom—especially one of the traditional type. The children sit still for hours, until at last there may be a session of physical education; and even then the children may spend most of that time standing still, waiting their turn for the various activities.

If these same children could run and play and climb and jump after the school day ended, their long inaction might prove innocuous, but for the urban child there is rarely space for him to play freely and securely. He is deprived of the natural exercise needed for him to become aware of his body and of the relationship of his body to the environment.

The first handicap resulting from lack of movement is a depreciated joy in living. Each year many papers are written discussing the relationship of various activities to reading; very few are written discussing the relationship of school activities to the experience of joy and well-being. The result of our lack of concern with how children feel is that some of them try to burn down the schools almost as soon as they are able to strike a match.

In this age of seeming comfort, in which we can supposedly adjust the physical climate to our needs by turning a switch—at least, indoors —in which new foods to please our palates appear in the markets daily from all over the world, and household machinery frees the housewife from much labor, our emotional climate is uncomfortable, including the emotional climate in which millions of children grow up.

We are not so naive as to believe that the introduction of a good movement-education program—or even good education—will change this sad state of affairs. J. Bruner (1971, p. 98) is correct when he writes: ". . . the past decade has taught us that educational reform confined only to the schools and not to society at large is doomed to eventual triviality." But good education can certainly help to bring about needed and beneficial social reforms.

Significance of Movement Education

A more general use of movement education is only one aspect of the many changes needed to provide a healthy and happy school environment, but it is an extremely important one, because movement, especially self-directed movement, like no other aspect of the curriculum, can make children aware of themselves as individuals able to perform feats of speed and skill, to master their own bodies, conquer space, and joyfully interact with each other. Movement education can thus improve a child's self-concept. Body awareness leads to body control, which requires concentration and self-monitoring, and body control leads to greater self-mastery. If these abilities are transferred to the classroom, movement education can be a powerful tool in promoting a more serene classroom environment. The self-awareness that movement education fosters is paralleled by a greater awareness of the outside world, most significantly of other children. When children move in pairs or small groups, they become sensitive to each other. Whether they move in unison or work together to solve a movement problem, they have to adapt the strength, tempo, and extension of their movements to each other. Awareness of another is the first step in cementing cooperation, understanding, and friendship, and—needless to say—goes a long way in ameliorating behavior problems.

These girls enjoy their awareness of each other's movements as they run in a circle retaining their grasp of the hoop. Such an exercise also promotes perception of spatial relationships, force, tempo, and one's own body.

Every child should have at least one half-hour daily of supervised play and movement education, but children with learning problems may need additional intensive structured and guided movement education. Some may also need a special program of manipulatory activities or occupational therapy.

Manipulation

Training in manipulatory activities is usually adequately provided for in preschool and kindergarten curricula, and later through arts and crafts programs, scientific experiments and workshop activities.* It should certainly not be neglected. It is in handling objects that the child learns to differentiate between textures, forms, and sizes, and discovers that a thing looks quite different when seen in different positions and from different angles. He also acquires skill in fine motor coordination.

Body Awareness

Body awareness may be defined as a combination of the sum of all feelings concerning the body (body image), the automatic adjustments of bones and muscles necessary for posture and movement (body schema), and factual knowledge concerning the body (body concept). (See Frostig, 1970, pp. 43–65.)

Body awareness is intimately connected with the child's whole physical and emotional adjustment (Ajuriaguerra, 1965; Schilder, 1964; Johnson, 1962; Wapner and Werner, 1957). Although all the child's experiences are reflected in his feelings about his body, movement education can be a highly effective way of influencing these feelings.

One aspect of training a child in body awareness is to ask him to concentrate on particular parts of his body. For example, the teacher might say, "Lie on your back on the floor. Relax completely. Feel as if you are melting into the floor. Good. Now concentrate only on your right knee. Can you sense where it is? Now turn it slightly inwards;

---

* Suggestions for craft and workshop projects using inexpensive or free materials may be obtained from any public library. The project sponsored by Arizona State University, Arizona Center for Early Childhood Education, Tucson, has many useful ideas.

now outwards again. Keep repeating that. Fine. Now relax again." Another exercise might be, "Lie on your stomach on the floor with your hands under your chin. Good. Now see if you can raise your elbows from the floor a bit. Keep your hands where they are. Good." Tactile feedback may be given in the exercises; for example, the teacher might gently touch the child's knee or elbow and exert a slight resistance to the movement.

Practice also needs to be given in perceiving the body in relation to space. For example, the child might be told: "See how far you can reach out in each direction from where you are standing. First, reach out with your arms. Good. Now with one leg and both arms, standing on the other leg."

Exercises should be given frequently to promote perception of the body in relation to others, and to promote interaction with others. For example, one child may be required to pull another across the room. The child who is pulled should offer just enough resistance for his partner to have to exert effort, but not so much that he cannot be pulled. The exercise requires mutual cooperation, and each child's awareness of both his own and his partner's efforts.

It is essential to develop social contacts through activities requiring cooperation. All children enjoy them, and there are no unhappy losers as too often there are in competitive activities.

Training Movement Skills

Factor analytical studies generally agree that the abilities that can be differentiated in movement are coordination, agility, balance, flexibility, strength, speed, endurance. These attributes of movement have been defined by Orpet and Heustis (1971) as follows:

Coordination and Rhythm
Gross motor: The simultaneous and coordinated use of several muscles or muscle groups. Rhythm denotes flowing, measured, balanced movement.

Agility
The ability to initiate movement, change direction, or otherwise adjust position speedily.

Flexibility
The ability to move parts of the body easily in relation to each other with maximum joint extension and flexion.

Strength

The force exerted with the whole body or with parts of it.

Speed

The tempo achieved during a movement sequence.

Balance

The ability to maintain a position with minimal contact with a surface.
Static: Balance in which the surface is stable and the person is not moving.
Dynamic: The ability to maintain a position on a moving surface.
Object: The ability to use a minimal surface to support an object without letting it fall.

Endurance

The ability to sustain physical activity and resist muscular fatigue. (Do not rate children under eight years of age.)

Training in these skills is important for all children but especially for children with learning difficulties who are characteristically deficient in movement skills. For instance, the mean scale scores on the Frostig Movement Skills Test Battery (Orpet, 1972) for three classes of children with learning difficulties were all below the mean-scale score of the normative sample of 744 public school children (Frostig, 1971). The six- to eight-year-old children with learning difficulties had particularly low scores in tests involving agility, speed, and balance, as well as in tasks requiring transfer of objects across the midline of the body (e.g., transferring marbles from one hand to another).

Training in basic movement skills is essential for these children. They may need help and practice in the basic forms of locomotion, such as running, galloping, hopping, skipping, and so on. They also need exercises in throwing and catching. These exercises can be adapted so that in doing them each child can experience success. In catching and throwing beanbags (in which the primary ability required is coordination), for example, some children may need to stand still and throw their beanbag gently into the air in order to catch it; others can walk while tossing their beanbag into the air and catching it; still others can toss their beanbag back and forth to a partner or among a group of children; while others with severe difficulties may have to stand with their hands forming a bowl and learn to grasp the beanbag that the teacher throws gently.

To walk a balance beam, some children may need the help of another child; others will be able to walk unaided; while still others may be able to introduce variations in movement, position, body support, and tempo as they move along the beam.

Children with learning problems often have great difficulty in learning movement sequences, which requires the child to pay attention and to keep the total sequence in mind while doing the various movements in the correct order. Suggestions for helping the child to learn a sequence of movements follow.

The teacher can structure an exercise or movement sequence by clarifying the temporal, spatial, and causal relationships of the task step by step. Learning to run a relay race, for example, can be structured step by step. The teacher first shows the children where each should stand in line, thus making them aware of spatial relationships. She might then suggest the following as an introductory game: "When I say 'Run!' you run to your places. See if you can get there before I repeat the word 'run' four times. It will sound like this: 'Run . . . run . . . run . . . run!' All ready? 'Run . . . run . . . run . . . run!' " In waiting for the signal, running immediately after hearing it, and in keeping track of the number of times the word "run" is said, the children learn to perceive temporal sequences.

After the children have learned to run to a goal, the teacher should ask them to take turns in walking to a designated place on a given signal, pick up a beanbag, and return to the end of the line, handing the beanbag in passing to the child at the front of the line. Finally, the children repeat the sequence as a relay race, but running instead of walking. In such a step-by-step sequence, the temporal relationships can be emphasized by telling the children, "*First* you do this; *then* you do this; *finally* you do this." The spatial relationships can be emphasized by pointing out, "You go from your place to the goal, then back to the first child in line, and then to the end of the line."

The teacher may, however, have to divide the task into further steps for some children—for example, it might be necessary to teach the children how to hand the beanbag to the next child.

Children with learning difficulties should be required to overlearn each segment of an activity through repetition until they can complete the entire sequence without mistake. Clinical experience indicates that many children otherwise unable to reproduce movement sequences are helped if they are able to observe them repeatedly, as well as experience them. They should therefore, have ample opportunity to observe the teacher and each other. Teaching all the steps of an exercise, such as the relay race, may take days or even weeks, but the children will learn in this way to engage in sequential behavior and become more aware of time, space, and causality.

Structured movement exercises should be presented verbally, pictorially, and in writing.

FIGURE 1

Figure 1 is a pictorial presentation of an exercise for younger children. The oral and written instructions might be:

1. Stand straight.
2. When I clap, run to the gate.
3. Run back.

FIGURE 2

Figure 2 is a pictorial presentation of an exercise for older children. The written instructions might be:

1. Hands and feet on the floor like a dog.
2. Hands off the floor, weight on legs.
3. Stand straight.
4. Bend knees and stretch arms forward.
5. Be a "dog" again.
6. Repeat three times.

Spatial and temporal structuring, especially when frequently verbalized by both the teacher and each child, is most helpful in making children aware of sequences in time and space and of cause and effect. It is an important aid to ameliorating global disturbances because it helps children to formulate and internalize a plan of action, to learn it, to execute it, and to repeat it.*

Structuring Movement Education

The effectiveness of movement education is enhanced if the time is structured so that relaxation exercises follow lively or stimulating ones. Children with learning difficulties frequently require a different tension level from the majority of their classmates. Movement education offers an opportunity for these children to adjust the tension and tempo of activities to their own needs. If the teacher varies the activities and permits a child to rest—or to punch a punching bag, for example—when he wants, the child will regulate his own tension level.

Each session should begin with a "warm-up exercise"—running, hopping, or some other lively action. Exercises to improve body awareness and attributes of movement (coordination, agility, balance, flexibility, speed, strength, and for older children, endurance) should be included.

In some schools playground activities are tightly structured. All the children using the playground are told in what activities they are to engage. In other schools, playground activities are undirected; children entertain themselves as best they can. This freedom is detrimental to children who are anxious, feel friendless, have little imagination or a poor self-concept. Those children are often unoccupied; they become bored, mischievous, and aggressive as a result.

Teachers help children best when they suggest games, teach playground activities, and interact with the children, thus providing a model. Age-old children's games and activities and the use of playground equipment** can provide a great deal of fun as well as enhancing the children's skills.

* From *Movement Education: Theory and Practice* (Frostig, 1970), pp. 140–142 and the Teacher's Guide to *Move-Grow-Learn* (Frostig, 1969), pp. 39–41.

** Designs of two playgrounds equipped with inexpensive materials, such as wooden poles, ropes, and pipes, are shown on pages 158–159 of *Movement Education* (Frostig, 1970).

Visual Perception and Movement Education

As discussed earlier, the sensory-motor phase, during which the child's world is explored by all the senses and movement simultaneously, lays the foundation for later perceptual skills.

The child learns to recognize distances and spatial relationships while moving in space, and children who are handicapped in movement or lack experience in playing in open spaces may lag in the development of such visual-perceptual skills as perception of position in space and spatial relations.

Movement education can ameliorate these problems by providing motor and tactile experiences that guide visual perception during such activities as climbing, throwing and catching balls, rolling hoops, and so on. Movement education also provides the child with experiences of the temporal and spatial aspects of the world and of his own actions within it. The example of learning to run a relay race, given above, illustrates this. Learning to perceive temporal and spatial sequences is of subsequent help in academic learning.

Auditory Perception and Movement Education

Auditory perception is trained when the child attends to verbal directions, translates music into movements, or responds to rhythms played on percussion instruments.

The use of music and of percussion instruments is useful in stimulating and sustaining movement. But music should not be used excessively, because it is important for children to become aware of their own body rhythms. If the child's own rhythm occasionally directs the beat of the instrument, rather than vice versa, his awareness of it is enhanced.

Children can be made aware of various aspects of sound, such as pitch and volume, by adapting movements to them. For instance, children may move low to the floor when a deep note is sounded and as high as possible (on tiptoes with uplifted arms) when a high note is sounded. Attention to sound can also be enhanced by using a change in tone or loudness or rhythm as a signal for shifting the direction, kind, or tempo of movement. For example, "When the music is fast, run in a circle; when the bell rings, 'freeze'; when the music is soft and low, lie on your back." Such activities also help promote intersensory integration; kinesthetic, auditory, and visual channels are used simultaneously.

Language and Movement Education

In regard to language, movement education enhances the ability to follow simple directions, and also teaches a spatial and temporal vocabulary; e.g., such words as *in between, fast, sooner.*

Expressive language can also be developed by having the child describe the movements he plans and those he has completed. The verbal expression of an activity heightens awareness of it. For example, a young child may explain a movement sequence that he has planned as follows: "I will run in a circle, and when I pass the window, I will jump, pulling my knees up as high as possible." A more advanced child may be able to lengthen this sequence, and add: "I will make a half turn in the air, and when I land, run in the other direction, completing a circle. I will repeat this exercise twice more." In having the children verbalize their activities routinely,* the teacher promotes expressive language, sequential thinking, and motor planning.

These abilities are also promoted when children become involved in planning and evaluating movement education sessions, and when they take turns in giving directions and being the teacher.

Movement Education and Association

During movement education the child learns to follow directions, which requires him to make associations between auditory stimuli and a movement response. He learns to imitate movement sequences, which require him to make associations between visual stimuli and movement.

He also learns to integrate the perceptions of more than one sense modality. All movement requires the association of various kinesthetic perceptions and other sensations emanating from the body (proprioception). In climbing, for example, tactile and proprioceptive input is integrated; in dancing to music, auditory, visual, and proprioceptive stimuli are associated.

Associating present movement with previous experiences occurs when the child reproduces a movement he has seen, and whenever movement skills are all taught in a gradual step-by-step fashion.

---

* Care should be taken, however, not to slow down the tempo of the movement-education period.

Movement Education and Imagery

As already discussed (see Chapter 8), imagery is indispensable for the formation of associational nets. Bruner (1966), Hebb (1968), and Piaget and Inhelder (1971), among others, have discussed the importance of imagery in associative processes. Imagery is also necessary for planning (Abravanel, 1968).

Exercises that require the reproducing (as opposed to copying) of movements and movement sequences give practice in visual imagery. The same is true when the child translates into movement a pattern that the teacher has drawn on the board, or executes an activity indicated by pictures of stick figures.

Movement Education and Thought Processes

Thought processes can also be developed by movement education. Movement education can help the child learn to keep several ideas in mind simultaneously and help develop his memory for sequences as when he is following such complicated directions as, "Take two steps forward on tiptoe, then take three hops forward, followed by twelve running steps on the spot. Then run forward until you reach the opposite wall."

Concepts of time, space, force, and resistance can be taught through providing movement experiences that vary according to these dimensions.

Problem-solving is a most important aspect of movement education. To give a simple example, the child might be instructed: "Find three ways of jumping over a low beam, changing the direction of your body while jumping." Problem-solving through movement education simultaneously involves the child in seeking creative solutions and new avenues for self-expression.

Creative Movement

Movement education should provide opportunities for creative movement, as well as training the specific attributes of movement. Creative movement involves the individual in finding his own solution to movement problems, in self-expression, and in creating a free flow of movements. The teacher's role in creative movement is to stimulate the children's inventiveness and provide assistance, not to demand set responses. The goal is to help children to be able to think, feel, and act for themselves, not merely to be mechanically able to perform a set task.

Children should be encouraged to form movement sequences to explore space, changing their direction of movement (forward, backward, and so on), the extension of their bodies (tiptoes, crouching, rolling, and so on), their speed and flow of movements (smooth, abrupt, and so on), the weight of movements (heavy or light); the points of support of the body (touching the floor with the hands, head, elbows, buttocks, and so on, as well as the feet); and the shape of the body (twisting it like a screw, spreading it like a wall, and so on). These basic dimensions of movement have been drawn from the work of Rudolf von Laban (1968).

Initially the children are given relatively simple tasks that can be solved in different ways (e.g., to find how far they can extend themselves in any direction without moving from their place), but gradually the tasks and their solutions become more complex (e.g., the children may be told: "Move in any way you like, in any direction you like, while I play a rhythm on the tambourine. Keep your bodies high. Alter speed when the rhythm alters. Be careful not to bump into each other."). After performing their movement sequences, the children and teacher discuss the solutions that various children have found.

Some of the activities should involve cooperative movement, as when two children are required to move from a sitting to a standing position while holding hands. Or the group may move together in a circle trying not to alter the circular shape.

The activities may also include mimetic play, in which the children "move as lightly as birds," imitate the tread of elephants, or invent a movement expressing happiness.

Creative movement may be used to express and channel both positive and negative emotions. The clarification and symbolic "acting out" of various feelings helps the child understand both himself and others.

If children are encouraged to use their imagination and care is taken to diminish their self-consciousness, they will develop their own ideas. Self-consciousness may be diminished by the use of simple props (such as a piece of net for a veil, or a mask, or a hat), and by the teacher's joining in the children's play-acting until they have overcome their shyness. Then suggestions from the children will come fast and frequently.

In one movement-education session, one child said, "I love the sun. I want to dance a dance catching the sun's rays." Another said, "I want to catch the stars." Both children danced their dance, which carried them in imagination to the sun and the stars, and the other children joined in.

Movement Education and Academic Skills

As movement education influences all psychological functions, it necessarily indirectly affects the learning of academic skills. Movement education can help the child to pay attention, to direct attention, to concentrate, to react promptly to stimuli, to quicken a usually slow tempo of response, to control impulsive reactions, to remember a sequence, and to follow directions. All these abilities are prerequisite for academic success.

But training academic skills through movement education need not necessarily be indirect. Academic skills can also be trained directly, through such activities as keeping score, reading written directions given by the teacher, playing number-line hopscotch, and so on. Some beginning number-line games* are given here as examples:

Number Line Games—Arithmetic Hopscotch
The number line is made up of ten 24-inch squares painted on the surface of the playground and numbered from "Start" (or 0) through 10. It is used for Arithmetic Hopscotch games. Since children should not have to wait in line for any length of time but should be active, it is best to use more than one number line if there are more than eight to ten children in a group.

Game 1: Hop a Number
This game helps children grasp the equivalence of numbers and also makes them aware of the sequence of numbers (seriation).

A child is told by the teacher to hop to a certain numbered square on the number line. The child, who begins at the "Start" square, then finds out that to land on the square marked with a certain numeral he must make an equal number of hops—four hops to reach the square marked 4, five to reach the square marked 5, and so on.

Game 2: Find Your Number
This game, like the preceding one, helps children become aware of the sequence of numbers.

The teacher first covers the numerals on the number line with cards big enough to cover the numeral on each square. She then gives each child a card bearing a numeral corresponding to one on the number line. Each child in turn runs to the square that he thinks corresponds to his number and removes the cover card to see if the numerals match.

The teacher should continue the game, giving the children different numerals each time, until they are thoroughly acquainted with the position of each number.

* From *Movement Education: Theory and Practice* (Frostig, 1970), pp. 115–116.

Game 3: Find Your Neighbor

In this game, the children learn to find the next number. They also become acquainted with partial counting and the concept of adding one.

The teacher tells the children that the square next to a given square is called its "neighbor." Each child in turn is then "given" a number. One child, for example, is given the number 3. He runs to the square numbered 3, and then he makes a single jump and "finds his neighbor," number 4. As he jumps, he shouts, "3 and 1 are 4," looking at the numbers as he does so. If a child has no difficulty in verbalizing number facts, such as "3 and 1 are 4" or "6 and 1 are 7," he may practice variations in jumping, such as landing on one foot or clapping while jumping, in order to avoid boredom and further his movement skills.

Game 4: Find the One Before You

This game introduces children to the concept of subtracting one, and it teaches them to count backward.

The teacher points out that each number has two neighbors, one of which is before it and one after it. Each child is asked to stand on a square and then jump backward, saying first the number from which he starts and then the number on which he lands—for example, "4, 3."

The teacher should explain the meanings of the words plus and minus. Games 3 and 4 can then be played again with the children saying "plus one" as they jump forward and "minus one" as they jump backward. This step prepares children for addition and subtraction with numbers other than 1.

Movement Education and Social and Emotional Development

As discussed earlier in this chapter, movement education can promote not only cognitive and communicative functions, but social and emotional development as well. Movement itself is almost always pleasurable to children, and when combined with feelings of mastery and success, gives rise to a sense of self-worth and an enhanced self-concept. Movement education can also lead to heightened self-control and to better interaction with others.

The type, duration, and intensity of physical and social contact between and among children can be easily and naturally adjusted in movement education. A child can progress in steps that are comfortable for him from doing exercises by himself, to working with a partner but without touching him, to hand contact, to more sustained and involved contact, to group games and dances. Competition, at least in the early elementary grades, can be kept at a minimal level. The increased awareness of the self and others promoted by movement education helps the child decentrate, to understand his social, as well as spatial, relationships with other children.

The importance of movement education in establishing self-control has usually been underestimated in this country. "Psychomotor education"—the European term for what we call "movement education"—is based on neurophysiological and developmental foundations (Naville and Ajuriaguerra, 1967); it lays great stress on inner controls.

Movement education necessarily teaches control of movements, because movements have to be performed in a certain order within a designated space. Movements have to proceed according to a plan, and disruptive movements have to be inhibited. For instance, a child in walking the balance beam must be guided by sensations arising from his muscles and his visual sense, and he must inhibit his awareness of shouts from the other side of the playground.

The control and concentrated attention mastered in movement education may be transferred to the home and classroom, particularly if the teacher helps the child become aware of the ways he has achieved success—planning, visualizing, keeping the goal in mind, concentrating, inhibiting disruptions, and self-evaluating his performance.

A well-rounded program of movement education can influence all the child's psychological abilities, and is particularly effective in helping him focus attention, achieve self-control, and develop creativity.

WORKS CITED

Abravanel, E. The development of intersensory patterning with regard to selected spatial dimensions. *Monograph of the Society for Research in Child Development*, 1968, 33(2), (Serial No. 118).

Ajuriaguerra, J. Discussion. In S. Wapner & H. Werner (Eds.), *The body percept*. New York: Random House, 1965.

Barsch, R. H. *A movigenic curriculum*. Bulletin No. 25, Bureau for Handicapped Children. Madison, Wisconsin: State Department of Public Instruction, 1965.

Berry, M. F. *Language disorders of children: The bases and diagnoses*. New York: Appleton-Century-Crofts, 1969.

Bruner, J. S. *The process of education*. New York: Random House, Vintage Books, 1960.

Bruner, J. S. *Toward a theory of instruction*. Cambridge, Mass.: Harvard University Press, 1966.

Bruner, J. S. *The relevance of education*. New York: Norton, 1971.

Bush, W. J., and Giles, M. T. *Aids to psycholinguistic teaching*. Columbus, Ohio: Charles E. Merrill, 1969.

Dubnoff, B., Chambers, I., and Schaefer, F. *Dubnoff school programs: Experiential perceptual-motor exercises*. Boston: Teaching Resources, 1968.

Fairbanks, J., and Robinson, J. *Fairbanks-Robinson program 1: Perceptual-motor development.* Boston: Teaching Resources, 1967.

Fitzhugh, K., and Fitzhugh, L. *The Fitzhugh plus program.* Galien, Michigan: Allied Educational Council, 1966.

Frostig, M. *Movement education: Theory and practice.* Chicago: Follett Educational Corporation, 1970.

Frostig, M. The psychoeducationl test battery, with particular reference to assessment of movement skills. *Syllabus of instructional courses, 25th annual meeting.* New York: Academy of Cerebral Palsy, 1971.

Gagné, R. M. *The conditions of learning.* New York: Holt, 1965.

Godfrey, B. B., and Kephart, N. C. *Movement patterns and motor education.* New York: Appleton-Century-Crofts, 1969.

Hart, N. W. M. The differential diagnosis of the psycholinguistic abilities of the cerebral palsied child and effective remedial procedures. *Special Schools Bulletin* (Brisbane, Australia), 1963, 5(2).

Hebb, D. O. Concerning imagery. *Psychological Review*, 1968, 75, 466–477.

Johnson, W. Some psychological aspects of physical rehabilitation: Toward an organismic theory. *Journal of the Association of Physical and Mental Rehabilitation*, 1962, 16(6), 165–168.

Kephart, N. C. *The slow learner in the classroom* (Rev. ed.). Columbus, Ohio: Charles E. Merrill, 1971.

Kirk, S., and Kirk, W. *Psycholinguistic learning disabilities: Diagnosis and remediation.* Urbana, Ill.: University of Illinois Press, 1971.

Laban, R. *Modern educational dance* (2nd rev. ed.). New York: Praeger, 1968.

Levi, A. Remedial techniques in disorders of concept formation. *Journal of Special Education*, 1966, 1, 3–8.

Minskoff, E. H., Wiseman, D. E., and Minskoff, J. G. *The MWM program for the remediation of language learning disabilities.* (In press).

Naville, S. and Ajuriaguerra, J. H. Rééducation psychomotríce. *Revue Belge de Therapeutique Physique*, 1967, 34, 3–14.

Orpet, R. *Frostig movement skills test battery.* Palo Alto: Consulting Psychologists Press, 1972.

Orpet, R. and Heustis, T. *Move-grow-learn movement skills survey.* Chicago: Follett Educational Corp., 1971.

Piaget, J. and Inhelder, B. *Mental imagery in the child.* New York: Basic Books, 1971.

Schilder, P. *The image and appearance of the human body.* New York: Wiley, 1964.

Semel, E. *Sound, order, sense, level I.* Chicago: Follett Educational Corporation, 1970.

Wapner, S. and Werner, H. *Perceptual development.* Worcester, Mass.: Clark University Press, 1957.

13

VISUAL-PERCEPTUAL ABILITIES*

Education promotes the development of the child's psychological functions. Like any other aspect of education, visual-perceptual training** includes training in the abilities to think, to learn, and to remember, and it should help the child in his social and emotional adjustment.

Without perception, a human being cannot receive any message from his environment or respond to it. In fact, all consciousness involves perception. The richness and depth of our experience depends on the richness and depth of the stimuli in our environment and our response to them. The enjoyment of art, of nature, of the world around us, depends on the refinement of our perceptual skills—auditory, visual, kinesthetic, tactile—but it is visual perception that is primarily the medium through which human beings encounter their environment. Getman (1962) has estimated that 80 percent of our perceptions are visual.

Montessori, Froebel, and many educators in this century have based education on the quality of the experiences that provide the child with direct contact with his environment—color, shape, size, texture—not only for training his perception, but also as a first step in training higher cognitive functions: classification, seriation, categorization, and so on.

---

* This chapter is based in part on the *Teacher's Guides to Pictures and Patterns: The Developmental Program in Visual Perception* (revised to include basic readiness concepts), by Marianne Frostig, David Horne, and Ann-Marie Miller, 1972. It is used with the permission of Follett Publishing Company, Chicago.

** Visual perception is here defined as the ability to recognize and discriminate between visual stimuli and to interpret those stimuli by associating them with previous experiences.

Purpose and Value
of Visual-Perception Training

Although language training, auditory-perceptual training, and training in cognitive functions have now become specific educational goals, the question, Which children need visual-perceptual training? continues to be asked. It is the firm contention of the authors—and one already emphasized—that *all* children need training in all developmental abilities, although the emphasis will depend on the age level of the child and on his specific needs (language or visual perception or higher cognitive functions).

Visual-perceptual programs will only be fully effective if the training is not solely directed toward visual-perceptual functions, although it should focus on perception. The authors suggest more specifically that it should focus on the five perceptual skills evaluated by the Frostig Developmental Test of Visual Perception, because both classroom observations and experimental studies indicate that these abilities are relevant to a child's school progress.

Figure-ground perception has been regarded as the main visual-perceptual deficit in children with neurological handicaps (Strauss and Lehtinen, 1949). Perception of position in space is thought to be essential to reading by many educators because without it children cannot differentiate between such letters as *b* and *d*. Perception of spatial relationships is essential for spelling; a child has to perceive the sequence of letters in order to be able to place them in their right order. Perceptual constancy (form perception) is important for the ability to discriminate minute details, as, for instance, an *r* from an *n*, or an *a* from a *d*. Visual-motor coordination is not a visual-perceptual ability per se, but is important for manipulative activities and for drawing, writing, and copying, all of which are needed for school achievement.

The examples given are not intended to convey the impression that the authors regard visual-perceptual training solely in the context of its relation to academic learning. Surely most people do not consider language training only in relation to reading. The child who masters his own language will, however, be able to communicate better with others, and this communication will assist his adjustment in the group in which he lives and allow him to play a more effective part in the affairs of the larger community. Mastery of language helps to free a child from egocentric restrictions, and permits him to enter into discourse with individuals and groups extended over time and space; it enriches his life and thereby helps him to enrich the lives of others. In the same way, visual perception is necessary for living a fully satisfactory life. A person who is deficient in visual-perceptual abilities will be deprived of much pleasure in and understanding of the world around him. (See Arnheim's book, *Visual Thinking*, 1969, for examples of how art can give meaning and direction to thought, as well as express emotions.)

Even at a very young age, children need guidance to become aware of their environment. To give an example, every day Doris, aged two and a half, walked quietly to the playground with her mother. One day her mother pointed out a bed of marigolds planted at the edge of the sidewalk. She discussed the colors, the delicate tracing in the leaves, the pungent smell. The little girl listened, looked, touched, and smelled. On the way home from the playground, Doris made many remarks about things she had apparently never noticed before, using words her mother had not heard her say previously, such as, "Some of the leaves on this tree are shiny and green, but some are brown and wrinkly." This example illustrates how conscious focusing on the perception of specific aspects of the environment provides the basis for learning, including the learning of language and concepts.

The question is often raised as to how helpful visual-perceptual training can be. Training in basic abilities has proved invaluable when it is not presented as isolated activity. Giving a child a sheet on which to draw lines or complete a pattern will not often lead to transfer to other situations, unless the paper-and-pencil work is done to master a specific task and is accompanied by planning and verbalization. Many research studies have shown that visual-perceptual training can be highly effective in enhancing the child's ability to learn when it is integrated with training in other abilities. (See, for example, Cowles, 1969; Faustman, 1968; Friedman, 1967; Karnes et al. 1968; Kost, 1964-66; Linn, 1967, 1968; McConnell et al., 1969; Marshall, 1970.)

Integration with Other Psychological Functions

The use of *movement* in combination with visual perception is an important aspect of developing a child's basic abilities and helps him to sustain attention, to come less restless, and to channel his energies. This is especially important for a hyperactive child.

Training in *body awareness* has been discussed in the previous chapter on sensory-motor training. It should either be taught separately, or as part of the visual-perceptual training program. (Examples are given in *Teacher's Guides to Pictures and Patterns*, pp. 16–20.) The more time the teacher is able to use for training sensory-motor functions, the better.

Special care has to be taken to develop laterality if it is not already established. [Examples are given in *Movement Education* (Frostig, 1970), p. 59.]

Both *language* and visual-perceptual abilities are needed for a child to develop optimally. To learn about the world outside, the child must have experience and must be consciously aware of what he is perceiving. When his perceptions are given a label, he is better able to store perceptions in his memory and later retrieve (remember) them. He can also begin to form concepts; that is, he can begin to structure the world in a similar way to the other members of his social group. Concepts of relationship, such as *in, under, over,* and so on, are readily learned when the child associates movement with perception and language, as when he shows how a boat sails *under* a bridge. Learning such relationships is particularly important for economically deprived children, who may not have had enough opportunities for adult-supervised play in the course of which the adult supplies the relationship word.

Memory training is also always integrated with visual-perceptual training. Penfield (1970, p. 121) states, "The sequential record of experience is, in a sense, the record of succeeding perceptions." In perceiving events in sequence, in perceiving sequences in space, and in perceiving events as connected in space and time, memory functions are involved. Thus when a child reproduces bead patterns or peg designs, for example, and later letters, numbers, and words, he is receiving training in both visual perception and memory.

Early Visual-Perceptual Training*

Visual-Motor Coordination**

Such common preschool activities as cutting, painting, pasting, tracing, coloring, model making, bead stringing, and building with blocks provide excellent training in fine motor coordination.

FREE PASTING. Scraps of torn paper, cloth, and other materials can be pasted on large sheets of paper in any way the children want to do it.

PLACING AND PASTING. Placing and pasting exercises train children in many skills in addition to visual-motor coordination: sorting, alternat-

* Material in this section has been excerpted from *Teacher's Guides to Pictures and Patterns*, pp. 21–22, 26–33.
** Some exercises for training eye movement are given in Chapter 18.

ing, following a pattern, and remembering motor sequences. Placing exercises should precede pasting. A placing activity consists of putting three-dimensional objects on an outline and later doing the same thing with cardboard cutouts. For example, the teacher might say, "Let's make some cookies," and ask the children to cut out from modeling dough simple shapes, such as squares, triangles, circles, and hearts. Have them put the cookies on a "cookie sheet" on which the same shapes have already been drawn. Finally, ask them to paste matching construction-paper cutouts over the shapes drawn on the paper.

This activity can be adapted to other geometric shapes as the children learn to recognize and name them.

For example, give the children a diagram like Figure 1.

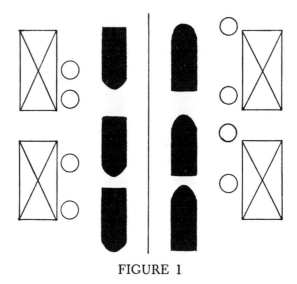

FIGURE 1

Tell them that it is a picture of a street, with houses, trees, and cars. Ask them to put rectangular blocks on the outlines of the houses, toy trees on the circles, and toy cards on the solid black shapes. Then give each child an envelope containing cutouts of the same shapes as those on the diagram, and have them put the cutouts on the appropriate outlines. When the children can place the cutouts accurately, ask them to paste them down.

FINGER TRACING. Both form sense and visual-motor coordination can be enhanced by having children trace geometric shapes and other forms with their fingers. Tracing around shapes and objects with a crayon is usually too difficult for nursery school children, but many may be suc-

cessful in tracing around the inside shape of plastic inserts or of Montessori stencils (available from Creative Playthings, Inc.).

For children who have a motor handicap or whose fine motor coordination is extremely immature, it is often necessary to introduce an
intermediate step between simple finger-tracing activities and the
paper-and-crayon exercises. This can be done by having such children
trace the worksheet exercises with their fingers or push small blocks
(½-inch by ½-inch by 2-inch), representing cars or trains, along the
paths they will subsequently make with their crayons.

FINGER GAMES. Finger games provide exercises in fine muscle coordination and may also be adapted for training in verbal expression,
counting, and remembering sequences. There is an excellent collection
of finger games in *Finger Plays.**

ACTIVITIES WITH CONSTRUCTION AND MANIPULATIVE TOYS. Most of the
toys known as educational toys, such as color cones, interfitting barrels
and cups, beads for stringing, graded blocks, plastic nuts and bolts,
and simple models, can be used for practice in visual-motor coordination. (It should be remembered, however, that the interest of some
nursery school children in bead stringing and working with manipulative toys develops only gradually.) Activities with such toys also provide training in perception of position in space and discrimination of
shape, color, and size. Appropriate words should always be given for
the shapes, colors, sizes, and positions of the components of the toys.

BEAD STRINGING. Bead stringing not only trains fine motor coordination, but it can also be used to train shape and color discrimination
and memorization of sequences.

First, tell the children which color and shape of bead you want each
of them to put on his string. Next, ask each child to string beads of
given colors and shapes in sequences of two, then three, then four.

TRACING AND COLORING. Tracing and coloring should be done concurrently. The children should trace and then color shapes that gradually increase in complexity of outline. The degree of precision required
of the children becomes greater as the outlines become smaller and
more complex.

SELF-HELP ACTIVITIES. All children should be encouraged to develop
visual-motor skills necessary in everyday life, such as buttoning and

* Holl, Adelaide, New York: Golden Press, 1964.

unbuttoning jackets and coats, lacing and tying shoelaces, opening and closing snaps and zippers, using simple tools, carrying objects, and pouring liquids from one container to another. Practice in performing such skills helps to develop a healthy self-reliance.

Montessori suggested that children "sweep the rooms, dust and wash the furniture, polish the brasses . . ." (1965, p. 44). In many modern households there is little brass to be polished, and the rugs are tacked to the floor and cleaned with a vacuum cleaner. But the principle of having children undertake self-help activities is as valid now as it was in 1907 when Montessori worked in *Case dei Bambini* (Children's Houses) in the slums of Rome. Present-day children can at least be encouraged to perform such tasks as setting the table, arranging chairs or rugs, finding and fetching objects, helping in the garden, keeping their room and their clothes tidy, and looking after their personal cleanliness. They should all help in keeping their schoolroom tidy, and in cleaning up both themselves and the utensils after messy activities such as finger painting. A first grader should be quite proficient in these activities.

The importance of self-help activities cannot be too strongly emphasized. Without mastery of such skills, children's awareness of their environment, their ability to observe, and their sense of responsibility will not fully develop. Of special importance is the development of children's ability to plan. For example, the teacher may say, "We will finger-paint at the table. What will we need?" The children will have to remember that they need such things as newspaper to cover the table, aprons or smocks, paints, and special paper. With children for whom planning is difficult, as it frequently is for children with learning difficulties or who come from disorganized households, each activity should be discussed and planned beforehand, and evaluated afterward.

Figure-Ground Activities

Training in figure-ground perception should result in improved ability to shift attention appropriately, to concentrate upon relevant stimuli and ignore irrelevant stimuli, to scan adequately, and in general to show more organized behavior.

DISCRIMINATION ACTIVITIES. Ask the children to point out various categories of objects, such as round things, red things, wooden things, and so on, in a room or play yard. Then ask the children to pick out specific objects, such as a particular book, picture, or toy. As the game continues, the objects the children choose should be less and less conspicuous.

"Policeman, Find My Child!" is a game that the younger children like to play and is valuable in helping them to learn to discriminate. The teacher should play the part of the mother and ask one of the children to be the policeman. The mother then tells the policeman that her child is lost and asks him to help her find the child. The mother describes the child, telling the policeman whether the child is a boy or a girl, the kind and color of clothes he or she is wearing, and other details. The policeman should be able to find and point to the child in the room who fits the mother's description.

At another time, ask the children to find a square button in a box of round ones, a large block among smaller blocks, a green marble among blue ones, a piece of rough paper among smooth pieces, and so on.

A variation of this activity is to put a number of objects of various shapes into a large brown-paper bag and let the children reach into the bag without looking into it. The teacher should ask each child to take hold of an object and try to identify it by touch alone.

EVERYDAY ACTIVITIES. Teachers can help their pupils to improve in figure-ground perception if they use everyday opportunities for practice. While out walking, for example, the teacher may ask, "Do you see the white house?" "Do you see the little bird in the grass?" "Do you see the colored stone?"

In the schoolroom, the teacher may ask a child to pick out a particular crayon from the box or to sort and put away the toy dishes according to size and shape. She might also ask the children to help during clean-up time, telling the children to be sure not to overlook any object.

While the teacher is reading a story aloud, she might hold up pictures that have considerable detail in them and ask the children to look carefully at them and identify separate objects in each of the pictures.

Such activities involve other perceptual abilities, but they are particularly helpful for training figure-ground perception.

SORTING. Sorting is perhaps the most useful exercise in developing figure-ground perception. It helps children to concentrate upon particular stimuli and to shift attention when the principle of sorting is changed. And because sorting involves the correct identification of such qualities as size, shape, and color, it helps improve perceptual constancy, as well as figure-ground perception.

The teacher should mix objects of two or more types together, and ask the children to sort them. Or, she might ask the children to pick out certain objects from a box containing many different objects. At first the objects in the box should differ greatly from each other, but later they should differ less. The children might be asked, for example, to pick out from a box of toy houses all those with flat roofs, all those with pointed roofs, and then all those with painted roofs.

Subsequently the children can be asked to sort shapes. Provide cubes and spheres, for example; then provide cubes, spheres, and three- and four-sided pyramids. Next add more irregular shapes. Objects may be sorted according to size, color, and texture, as well as shape. The more variables among the objects, the more difficult the exercise. It is more difficult to sort out the round black buttons than simply to sort out the round buttons; and it is more difficult to sort out the large, round black buttons than to sort out those that are round and black.

Perceptual-Constancy Activities

Perceptual-constancy activities help children discriminate size, shape, and color, and also help them recognize three-dimensional objects drawn in a two-dimensional plane, and vice versa.

Development of visual constancy depends upon learning. Experience indicates that the ability to perceive constancy can be acquired through training, and that training should first take the form of gaining familiarity with simple shapes of various sizes.

Children should have frequent opportunities for handling objects and materials, fitting them together, taking them apart, and creating structures with blocks of different shapes and sizes. But perception of three-dimensional objects does not necessarily carry over to perception of two-dimensional shapes. Transfer can be increased by having children trace objects and templates and later draw simple shapes.

Templates of simple figures—circles, squares, and rectangles—are available in the Winter Haven program (Sutphin, 1964), or they can easily be made from cardboard, wood, or plastic. For example, in a piece of cardboard, cut a circle about 8 inches in diameter; in another, cut a circle about 3 inches in diameter. (See Figure 2.)

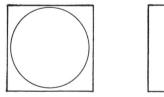

FIGURE 2

Similar sets can be made of squares, diamonds, and rectangles, with the sizes of the cutout portions in about the same ratio to each other as the two circles. Children may also draw around poker chips, blocks, and pieces from parquetry sets.

RECOGNIZING AND NAMING PLANES AND SOLIDS.   Children are usually eager to learn the names of people, objects, and concepts. Names enable them to classify and organize their world, to remember concepts, and to have a means of communication. The names of geometric shapes are no more difficult for children to learn than any other names. They are the labels that help them recognize and classify objects and the attributes of objects that they constantly see and handle.

The names of *circle, square, triangle, cross, star, semicircle, oval, rectangle, diamond,* should gradually be taught. Present each figure by showing blocks of the appropriate shape. Have the children handle the blocks as they learn the names of them. Show only one or two at a time. Each figure should be presented to the children in many positions so that they do not learn to recognize it in one poisition only.

Compare the oval with the circle and the rectangle with the square so that the children understand the differences. Show how the diamond differs from the square.

Have the children use form-boards that include these shapes. If other shapes are on the board, identify them.

When the children know a few of the shapes, play games in which they have to identify the shapes quickly as they are displayed in a variety of positions.

Sphere, cube, cone, cylinder, pyramid, prism: Identify each solid, as was done with the plane shapes, and play games of identification.

PICTURE-RECOGNITION ACTIVITIES.   Some children are unable to recognize pictures of objects even if the objects are familiar. Other children have the reverse problem: because photographs, pictures, and schematic drawings are used in many textbooks, they can recognize a drawing of a square without being able to recognize the squareness of a tabletop or picture frame.

To help develop the ability to translate the visual image of a three-dimensional object to a two-dimensional plane, and vice versa, these activities are useful: Set aside spaces on shelves for blocks of specific shapes. Directly above each space, tape or tack a small drawing of that shape. When the children put away the blocks, ask them to be sure to put each block in the correct space, thus matching the block with the picture. In the reverse process, give a child a drawing of one of the blocks and ask him to find a block of that shape on the shelves.

FINDING AND SORTING ACTIVITIES

Finding different sizes. Show the children two objects of radically different sizes, and ask each child to point out the larger. (Montessori weights, available through Creative Playthings, Inc., are useful in this activity.) Then show the children two more pairs, the difference in size between the objects in each pair becoming less with each pair. Some of the objects should vary only in height, in width, or in depth so that the children, with the teacher's help, can learn to discriminate differences in size in each of the three dimensions.

Sorting according to size. An object of a third size should be added to each of the pairs used in the activity above, and each child should point out which is big, which is small, and which is medium-size. Explain and demonstrate the concept of medium-size.

Then extend the range of sizes and ask the children to arrange the objects in ascending or descending order. Because it is difficult for young children to perceive gradations of size, this exercise may need to be done repeatedly, with reinforcement from work with nesting toys —cubes, cups, eggs, and barrels.

Some Montessori materials can also be used to teach differences in size and shape. For instance, there are long wooden blocks containing series of cylindrical holes that decrease in diameter, in depth, or in diameter and depth. The children should fill the holes with cylinders of the appropriate size.

FINDING THE SAME SIZE. Give each child an object, such as a disk, stick, or ball. Place objects of the same shapes but of a variety of sizes at various distances from the children. Some of these objects should be larger and some smaller than the ones the children have in their hands; some should be of the same size. Ask each child to indicate the objects that are the same size as the one he holds. When he has pointed one out, he should place it on or next to the object he has so that he can see if his choice was correct.

WORDS DENOTING SIZE. Different ways of expressing the same concept, such as *tall* and *high*, should be used. Opposites should be juxtaposed, such as "This block is *thick*; that block is *thin*." Many examples should be pointed out to illustrate such concepts as *tall, long, wide*—a *wide* chair, desk, or margin, contrasted with a *narrow* chair, desk, or margin. The same concepts should be illustrated with pictures showing objects in perspective, such as a *tall* lamp, *tall* building, and *tall* tree.

As the children learn to determine which object or shape is bigger and which is smaller, they should be taught the words for the different dimensions and their comparatives. Say, for instance, "This block is *wide*; that block is *wider*. This block is *tall*; that block is *taller*. It is much *higher*. This block is *thick*; that block is *thin*. It is not as thick as the other one. It is *thinner*."

Finding the same shape. The teacher should show the children a geometrical form and ask each child to identify all the similar shapes in the room. If a rectangle is shown, for example, a child might point out a tabletop, a crayon box, and a book; if a circle is shown, he might point to a clock face, a telephone dial, and a hoop. The teacher may have to make and place in various positions in the room some objects of less common shapes, such as triangles, diamonds, semicircles, and hexagons.

Sorting according to shape. Square, round, and triangular objects should be used to teach recognition of square, round, and triangular two-dimensional shapes. For example, the children may be given cubes, balls, and pyramids and asked to match them with corresponding drawings.

The teacher may also give the children a number of objects of two distinct shapes. The children should be asked to sort the objects into two groups, according to shape. Add shapes that are successively less readily distinguishable from each other.

Position in Space Activities

The exercises for body image, body concept, and body schema, as well as those that follow, all contribute to the development of perception of position in space and spatial relationships. They should on no account be omitted.

BODY-OBJECT RELATIONSHIP ACTIVITIES. The children should do exercises involving the recognition of the position of their bodies in relation to objects. They should climb *on* a chair, jump *over* a block, crawl *under* a table, go *around* a desk, stand *in* a box, step *out* of a circle, and so on. These activities can be carried out in the form of a game, such as an obstacle race, or by command. Sometimes the children should say or shout what they are doing as they do it so that word, action, and position become firmly associated.

The following example shows how large rectangular blocks may be used to help children recognize relative positions.

First, the teacher may ask the children to cooperate in building a large house with an entrance big enough to allow a child to go *through* it. As the children build together, describe the relative positions of the blocks. For instance, "That block goes *on top* of the two upright blocks; that block should go *beside* the doorway," and so on. When the house is finished, ask the children to go *in* and *out* of it, *through* the door, *over* the wall, and stand *in front of* and *behind* the house. As each child takes the position indicated, he should say what the position is.

Activities like this are particularly effective in teaching perception of position in space because they involve the movement and placement of the child's own body in relation to objects.

DIRECTIONALITY. Establishing left and right orientation is necessary if children are to perceive position in space and spatial relationships correctly.
Differentiating left and right on oneself.

1. Have the children sing a song, such as the following, and act it out as they do so. In demonstrating the movements, be sure to face the same way as the children so that you do not confuse them as to their left and right.

> I shake my *right* hand in the air,
> In the air, in the air.
> I shake my *left* hand in the air,
> And try to touch the sky.
>
> I stamp my *right* foot on the floor,
> On the floor, on the floor.
> I stamp my *left* foot on the floor,
> And jump with both together.

2. Using illustrations, say, "Here is a picture of a hand, just like one of yours. Can you tell me which hand it is? Is it the left hand or the right hand?" If the children cannot answer correctly, continue, "Put your hand near the picture, so that it looks just like the hand in the picture." Be sure that the children place their hands palms up or down to match the hands in the pictures. Ask, "Now is that your left hand or your right hand?"
3. Have the children put their right hand over their left hand; their left over their right.
4. Have the children touch or move parts of the body designated as left or right: "Hold your right arm up in the air. Stretch as high as you can. Put it down and raise your left arm."

Differentiating between the left and right positions of objects in relation to oneself. Indicate various objects in the room or on the playground and ask the children to say whether the objects are to their left or to their right. Then tell them to walk and change direction as you direct them. For instance, "Walk forward; turn left; walk forward; turn right; walk forward. Now walk sideways toward the left. Now walk backward and then turn right."

Ask two children to stand opposite each other and take turns moving different body parts. One child should stretch his right arm out to the right side or stamp his left foot on the ground, for instance. The other child should tell whether the body part moved is on the owner's left or right.

Use Figure 3: "Here are two boys. One is facing you and one has his back to you. Show me the *right* leg on each boy." Continue in a similar manner, naming hands and other parts of the body. To reinforce the pictorial impression, ask the children to stamp the right foot, raise the left hand, touch the right knee, and so on.

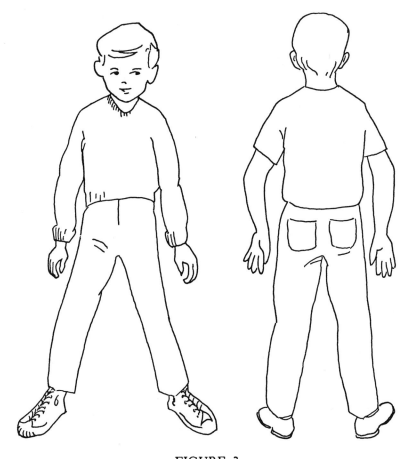

FIGURE 3

Demonstrate with two children working together. Say to them, "Stand side by side. I am going to give you each a stick (or ball or cardboard circle) to hold in your outside hand. We are going to pretend that you are a picture folded in half. So turn to face each other. Do you see what has happened? The sticks are both at the same side. Your right hand (indicate one child) is at the same side as your left hand (indicate the other child)."

Recognition of directions should be practiced throughout the school day. The teacher should say, for example, "Write the date in the upper right corner of your paper." "Draw a horizontal line from left to right." "All children stand at the left of their desks."

Differentiating the left and right positions of objects in relation to each other. After a child has learned to differentiate between right and left in relation to his body, he should learn to differentiate the left and right position of objects in relation to each other. The teacher should realize, though, that many children learn this task only when they are older—in third grade or even later.

An example of how the relative position of objects can be taught is the following: Place two different colored blocks in various positions and ask the children to tell which is to the left of the other; which is to the right. Add a block of another color and discuss the relative positions of all three.

Also ask the children to place blocks to the left or to the right of each other according to your instructions.

REVERSING AND ROTATING. The following three-dimensional activities are designed to help children perceive reversals and rotations of figures.

Squares and diamonds. Place several identical squares of cardboard in front of each child, in random order. Then ask the children to place all the squares so that the sides are horizontal and vertical, like this: □ □ □ . Scatter the squares and tell the children to turn them so that they all stand on a corner, like this: ◇◇◇ . Then give the children diamond shapes so that they can compare them with the squares and see the difference. Ask them to turn the diamonds so that they look like this: ◇◇◇

Triangles. Repeat the procedure above with equilateral triangles. First, have the children turn the triangles so that each stands on a side; then so that each stands on a corner. Next, introduce isosceles triangles. Place one in any position—like this ▽ , for instance—and ask the children to turn their triangles to the same position. Then vary the position to be copied. Repeat with right-angle and scalene (unequal-sided) triangles, and teach the difference between them.

Rectangular blocks. Give the children rectangular blocks and ask each child to place his block in the same position as that demonstrated. With children of nursery school age, this activity and the one following should be done individually rather than in groups.

Block patterns. Two, three, or four blocks may be arranged in patterns for the children to copy. See examples in Figure 4.

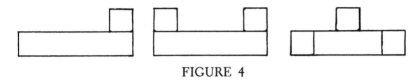

FIGURE 4

At a more advanced level the children can be asked to place their blocks according to designs presented in pictures. They should also be encouraged to make their own designs.

Block pattern exercises promote perception of spatial relationships as well as perception of position in space.

Spatial Relationship Activities

It cannot be emphasized too strongly that training in perception of spatial relationships must begin with and continue to involve the use of three-dimensional objects, including the child's body. Informally, both at school and at home, children may be helped to make simple models, fashion small objects from wood or other materials, and build according to a pattern. Even work in the yard or in the house can involve practice in perception of spatial relationships.

The following activities and games are appropriate for the classroom, but whether presented formally or informally, they should be enjoyable for the children.

BLOCKS. Give each child colored blocks and say, "I want everybody to put a green block *on top of* a blue one. Good. Where is the blue block? That's right—*under* the green one. Now put a green block *in front of* a blue one. Now *behind* it. Good. Now put a yellow block *between* two blue blocks.

"Make a bridge with three blocks. Where is the *middle* block? That's right. *On top.* Let's get another block and pretend that a train is going to go *under* the bridge. It is far away, but here it comes—*nearer* and *nearer.* Now it is *under* the bridge. Make it go *farther* and *farther away.* It is *far away* now.

"Can you use your fingers and pretend to *cross* the bridge? Careful! Fine."

Objects such as colored pegs or marbles can be used similarly to teach relative positions. The children should take turns in giving the instructions to ensure that they use the correct vocabulary.

PATTERNS. Design any number of patterns [with pegs, marbles, poker chips, and so on]. Block patterns may also be reproduced on chess boards. The teacher might build a "village" on his board, for example, and ask the children to build similar villages in the corresponding squares on their boards. Children should not only reproduce patterns but also design some on their own.

Paper and Pencil Exercises

As this book has already discussed, in the chapter on development, the ability to accurately perceive symbols and pictures presented in the two-dimensional plane (on paper), develops in children *after* they have learned to perceive objects and their relationship to each other in three dimensions.

It may, however, be a mistake to wait for the child to master three-dimensional materials before introducing paper-and-pencil exercises, because accurate visual perception in three-dimensional space does not guarantee the ability to work on a plane surface. Work in two-dimensional space does not necessarily depend on good manipulatory skills or on accurate perception of three-dimensional materials. More important, adequate visual perception in two-dimensional space is needed in many academic tasks, such as reading and writing, and must be developed even in children who are clumsy in their handling of three-dimensional materials. Paper-and-pencil exercises should not be delayed beyond the first two weeks of kindergarten at the latest. The activities and work suggested in the preceding section should in any case accompany, as well as precede, two-dimensional work.

There are a number of other visual-perceptual training programs on the market besides that from which we have quoted so extensively, such as those by Belle Dubnoff (1968) (Dubnoff Experiential-Perceptual Motor Exercises), the Fitzhugh *Plus* Program Materials (1966), and Fairbanks and Robinson (1967).

Individualization and Personalization of Training

Visual-perceptual training, like all learning, should begin at the level appropriate for the individual child and proceed step by step. Failure indicates that the task was too difficult, and some intermediate measure is needed. If, for example, a child is able to distinguish three sizes of circles on a worksheet designed to train constancy of size perception, but becomes confused with four sizes, he may need additional practice with three sizes which become gradually more similar. He may also need practice in sorting shapes in order of size (seriation).

Individualization and giving additional help is made possible in a classroom by teaching in small groups based on visual-perceptual ability; by teaching the class as a whole and giving additional practice to individuals; by helping children who have difficulties; by preparing additional self-correcting material at the same level as that already mastered by the child for "extra" work or for homework; by pairing children (e.g., one who is good in language but poor in perception of spatial relationships, with one good in perception of spatial relationships but who has difficulty in verbalizing the relationships); by assigning tasks in a group project that will help each child in the area of his difficulty (e.g., a child with poor figure-ground perception may be asked to sort and put away blocks according to shape during classroom cleanup); and so on.

Whenever possible perceptual training should take into account the special interests of the child. If a child is caught up in the excitement of football, or minibikes, or mythology, for instance, the worksheets may be adapted accordingly. Instead of drawing a line "to show the path a boy takes to meet his friend," he can be asked "to trace the path a football star runs in scoring a touchdown." If such an adaptation requires altering the worksheet picture, artistic skill will not be important; the children will accept even the sketchiest stick figures, or a large X, square, or circle as symbols for the objects that interest them.

Teaching Principles

Feedback

Feedback is necessary in visual-perceptual training, as in all other learning. To get immediate feedback, the children can be required to hold up their papers after completing them so that the teacher can easily perceive any mistakes; or the children can check each other's work; or they can be taught to compare their work with a standard model. Corrections must be made immediately if faulty learning is to be avoided. Homework should therefore be self-correcting, and the assignments selected from tasks that the child has already mastered in the classroom.

Whenever possible correction should be given in a positive form. To say "John, this is wrong" may confirm a child's poor self-concept. But if he is told, "John, look at this part of the page. Why don't you play detective? Push this cutout shape along the row and see if you can find another one just like it!" he may be led to discover the correct solution for himself, and his feelings are more likely to be of enjoyment and accomplishment.

Ensuring Success

Sometimes "crutches" are needed to improve perceptual skills. For instance, the child may first attempt a new worksheet by making crayon marks on a plastic overlay, so that incorrect marks can easily be wiped away and the exercise repeated.

Paper cutouts of an identical shape as the figure to be found or compared may be used. (See Figure 5.)

Repetition is often necessary. In eye-hand coordination exercises, "rainbow tracing" may be used. The child draws the same line repeatedly with different colored crayons.

The child may rehearse the exercise. For instance, he may trace a line with his finger before using a crayon or pencil, or indicate the solution on an overhead transparency before drawing on his own sheet.

Match a cutout with the original.

Slide the cutout across, matching its position with each figure.

Find the figure which is in the same position as the original.

FIGURE 5

Children often develop their own "crutches." For example, a child may point with his finger or use a marker to follow along a line. During the standardization testing with the Frostig test, one little girl could not draw vertical lines. On her second attempt, she was observed folding over the page in such a way that the edge served as a ruler—an excellent example of thought processes compensating for a deficit in eye-hand coordination! Crutches should be permitted as long as the child needs them, but training should be given in the skill for which they substitute until gradually there is no longer the need for them.

Remedial Visual-Perceptual Training

Remedial visual-perceptual training should be started as early as possible. It seems unwise to postpone school entrance because a child is immature in visual perception—or in any other ability—because an immature child is usually the one who most needs stimulation. Special classes or tutoring with emphasis on ability training will provide the best readiness program for such a child. Sabatino and Hayden (1970) state, "The direct relationship between perceptual behaviors and academic achievement suggests that more concentrated classroom and resource room work must be applied directly to these skills in the primary grades."

Remedial training is necessary despite the fact that many children learn to compensate for or develop lagging skills later without special help. At the moment, however, there is no way to predict which children will improve without training. Moreover, those children who do overcome their deficiencies in later grades may suffer considerable feelings of inadequacy and stress during the time they experience difficulty.* The cause and experience of failure may affect their overall ability to learn and their later attitude toward learning. One little girl, who was retained in kindergarten because of her clumsiness and perceptual inadequacies, remarked sadly to one of the authors: "I will be in kindergarten again; I failed in coloring."

Visual-perceptual disabilities are often found in children with learning difficulties. (See for example, the review by Chalfant and Scheffelin, 1969). In a sample of eighty-nine children of nine years of age or older who were referred to the Frostig Center because of learning difficulties, 78 percent had deficits in visual perception. Training in

---

* Such stress is reflected in the high correlation found between low scores on the Frostig test and teacher ratings of classroom maladjustment. (See Maslow et al., 1964, p. 392; McBeth, 1966.)

visual perception at the preschool or early primary level might have prevented or ameliorated their continuing school failure.

The materials and methods used for remedial visual-perceptual training differ from those used in developmental or readiness programs only in that remedial work focuses more strongly on the area of deficit. Integration with other areas of visual perception and especially with training in sensory-motor abilities, language, and higher cognitive processes, as well as with academic subjects, must, however, be equally emphasized.

Visual-Perceptual Programs

for Older Children

Many youngsters with disabilities in visual perception have experienced years of school failure. A fourth grader with learning difficulties, for example, has spent more than half his life in what has frequently been for him a stressful situation, which has made him feel inadequate, "dumb," unable to live up to his parents' or teachers' expectations. He cannot escape school: he will have to endure for another seven years. An adult can readily empathize with these children by imagining how he would feel if he failed at his job year after year.

It is most imperative that these youngsters experience consistent success if they are to develop a positive attitude toward learning. But they are quick to resent the use of elementary material, which they consider "baby stuff." At the Frostig Center we have found it indispensable to explain to the student as simply and directly as we can what visual perception is and how it affects his performance; we reassure him that he is not stupid. Such a discussion is normally effective in relieving anxiety. The student can then view the visual-perceptual tasks as helping him to become more competent. The teacher can then frequently use a number of the exercises from material originally designed for younger children without adjusting them, although very often older children are required to do them at a certain rate of speed. If necessary the pictures may be somewhat altered so that the stick figures are engaged in more interesting activities. The Fitzhugh program (1966) is a good addition for perceptual training of the older child.

The integration of visual-perceptual training with the teaching of academic skills and content is crucial for older age groups. These children often need extra help in academic tasks that require visual perceptual abilities, such as beginning geometry or long division or the use of a dictionary. Material drawn from such subjects as astronomy, geography, and science may be adapted and used as visual-perceptual training exercises per se. (See Figures 6 and 7.)

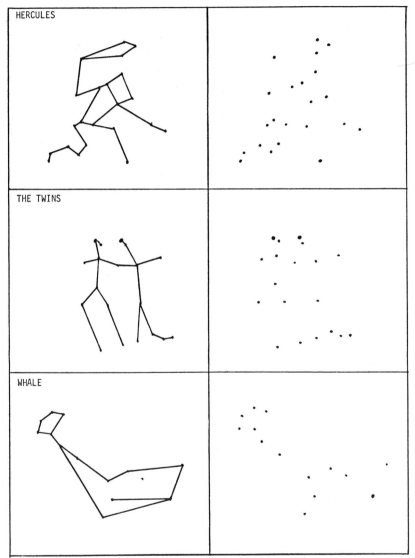

HERCULES

THE TWINS

WHALE

Connect the stars in each constellation in the right column as they are shown in the left column.

FIGURE 6

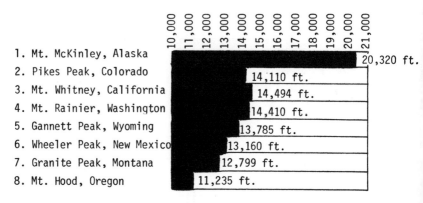

1. Mt. McKinley, Alaska   20,320 ft.
2. Pikes Peak, Colorado   14,110 ft.
3. Mt. Whitney, California   14,494 ft.
4. Mt. Rainier, Washington   14,410 ft.
5. Gannett Peak, Wyoming   13,785 ft.
6. Wheeler Peak, New Mexico   13,160 ft.
7. Granite Peak, Montana   12,799 ft.
8. Mt. Hood, Oregon   11,235 ft.

Using the information in the bar graph above, make a line graph:

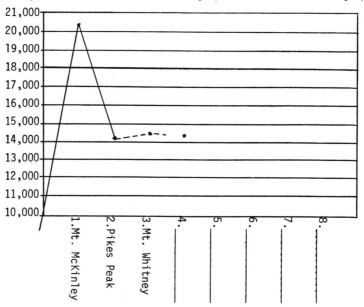

FOLLOW UP: Using an outline map of the United States, write
the number of each mountain in the correct state.

FIGURE 7

Transfer of Perceptual Skills

The effectiveness of visual-perceptual training should be assessed as broadly as possible: Is the child better adjusted in the classroom? Can he pay attention better? Is he more aware of his surroundings? Does he get more information from a picture? Can he describe what he sees? And so on. Too often the effectiveness of visual-perceptual training is judged by its effects on academic achievement alone, particularly reading.

If visual-perceptual training is to help the child most effectively, the teacher must "teach for transfer." That means that she must (1) point out to the child the similarities between the games and tasks he uses during perceptual training and those he undertakes during academic work, and (2) develop exercises that help to make the transfer easier. (For concrete examples, see the chapters on teaching math and reading.)

WORKS CITED

Arnheim, R. *Visual thinking.* Berkeley, Calif.: University of California Press, 1969.

Chalfant, J. C., and Scheffelin, M. A. *Central processing dysfunctions in children: A review of research.* NINDS Monograph No. 9. Washington, D.C.: U.S. Government Printing Office, 1969.

Cowles, J. D. An experimental study of visual perceptual training and readiness scores with certain first-grade children. Paper presented at American Educational Research Association, February, 1969. ERIC Document No. ED 032 921.

Dubnoff, B., Chambers, I., & Schaefer, F. *Dubnoff school programs. Experiential perceptual-motor exercises.* Boston: Teaching Resources, 1968.

Fairbanks, J., and Robinson, J. *Fairbanks-Robinson program 1: Perceptual-motor development.* Boston: Teaching Resources, 1967.

Faustman, M. N. Some effects of perception training in kindergarten on first grade success in reading. In International Reading Association. *Conference proceedings.* Vol. 12. *Perception and reading.* Newark, Del.: International Reading Association, 1968.

Fitzhugh, K., and Fitzhugh, L. *The Fitzhugh plus program.* Galien, Mich.: Allied Education Council, 1966.

Frostig, M., Horne, D., Miller, A. *Pictures and patterns;* and *Teacher's guides to pictures and patterns.* (Rev. ed.) Chicago: Follett Educational Corporation, 1972.

Getman, G. N. *How to develop your child's intelligence.* Luverne, Minn.: Research Press, 1962.

Kost, M. L. Experimental study—a program to meet the needs of first grade children, 1964–65. Continuation, 1965–66, Maturity training program. Unpublished reports, Dry Creek School, Rio Linda (California) Union School District.

Linn, S. H. A follow-up: Achievement report of first-grade students after visual-perceptual training in kindergarten. *Academic Therapy Quarterly,* 1967, 3 (3), 179–180.

Linn, S. H. Visual-perceptual training for kindergarten children. *Academic Therapy Quarterly,* 1967, 2 (4), 255–258.

Marshall, H. R. Effect of training on visual perception skills and reading achievement of deaf children. Experimental Publication System. October, 1970, 8, MS. No. 281–283.

Maslow, P., Frostig, M., Lefever, D. W., and Whittlesey, J. R. B. The Marianne Frostig development test of visual perception. 1963 standardization. *Perceptual and Motor Skills,* 19(2), 463–499. Monograph Supplement 2–V19, 1964.

McBeath, M. Behavioral characteristics of visually perceptually handicapped and non-handicapped kindergarteners. *Psychology in the Schools,* 1966, 3(3), 264–266.

McConnell, F., Horton, K. B., and Smith, B. R. Language development and cultural disadvantagement. *Exceptional Children,* 1969, 35(8), 597–608.

Penfield, W. Memory and perception. In D. Hamburg, K. Pribram, & A. Stumkard (Eds.), *Perception and its disorders.* Baltimore: Williams & Wilkins, 1970.

Sabatino, D., and Hayden, D. L. Psychoeducational study of selected behavior variables of children failing the elementary grades. *Journal of Experimental Education,* 1970, 38, 40–57.

Strauss, A., and Lehtinen, L. *Psychopathology and the education of the brain-injured child,* Vol. 1. New York: Grune & Stratton, 1947.

Sutphin, F. E. *Perceptual testing-training handbook for first grade teachers.* Winter Haven, Florida: Winter Haven Lions Research Foundation, 1964.

14
AUDITORY
PERCEPTION

Auditory perception is the ability to interpret auditory stimuli, to associate them with stimuli earlier perceived, and to discriminate among them. Auditory perception is of the utmost importance in developing the ability to understand and communicate through oral and written words. It is also necessary for an optimum adjustment to the environment. We should be able to recognize such sounds as a siren or a policeman's whistle, the water running into the bathtub (or we might forget to turn it off), the teakettle's whistle. Sound also enriches our lives and adds to its meaning. Auditory perception is necessary to appreciate the music of either a brook or a symphony orchestra.

Comparison of Visual
and Auditory-Perceptual Abilities

The differences between auditory and visual perception have been often discussed. Visual perception has spatial dimensions; auditory perception has temporal ones. Visual perception can be immediately stopped by voluntarily closing the eyes; the auditory channel cannot be so easily eliminated. Since our gaze is essentially always directed in the direction in which the head is turned, visual perception can only encompass a portion of the space that surrounds us; there is far less limitation to the range of auditory perception.

Visual and auditory perception also have a number of common characteristics. First, both the ear and the eyes are distance receptors; they can register stimuli from distant points in space. Less apparent is the fact that there is also much similarity between the various auditory- and visual-perceptual functions. The following list of juxtaposed auditory- and visual-perceptual abilities indicates the similarities between auditory- and visual-perceptual functions; it is not intended, however, to offer more than an analogy.

TABLE 6
Similarities Between Visual
and Auditory-Perceptual Abilities

Visual-Perceptual Abilities	Auditory-Perceptual Abilities
1. Awareness of stimuli	1. Awareness of stimuli
2. Attention to stimuli	2. Attention to stimuli
3. Eye-motor coordination	3. Auditory-motor association
4. Visual figure-ground perception	4. Auditory figure-ground perception
5. Visual constancy of perception	5. Auditory discrimination
6. Perception of position in space	6. Perception of sound location
7. Perception of spatial relationships	7. Recognition and discrimination of auditory sequences
8. Analysis of complex patterns	8. Auditory analysis of words
9. Synthesis of patterns	9. Sound blending, necessary for word synthesis
10. Visual decoding (reception)	10. Auditory decoding (reception)
11. Visual closure	11. Auditory closure
12. No corresponding ability to grammatic closure	12. Grammatic closure
13. Visual memory for sequences	13. Auditory memory

Disabilities in Auditory Perception

Among children with learning problems are many who have inadequate auditory skills. This inadequacy may be caused by poor auditory acuity (what we commonly term "poor hearing"). Auditory acuity should therefore always be evaluated. Usually the school nurse does the preliminary screening of auditory acuity and refers children with acuity problems to their family doctor. But auditory difficulties also occur because of a disability in auditory perception, which is not a function of the sense organ but of the brain's interpretation of incoming auditory stimuli. It is possible for the teacher to make an informal assessment of a child's auditory-perceptual abilities, because many methods of evaluating auditory perception are observational or consist of informal or nonstandardized tests. But whenever auditory-perceptual difficulties are suspected, there should be further testing by a language pathologist or audiologist or psychologist. As discussed further in the chapter on language, auditory-perceptual deficiencies are frequently found in children who have defects in articulation. Such a child should always be screened as soon as possible for disabilities in both auditory acuity and auditory perception (Mange, 1960).

Auditory Awareness

Children are often assumed to have an adequately developed awareness of sound in the same way that it is assumed that they are aware of visual stimuli. If a child were totally lacking in auditory awareness, the handicap would soon be obvious: he would be diagnosed as deaf, and the appropriate educational measures would be taken. But there are degrees of auditory awareness, and a child may be significantly handicapped in this respect even though he is not deaf. If the difficulty is due to poor auditory acuity, it will be revealed by a hearing test. Medical treatment can help improve acuity in some of these children, and some may profit from a hearing aid, but many children with a neurogenic hearing loss cannot profit from amplification. The teacher must then take steps to ensure that the child can hear the directions she gives and can follow classroom discussions, lectures, film presentations, and so on. Such a child needs to sit near the source of the sound and watch the lips of the speaker whenever possible. Clear enunciation and slow speech heighten awareness of speech sounds, and are particularly important for a child with lowered auditory acuity.

Diminished auditory awareness is a cultural problem. City children have usually learned to tune out much sound because many city noises are intrusive or unpleasant. There are also many sounds that they have never heard because they are inaudible or nonexistent in an urban environment. These children need to experience a variety of auditory stimuli in an orderly learning situation. Sound films can bring to them auditory experiences ordinarily beyond their reach, such as the sound of a rushing waterfall, the noise of rain in the forest, the mooing of a cow, the cry of a whippoorwill, and so on,* and thus

* The Learning Center of the Centennial Public Schools, Warminster, Pennsylvania, under the direction of Dr. Henry Ray, has prepared pilot multimedia presentations that "surround" the child with the sights and sounds of the seashore, forest, and so forth. This group is also preparing to add the appropriate odors!

make them aware that many natural sounds are pleasant. The teachei can also heighten an awareness of everyday noises. Semel (1970) and Zigmond (1968) give many excellent suggestions.

Attention to Auditory Stimuli

If the child's auditory acuity is poor, his awareness of sound will be diminished, and as a further consequence, his attention to auditory stimuli will be also. Poor attention may also be caused by a disturbance in brain function, by preoccupation with inner stimuli, or by the need to escape from an unpleasant situation. Whatever the presumed underlying cause, one remedy—and the only one immediately available to the classroom teacher—is to create an environment more conducive to learning.

Some specific ways of increasing the child's attention to auditory stimuli include:

1. Reducing the amount of irrelevant verbiage. It is instructive to use a tape-recorder to record one's own teaching—the amount of unnecessary talking can be surprising. Most children respond best to clear, brief instructions—such instructions are essential for those with impaired attention to auditory stimuli.
2. Pausing, slowing, and/or speeding the rate of speech; changing tempo, intonation, expression, and loudness.
3. Attention-getting devices (such as snapping the fingers, or switching the lights quickly on and off) attract children's attention to the teacher, who can then give verbal instructions. But such devices are somewhat unpleasant and should rarely be used.
4. Lowering the voice periodically, so that the children have to strain to listen.
5. Providing adequate forewarning: "Now listen carefully. I am going to dictate an important word."
6. Making individual contact with each child as often as possible, especially one whose attention wanders. This may take the form of a nod, a smile, a gesture or actual touching with the hand, or some form of direct address.
7. The provision of reinforcing visual stimuli.

The teacher who tries to force the child to pay attention by using anything more than the mildest form of punishment will only cause the child to withdraw more and more from the situation. Examples of mild punishment are speaking in a slightly raised voice, asking the child a question to force him to pay attention, or saying something like: "Oh, John, your ears aren't good today. I'll have to say that again." But in the case of poor attention, as in every other instance in which the teacher wants to modify behavior, a positive approach is apt to be far more effective and conducive to the child's mental health.

Auditory Figure-Ground Perception

Auditory figure-ground perception is the ability to direct one's attention to relevant auditory stimuli and to ignore irrelevant ones.

Some people are deficient in this ability. They find it unusually difficult, for example, to follow a conversation when several persons are talking at the same time, or to follow a lecture when there is a noise in the next room or the sound of traffic outside the window.

It is important not only to be able to attend consciously to certain auditory stimuli while ignoring others, but also to be able to change at will the focus of attention. A mother listening to the talk of a neighbor should be able to hear the call of her child. A person who is telephoning should be aware of the doorbell ringing. A driver listening to the car radio should be able to hear the sound of the horn on another car. One student talking to another should be able to transfer his attention to the teacher's voice when necessary.

If a child has difficulties in this skill, his auditory figure-ground perception may be increased if the teacher gradually and systematically introduces increasingly distracting and complex background noises and at the same time requires attention be given to particular auditory stimuli. The goal is to help the child learn to work without strain in a room where there are other activities.

Another group of exercises to promote auditory figure-ground perception involves having the child make a response to an auditory signal without becoming distracted by other simultaneous (or preceding) stimuli. Such exercises may also serve as informal tests to gauge the child's ability to attend to and perceive auditory stimuli correctly.

1. A rhythm is played while a sentence is spoken or a direction given. The teacher may, for instance, beat on a tambourine while giving simple commands, such as "Hands in the air!" The child may be asked to attend to and repeat the rhythm or to carry out the teacher's instruction. (A series of instructions are not given because a child may be unable to carry those out because of a poor memory for auditory sequences, not because he has difficulties in auditory figure-ground perception.)

2. The children are told to jump or clap or move their arms when-
    ever the teacher says a particular word. For instance, they might
    play the game that follows, called "That's Not My Baby." Any
    number of variations of this game might be devised.

The teacher tells a story about a little bird that got lost. The word that
the children must listen for is *chirp*. The mother bird looks for her baby,
listening for its chirp, chirp. While looking, she hears different sounds—
a brook, children singing, paper rustling, the wind blowing. Each time the
mother bird hears one of these noises, she says, "That is not my baby. That
is——"; the children then repeat what it is—a brook, rustling paper, and
so on. When the mother bird finally hears the chirp, chirp, the children
flap their arms.

Discrimination of Sounds

The elementary-school teacher will rarely find children with gross deficits in the discrimination of nonspeech sounds. She may, however,
begin training in sound discrimination with nonspeech sounds in
order to develop in the children a feeling of mastery and self-assurance.
She may spend a little time with recognition of both gross and fine
differences of speech sounds, involving loudness, pitch, source, and so
on, but children above nursery-school age will soon proceed to the
recognition and discrimination of isolated speech sounds and speech
sounds in the context of a word.

Some children are able to discriminate single speech sounds, but are
unable to do so in the context of a word or sentence. Others may
understand a sentence spoken by their mothers or by television an-
nouncers, but may not understand the same sentence when spoken by
someone who uses an unfamiliar intonation or dialect. The ability to
recognize auditory stimuli as being the same under varying circumstances is known as auditory-perceptual constancy.

Exercises to help a child develop auditory-perceptual constancy may
include training in recognizing a musical note as being the same, although played by different instruments or in the context of different
melodies. But training with nonspeech sounds will very probably have
little or no effect on the child's ability to differentiate and recognize
speech sounds in isolation or in context.

Discrimination of speech sounds is of paramount importance in
reading and spelling. The child who has difficulty with speech-sound
discrimination will need systematic auditory training for an extended
period of time. Since he will most likely not be able to learn to read by

a phonic method, he must also be given extra help through visual-kinesthetic or linguistic approaches.

A formal test for discrimination of speech sounds is the Wepman Test of Auditory Discrimination (Wepman, 1958). This test, which takes only a short time, can easily be administered by a teacher after a brief period of training. Other tests include those by Goldman, Woodcock and Fristoe (1970) and Katz (1971).

Sound Localization

IN SPACE. An auditory ability that has survival value is locating the source of a sound (sound localization). It may be important to know from what spot the sound of a rattlesnake, a car, a scream, or a shot emanates.

Games in which the child is blindfolded and has to locate the source of a sound provide excellent training for younger children. The ability to locate the source of a sound is rarely severely disturbed in the elementary-school child. He is far more likely to have difficulty in locating the position of a sound in a sequence of sounds and this ability will be discussed below.

IN TIME. The reception of auditory stimuli always occurs in a given time sequence. Much of their meaning derives from maintaining this information in its proper order (Efrom, 1963). For example, the letters s-p-o-r-t have a different meaning than the same letters in the order p-o-r-t-s. Training in perception of auditory sequences is also concerned with the temporal order of words in a sentence and of sentences in a paragraph. The importance of such training cannot be overemphasized.

Recognition of Auditory Sequences

Deficits in the recognition and discrimination of auditory sequences occur very frequently. A child may perceive the temporal order of sounds in syllables and words correctly, and still be unable to reproduce an auditory sequence (de Hirsh, 1955).

Many children are unable to recognize and discriminate a sequence of sounds because they don't clearly understand the concept of *before* and *after*; others because they cannot keep a short sequence in mind. It is therefore often necessary to begin with training in reproducing non-verbal rhythms produced by clapping, stamping, ringing a bell, and so on. The child is first asked to count the number of sounds he hears, then to imitate short sequences of sounds; for example, two claps and then one stamp. (Movement is of great assistance in making the child aware of the temporal sequence of sounds.) The sequences can then be extended.

The child will be helped to recognize verbal sound sequences correctly if he is first made aware of the number of separate elements in the words and sentences spoken to him. He should count the words in sentences, first beginning with very short sentences and gradually progressing. He should then count in the same way the separate sounds in words.

The child can then be asked to identify the "same" or "different" pairs of words made up of the same sounds occurring in a different order (e.g., left–felt, ports–sport, please–sleep, top–pot, spill–pills, and so on). This game should be played with nonsense syllables (blod and dolb, for example), as well as with words. More difficult word-recognition games include selecting from words written on the board those that the teacher says out loud or recognizing which are the nonsense words in a story told by the teacher (which also provides practice in keeping an idea in mind). The story might take place on another planet, one on which there are imaginary objects, such as balls with an opening in the top, trees with branches wound around the stem, and so on, which have nonsense syllables as names (*frat*, *marb*, and so on). The teacher can make sketches of these objects and have the children point to the appropriate picture when the teacher says the nonsense word. Such a game also trains memory for auditory sequences.

Auditory Memory and Imagery (Auding)*

Auditory memory includes memory for sound sequences, words, sentences, and passages. The digit span subtest of the WISC and the auditory sequence subtest of the ITPA both check short-term memory for number sequences. Even when the results of these subtests are available, the teacher needs to find out if the child can easily remember such sequences as the days of the week or the months of the year.

Many researchers (e.g., Orton, 1937) have concluded that reading difficulties stem at least in part from an inability to recall sounds in the proper sequence.

As already mentioned, spelling mistakes often occur because a child cannot perceive or reproduce the proper auditory sequence. The differ-

---

* Auding is discussed also in the chapter on reading. Training in auditory memory is discussed also in the chapter on language.

ential diagnosis between difficulties in auditory perception and in memory for auditory sequences is not difficult. Children with difficulties in memory for auditory sequences are able to analyze a word or repeat a short sequence immediately, but are unable to do so later.

Auditory Analysis of Words

The auditory abilities that have been mentioned—discrimination of speech sounds, perception of the sequence of sounds, and attention to certain stimuli in a sequence—are all necessary for the auditory analysis of words. For example, when a child writes the word *top*, he has first to perceive each sound and the sequence in which it occurs. He must also pay special attention to those parts of the word that are more difficult to perceive auditorially. Such sounds are usually those in the middle of the word; for example in *top*, it would be the vowel *o*.

The auditory analysis of words therefore includes no new elements, but is a combination of the abilities previously discussed. If all the preparatory work with these skills has been practiced, then auditory word analysis should be relatively easy. Word analysis itself can be taught by color coding (see chapter on reading).

Auditory Synthesis—Sound Blending

Word analysis is necessary for sounding out a word in order to be able to spell and write and read it. But word analysis must be complemented by word synthesis. We do not say that we are going to see the new *p-l-a-n-t-s* in front of the *h-ou-s-e*, but that we will see the new *plants* in front of the *house*. After a word has been analyzed auditorially and the sounds indicated by the use of different colors (color coding), it should be pronounced as a whole word and also written in a single color so that it is perceived auditorially and visually as a whole (see pp. 309–310). Synthesis should always follow analysis.

Several sound blending tests are available: One is a subtest of the ITPA; another is the Roswell-Chall Sound Blending Test (1963); another comprises a section of the Spache (1963).

Associational Functions

In addition to the auditory abilities that have been discussed, the teacher needs to evaluate carefully and develop the association of auditory reception with motor responses (which involves responding appropriately to instructions) and the association of auditory- and visual-perceptual skills (evaluated by word recognition tests). Both these forms of association are very important for all learning.

Summary

There is no ideal curriculum for children at any given age level, and certainly the emphasis to be given specific auditory skills cannot be established by a curriculum designed for a certain region or school system. The amount and focus of auditory training provided for a child depends on the existence or absence of deficits. Awareness of sounds and of grammatic speech may be emphasized more in the language arts curriculum in congested urban areas than in the suburbs. When reading is taught at an early age by phonic methods, it may be necessary to emphasize the early discrimination of speech sounds.

Auditory training usually takes a long time, and auditory skills are often only acquired after great effort. When remedial work is necessary, it consists mainly of an emphasis on the methods described in this chapter and the chapter on language.* The periods of training should not be lengthy, stressful, or boring. They should last for from five to ten minutes and take place in the spirit, if not the form, of play and enjoyment.

References

de Hirsch, K. Prediction of future reading abilities in children with oral language disorders. *Folia Phoniatrica*, 1955, 7, 235–250.

Efrom, R. The effect of handedness on the perception of simultaneity and temporal order. *Brain*, 1963, 86, 261–284.

Engelmann, S. *Preventing failure in the primary grades*. Chicago: Science Research Associates, 1969.

Goldman, R., Fristoe, M., and Woodcock, R. W. *Test of auditory discrimination*. Circle Pines, Minn.: American Guidance Service, 1970.

Katz, J. *Kindergarten auditory screening test*. Chicago: Follett Educational Corp., 1971.

Mange, C. V. Relationships between selected auditory perceptual factors and articulation ability. *Journal of Speech and Hearing Research*, 1960, 3, 64–74.

* For additional suggestions see Englemann (1969), *Preventing failure in the primary grades*.

Orton, S. T. *Reading, writing, and speech problems in children.* New York: Norton, 1937.

Roswell, F. G., and Chall, J. S. *Roswell-Chall auditory blending test.* New York: Essay Press, 1963.

Semel, E. *Sound, order, sense, Level 1.* Chicago: Follett Educational Corp., 1970.

Spache, G. D. *Diagnostic Reading Scales.* New York: McGraw-Hill, 1963.

Zigmond, N. K., and Cicci, R. *Auditory learning.* San Rafael, Calif.: Dimensions Publishing Co., 1968.

15
DEVELOPING
LANGUAGE
ABILITIES

SECTION 1:
LANGUAGE, LINGUISTICS,
PSYCHOLINGUISTICS*

A characteristic of many children with learning difficulties is their restricted language code. Children who are neurologically handicapped, economically deprived, or emotionally disturbed often exhibit a stereotyped, limited language, with simple, often incomplete sentences and sparse use of subordinate clauses (Bernstein, 1961).

Various studies, as well as the authors' own clinical experience, suggest that improvement in the use of language takes place as a result of both highly structured formal training (e.g., Bereiter and Engelmann, 1966) and informal training arising in natural situations (e.g., Dawe, 1942). A combination of both approaches is recommended as ideal, the formal training being given for short periods of time.

Basic Concepts of Linguistics

The study of the structure and function of language is called *linguistics*. Linguistics seeks to discover the basic concepts that describe and contrast all languages. Every language is an orderly system of symbols arbitrarily and unconsciously agreed upon by a people in order to communicate. Language can be described and contrasted in regard to three variables: (1) the sound system (phonology), (2) the vocabulary and rules of word formation (morphology), and (3) rules for word combination (syntax). Linguistics tries to answer such complicated ques-

* The discussion in this section is presented as an attempt to help the teacher acquire the necessary vocabulary to read and evaluate the increasing number of professional articles and books dealing with language, linguistics, and psycholinguistics.

tions as, How do languages originate? How does a child learn language?*

Four to five thousand languages exist in the world today. All languages, however, have much in common (Bolinger, 1968, p. 18); e.g., all languages have classes of nouns and of verbs. The number of sounds in any language is not as great as one might expect: all four or five thousand languages can be transcribed with about fifty phonetic signs and about thirty diacritical marks.

Language is universal. Eric Lenneberg (1966) points out that language is a universal human characteristic, and that the child has an inborn capacity to develop language. But language has also to be learned, and the degree to which it is learned depends not only on the person's intellect, and special abilities for language, but—more importantly—on the language he hears.

The primary function of language is human communication. To achieve this end, there are words for everything that enters the realm of consciousness. Words and language structures refer to objects and ideas, to classes and categories, to qualities of things in the outside world, to the way things change, to the actions and feelings of others, and to one's own actions and feelings. One of the tasks of the teacher is to help the child to become more conscious of, and more knowledgeable about, his surroundings. Assisting the child to learn the right words or names for the people and objects and ideas in his environment is a most important part of teaching.

Language influences the feelings and, as a consequence, the actions of others. It can establish rapport, understanding, cooperation, and love, or conversely, hostility, anger, and distrust. As De Laguna (1927) has pointed out, applying such labels as thrifty, crafty, cruel, or tolerant influences the attitudes we form for or against another person's social group, rule, or country. Language affects all social action and therefore the course of history and the fate of humanity. Children need to understand that language can influence the way one person perceives others, to realize that language can be a powerful tool in helping or hurting another.

As previously mentioned, what we communicate and how we communicate—through words or through other symbols—depends on intel-

---

* Theories of language are diverse. The so-called cognitive view of language is based on a study of the role and importance of meaning (e.g., see Bloomfield, 1933). Most theories, however, are more concerned with form than with meaning; in part, no doubt, because exploration of the meaning of language is very difficult.

ligence.* Communication in turn influences the development of intelligence because language helps us to explain the environment to
ourselves and to others. Without language we are chained to the
present, but words allow us to communicate and think about both the
past and the future, about objects, characteristics, and relationships that
are not actually present. Problem-solving is therefore greatly facilitated
by language. Jerome Bruner (1966, p. 16) writes: "Language provides
the means of getting free of immediate appearance as the sole basis of
judgment." Similarly Piaget states that language helps in decentration.

Expressive language advances communicative functions in three
principal ways: (1) Language transmits information. The declarative
sentence is the form in which information is given, e.g., "It is time to
leave for the theater;"** (2) Language transmits a command, order, or
directive. A command is directed toward another person; it evokes the
listener's indirect response to the situation. Command is given in an
imperative sentence: "Leave immediately, Emma." (3) Language transmits emotions, having developed from cries, shouts, and grunts to an
infinite variety of verbal emotional expressions. When someone exclaims,
"What terrible weather!" the person he is talking to is someone who is
probably already well aware of the miserable state of the weather. The
exclamation conveys the speaker's feeling of annoyance, not information.

Three aspects in the use of language that need to be kept in mind
in teaching are: (1) understanding information, (2) giving and understanding instructions, and (3) using language to express and understand emotions. Examples of activities that will aid in developing these
three areas are reporting experiences, including telling and listening to
stories; following and giving instructions; and writing, reading, and
listening to poems and stories that evoke a variety of emotions.

Elements of Language

The medium of language is sound. The smallest unit of sound is
called a *phoneme*. The study of sound production is called phonetics
or phonology. The phonetic elements are articulation of individual
sound units and intonation (or change of pitch of the voice).

Most phonemes cannot be readily uttered by themselves but are

* Intelligence is here used in a Piagetian sense; that is, the active operative process by which a human being constructs reality, "knows" his environment.

** A special form of speech is the question, which is used to elicit an in-
formative response from another.

more easily sounded in syllables. Identification of each phoneme is therefore influenced by preceding and succeeding acoustic cues.

Phonics refers to teaching the correct use of sounds, their correspondence to letters, and the rules that govern the relationship of printed letter to the sound of that letter (or, as it is commonly referred to in the literature, the rules of grapheme-phoneme correspondence).

Phonics has implications for oral, written, and printed language. The correct formation of oral language sounds may be very difficult for many children. Children who have defects in articulation or intonation are usually referred to a speech therapist, as it is impossible for the teacher to give sufficient detailed practice in the careful discrimination of sound differences and consequent placement of the articulators for proper speech production. On the other hand, the speech therapist can spend comparatively little time with a child, while the teacher is with him for many hours a day. The teacher can therefore contribute significantly to the child's progress by providing correct models of sound production, and by repeating words or expanding and restating sentences that the child has had difficulty in formulating. In this way, she can avoid embarrassing a child by correcting him individually in front of the other children.

The smallest unit of language that conveys meaning is called a *morpheme*. In the word *boys* there are two morphemes: *boy* and *s*. The first can be defined as a group of sounds that evoke among English-speaking persons an image of a young male human being;* the second, which cannot stand by itself, conveys plurality—the sense of more than one. Another example of a word with two morphemes is *older*. *Old* evokes a state of being or quality; *er* indicates comparison with another object or category having the same state of being or quality as the initial morpheme; that is, of age or "oldness."

Making a child aware of the meaning of suffixes, prefixes, root words, and endings tends to improve his ability to form correctly a greater number and variety of words.

The study of how morphemes are put together to form meaningful sentences is called *syntax*, or the description of the structure of a language.

Teaching syntax is also the task of the teacher. Two methods seem to be used most often: (1) teaching the rules of grammar, including diagramming sentences; (2) practicing sentence formation.

As previously stated, language influences feelings and attitudes, understanding and concept formation; language thus indirectly affects total

---

* "Boy" is a "free" morpheme; it is an example of the smallest unit of language that in itself has meaning.

behavior. *Semantics* is the study of the meaning of language or of how language is used and affects the understanding and behavior of those who use it—a new field of study which is of importance for all human interaction.

Meaning refers to relationships; it ties events to former experiences, projects them into the future, and links them to each other. Meaning is always personal; no two events or objects have *exactly* the same meaning for any two persons because the experiences of no two persons can ever be exactly the same. For example, the word *apple* may have a variety of meanings depending on the context in which it occurs and the response of the person hearing the word. If someone says, "The smell of apples in my basket lured the squirrel to my whitewashed front porch," he is referring to an event in the past that has contributed to the personal meaning of the word *apples*. The speaker may be remembering the smell of the apples on that day. The word *apples* may also be associated with his realization that squirrels like to eat apples.

In the phrase, "You are the apple of my eye," the term has a symbolic value. The apple from the Tree of Life in the Garden of Paradise certainly has a meaning that is highly personal. To give another example, a black man may feel that the description of himself as black (in contrast to white) expresses the equal standing of the races, while the word *Negro*, because it was used for so long to denote a people who were suppressed and dominated, is often regarded as demeaning.

The history of a peoples' customs, mores, and ambitions load their words with shades of meaning not readily understood by those outside their culture. Semantics is a tool for understanding those shades of meaning, and thereby a means of achieving understanding of others and of learning to communicate so that one is understood. It is to be hoped that semantics will be accorded the status it deserves as an important area of study for both teachers and students.

In summary, the meaning of an utterance cannot be divorced from either the speaker or the listener. The entire experience of the person speaking and of the person listening, their knowledge, attitudes, and dispositions, affect the meaning of the words they hear. Knowledge is not a replica of the external world, but is influenced and changed by the personality of each individual. It is very difficult for many children to understand the less evident meanings of language, because both the imagery and the ability to abstract may develop at a slow rate. The result will be a learning difficulty because restriction in the acquisition of meanings has a cumulative effect. Children from a socioeconomically deprived background, whose experiences have been restricted, and whose language contains few precise descriptive and qualifying words, are at a disadvantage when they must start to acquire in school a knowledge of standard English.

Acquiring meaning is a process, an operative activity in which nets of connections are established. It develops from a fixed connection between two things or events, but meaning changes with usage. "I go to church" may mean the specific edifice on the corner of Third Street and Broadway. But "the Church regulated man's life during the Middle Ages" refers to a religious institution and its influence upon the whole life of the people during a particular period.

If learning is to have meaning, the teacher must relate everything that is taught in as many ways as possible to each child's life—to his home background, to his experiences in and out of school, and to past and future learning.

Psycholinguistics

Linguistic studies have traditionally focused on the analysis of the symbol system of language. This approach, however, does not explain how language is learned and understood by the individual. Studies focusing on relationships, in the broadest sense, between messages and the characteristics of those persons who receive and interpret them, are called psycholinguistic.

Psycholinguistics is a new science, about a quarter of a century old (Osgood and Sebeok, 1954). The definition of psycholinguistics is broader than that of linguistics. It includes the purposes of language and all aspects of communication, as well as the grammar of language (phonology, morphology, syntax) and semantics.

Communication involves both verbal and nonverbal forms, because people express ideas and feelings not only through words, but also through vocal intonations, facial expressions, and body movements. Information is thus received both by hearing the spoken word and by observation. Gestures and perception are therefore among the concerns of the psycholinguist.

Psycholinguistic analysis of communication involves three major processes: reception, expression, and association. The reader is reminded that receptive (decoding) functions refer to understanding messages and expressive (encoding) functions to the production or transmittal of messages.

Associative functions can only be inferred from observable events; they are not apparent. Imagine, for instance, that you are about to go out, and you are told that it is raining outside; you reply, "Well, then, please wait until I find my umbrella and coat before we go out." You must have had previous associations, such as, "If it rains, I will get wet. Usually when it rains, it is also windy and cold. I don't like to be either wet or cold. I must protect myself." Thoughts and feelings intervene, or *mediate*, between what is perceived and the verbal and motor reactions to the perception.

Psycholinguistics is also concerned with man's symbol-using capacities. The ability to use symbols is a necessary precondition of speech—the most important form of language—and for understanding printed or written language, in which letters are used to form a visual symbol for the spoken word.

A central problem of psycholinguistics is to account for the fact that every language contains a finite number of morphemes and syntactical rules, yet an infinite number of sentences may be generated by any speaker of a given language.

The stimulus-response theory of language (see, for example, Skinner, 1957, and Staats and Staats, 1964), is inadequate to account for this phenomenon. It also does not account for the fact that words are more easily recognized in sentences than in isolation. Information from the context supplements that from the discrete physical stimulus, and a word clearly understood in a certain context may be unintelligible or incomprehensible when heard in isolation. Understanding and expressing language is dependent on linguistic-cognitive rather than on external stimulus-response factors. This conclusion is borne out by the fact that we generally remember the meaning of what we hear and read, without remembering the exact words.

Chomsky's (1957) transformational grammar represents an attempt to explain this capacity of the human being to generate an infinite number of grammatically correct sentences. Chomsky's theory takes into account what is known about memory, logical meaning, and the importance of contextual relationships in understanding language.

According to Chomsky, the teaching of grammar is based on the postulate that all sentences may be generated from a kernel sentence (subject-predicate) by application of specific rules.

SECTION 2:
LANGUAGE TEACHING

Procedures for teaching language can best be derived from listening to small children and the way that their parents, or other close adults who converse with them, speak. Gleitman and Shipley (1963) have observed that such adults simplify their speech when talking to the child. They use (1) careful enunciation, (2) exaggerated intonation, (3) slow rate, (4) simple sentence structure, (5) concrete words, instead of substitute words, such as *it*. Bolinger (1968) adds a sixth point, repetition. These same procedures need to be applied by the teacher of children with language handicaps. Wyatt (1969) advocates essentially the same principles. Menyuk (1969) adds a discussion of the way in which adults expand children's sentences, as well as simplify their own.

Articulation

Language has already been discussed as having two aspects—structure and sound. It has also already been mentioned that if the articulation of letter sounds deviates from the norm, the child usually requires training by a speech therapist. The only way that the teacher can help is by reinforcing correct pronunciation. She may repeat more clearly a word which the child has uttered and call the child's attention to the correct pronunciation. But, as always, public correction needs to be held to a minimum, for otherwise it may only prove to be embarrassing to the child and disturbing to the class.

Although the teaching and testing of articulation, because they are matters for specialists, have not been included in this book, the teacher should know the tests of articulatory proficiency that are available. For example, among the frequently used tests are those by Templin and Darley (1960); see also Johnson, Darley, and Spriestersbach (1963) and Meyers and Hammill (1969, pp. 65-66).

Vocabulary Development

It is of the utmost importance to introduce new words to children before any lesson in which new vocabulary is used, and the words should be introduced in both written and spoken form. When an adult hears a new name, he often can not clearly recognize or remember it until he has seen it and spelled it, and thus analyzed it. This is especially true of a name heard over the telephone. Visual analysis is equally helpful for children with auditory-perceptual difficulties. Whenever possible additional visual aids to concept development, such as objects, pictures, and film strips, should be used.

When aspects of science and social studies are systematically taught, the vocabulary pertaining to these subjects tends to be learned systematically. Vocabulary is always best enriched as new ideas and relationships are explored. New concepts and the words denoting them are best remembered when presented as part of a general project or theme.

Concept Development*

There are many definitions of the word *concept*. A concept is here defined as having three main characteristics: the first is *discrimination*, or an awareness of those differences that set the concept apart (e.g., a leaf is not a stem or a flower.) A concept also involves *generalization*. There are all sorts of leaves of different sizes and shapes, textures and colors. The leaves of grasses, of a fir tree, of a philodendron, of a clover, all differ greatly from each other, but they have common qualities that make them leaves. The third characteristic of a concept is that it involves *representation* by a symbol. The word "leaves" stands for all leaves.**

The symbol or label aids in organizing experiences; in helping to store experiences in memory and to retrieve them ("Leaves on most plants in the semi-desert are small and grayish"); in finding relationships between concepts ("These are flowers, not leaves, but both are parts of plants"). The symbol or label is necessary for communicating the concepts and the mental processes concerned with them.

Training in concept formation must first provide concrete experiences (perceptual experiences), and then provide the vocabulary with which to denote the experiences. The acquisition of concepts involves continuous organization and reorganization. Continuous reintegration and restructuring takes place in order to achieve wider generalization, a higher level of abstraction, and clearer delineation from other concepts.

The following reading lesson conducted with children from eight to nine years of age, all with learning handicaps, illustrates how the teacher may develop concepts in children, even when most of the youngsters have language problems.

* The development of concepts will be discussed in this chapter because the semantic aspect of language cannot be separated from the formation of concepts. Other areas of higher cognitive processes (drawing inferences, estimating probabilities, etc.) will be discussed in Chapter 16. Cognitive development and language development interact, and neither aspect of development can be studied independently of the other.

** It may be necessary to clarify the relationship between the meaning of a term as individual label and as concept. The word *bottle* uttered by a baby may only refer to his personal particular bottle; it denotes an object. A concept also has connotations; it refers to many bottles of various kinds.

The children read the title of the story, "The Traveling Musicians." The teacher asked what *travel* meant.

Concrete experiences which are connected with the concepts.

CHILD A: "Travel means being in a car."
CHILD B: "Travel means a train."

Delineation from other concepts

TEACHER: "A train, a truck, a car are all for traveling. But when you see a car standing in front of a house, would you say it travels? No, not when it's still. So, when do we travel?"

CHILD: "Oh, when we go to another state."
TEACHER: "Yes, that is right. When we go to another state, that is travel. But do we always have to go to another state? When I fly to Sacramento, then go from there to San Francisco, and then return home to Los Angeles, I stay in California. Is it travel?"

CHILDREN: "Yes."

Generalization

TEACHER: "Then what is travel?"
CHILD: "When we go places."

Delineation

TEACHER: "Yes, you are right. But would we say we travel when we go to the grocer around the corner?"

CHILD: "No."

Delineation

TEACHER: "We only use the word travel for going quite a long distance. We can travel by car; we can travel by train or truck. Can we also travel without a car or without a train, just by walking?"

CHILD: "I don't know. . . . I don't think so."

Reorganization

Arriving at a definition

TEACHER: "Your story about the traveling musicians is about some animals who travel on foot. In the story they behave like people. People can also travel that way. Travel means moving considerable distances; and it is possible to go long distances on foot."

Fixing the concept in memory through verbalization

The children were then asked to give complete sentences using the word *travel*. They said, "I traveled to the city," "I traveled in a car," "I will travel to Mexico," and so on. Because this group was still egocentric, most of their sentences began with "I."

Relating con-
cepts to each
other

The expression of ideas from a less egocentric point of view could also have been carefully developed while teaching concepts (e.g., by asking the child to speak about somebody else). But the main approach taken was to utilize the children's previous experiences and relate them to each other in order to develop the concept of travel.

It is most important that the teacher refer back to new concepts on subsequent occasions. It is therefore absolutely necessary to keep a record of the new words and concepts that have been introduced, in order to be able to methodically illustrate them with new examples in later lessons.

Enriching experi-
ences

In this instance, the teacher could expand on the initial discussion by showing a travel film and then discussing how travel varies according to the time of the year, different climates, cultures, and civilizations, and how it is related to different purposes. The word *travel* leads to the introduction of concepts connected with the more abstract word *transportation*.

Often children will use the correct word merely as a label, without understanding the characteristics of the objects or relationships to which the word properly applies. The teacher must help the child form concepts, first, by providing concrete experiences, and second, by fitting the concept into a hierarchy. The child should be helped to understand how a particular concept is related to both supraordinate and subordinate concepts. In the above example, *travel* was related to the subordinate concepts of "going by car," "going by train," and the like; and to the supraordinate concept of "change of location by a person or object over greater distances by a conveyance or on foot." The "change of location over greater distances" must be differentiated from "change of location of an object or person over a short distance," such as putting a pencil in a box or visiting a neighbor next door.

Children often inadvertently learn incorrect meanings of words and concepts when using workbooks, because workbooks encourage guessing. It is not sufficient for the teacher merely to correct the answer in the workbook. If the concept is to be understood and retained it must be discussed with each child. (In this connection, it is astonishing to discover how often the use of a good dictionary can assist even a well-educated adult to clarify a concept.)

By relating different concepts, the teacher can enlarge the original concept and help the child build a coherent structure of knowledge into which new concepts can be fitted. This procedure is necessarily slow and repetitious. Concepts need to be accrued and interrelated very gradually, so that the child understands them, learns them, and can retrieve them from memory when he needs them. As a child learns new concepts he will also become more proficient in categorizing and generalizing.

Teaching Syntax

Nearly all children need a great deal of work in the formation of correct sentences. In order to be able to teach correct sentence formation we must ask ourselves how the child learns to use grammatically correct language.

Skinner (1957) and his followers have stated that language is acquired through feedback, the approval and disapproval of the adult. Roger Brown (1969) states, however, that the adult does not react to the child's grammar but rather to the content of the message—its "truth value." Approval and disapproval has therefore no effect on the development of correct syntax. The *sole* use of the operant conditioning model and the very structured teaching approach which follows from it has been found to be more appropriate for teaching children who are severely handicapped in language (aphasic) or mentally retarded or psychotic, or culturally different children who have to learn English as a second language, than in teaching the normal child who has spoken standard English from infancy on (Bricker and Bricker, 1970). Teaching solely by a structured method, such as that introduced by Bereiter and Engelmann (1966), may result in a relatively restricted parrotlike speech rather than normal flexible spontaneous language.

Brown and Bellugi (1964) originally stated the hypothesis that a child gains grammatical knowledge through expansion of his utterances by an adult. They believed that it was important to enlarge the child's telegraphic style by restating his one-word or short-phrase utterances in the form of complete sentences. But Brown's later studies did not corroborate this hypothesis. Instead Brown concluded that the child's development of syntax is due to copying an adult model, and that modeling leads to the greatest improvement in syntax. He and his co-workers observed in their experiments with preschool children that it was more important to add to the child's ideas and increase his information than to restate his utterances in expanded form. If Brown's suggestions are correct, then neither reinforcement nor restatement is the optimum approach. Rather, modeling correct speech by talking with the children and adding to their information are the avenues that a teacher should pursue.

Is the teacher's modeling sufficient to train large groups of children in correct sentence formation? There are usually thirty or more children in an elementary public-school class. Has the teacher the time to model speech? Or should the teacher restrict her speech because the children need time to do quiet work by themselves? Would she not encroach on the time the children need to express themselves orally?

Bereiter and Engelmann (1966) have introduced a method of teaching language, based on behavioristic psychology, that offers a solution to these problems. Their method advocates that (1) the teacher use the correct form of language; (2) the children repeat in unison what she has stated; they therefore all practice the correct form simultaneously; (3) then, with the help of pictures, other sentences of the same form are generated. In this way the children use a variety of words in well-formed sentences of the same structure. They learn to form affirmative kernel sentences (consisting of subject and predicate), negations, questions, and so on. The child thus learns the patterns (algorithms) for generating sentences.

Should grammar be taught formally? Some educators regard the systematic study of any kind of grammar, traditional or modern, as a waste of time. Others feel that emphasis on the mechanics of language hampers the development of creative skills (Torrance, 1961).

The present authors believe that many children, particularly children with learning difficulties and those from homes where nonstandard English is spoken, need assistance in developing and using the various transformations of standard English. But in teaching the mechanics of language, the stress should be on generating ideas (divergent thinking) rather than rules as such.*

Teaching generative and transformational grammar** is generally helpful to children with learning difficulties because they often have severe difficulties in syntactical competence (Rosenthal, 1970). They may be unable to complete sentences correctly, to formulate sentences of negation, and so on. As has been already mentioned, a formal approach to language through transformational grammar may also be helpful for children from homes where nonstandard English is spoken. If such a formal approach is presented in the spirit and manner of

* For an opposite opinion, see Shuy (1968), who believes that teaching rules of syllabification in great detail will enhance reading ability.

** When teaching generative grammar, the structure of the sentence remains the same, but the words change (e.g., "The man ate a fish. The boy flew a kite."). When teaching transformational grammar the structure of the sentence changes, but the same words are retained as far as possible (e.g., "John runs. Does John run?")

teaching a second language, rather than as correction of his customary language, the child's self-concept will be preserved. If his speech is corrected throughout the school day, he may feel that the language used at home—and with it, the behavior of his parents and himself—is considered inferior, and something that should be eradicated. Confused feelings about himself and negative feelings toward the school may be intensified as a result.

It is important to give psychological preparation before teaching standard English to such children. The teacher should point out that written language differs from oral language. She may explain that people speak many different dialects, even in the same region of the United States, and that these dialects help enrich the language as a whole. Norwegian, Czechoslovakian, French, and so on, were originally dialects that increasingly diverged from their parent language until they became recognized as independent languages of equal importance —like children growing up.

The caution with which standard English has to be presented to the economically deprived or culturally different child is emphasized by a number of workers in the field, including Bernstein (1961). Dialect psychologically unites the speaker with those with whom he lives and maintains close mutual support. The educational process increases the risk of separating the speaker of standard English from his family and group. If the direct honesty, vitality, and emotional expressiveness of the dialect is acknowledged and preserved, the child may more readily avail himself of the possibilities inherent in formal language.

As already noted above, the authors believe that the teacher can best help children with language problems or with lack of familiarity with standard English by modeling standard English and by providing instruction in speaking in complete sentences in various transformations —by teaching transformational grammar. The following outline provides an example of step-by-step procedures that can be used for teaching both generative and transformational grammar.

EXAMPLES OF TRANSFORMATIONAL GRAMMAR

Changing of Active into Passive Forms*

Regular verb, present tense:

> Mother washes the laundry.
> The laundry is being washed by Mother.

NOTE* The teacher should avoid using as examples verbs with prepositions, such as *tie up*. Such constructions are relatively infrequent in English.

Irregular verb, present tense:

> Jim rides a bicycle.
> A bicycle is ridden by Jim.

Regular verb, past tense:

> Dorothy knitted a sweater.
> A sweater was knitted by Dorothy.

Irregular verb, past tense:

> Jim rode a bicycle.
> The bicycle was ridden by Jim.

Changing Positive into Negative

Present tense, regular verb:

> I work today.
> I do not work today.

Present tense, irregular verb:

> I eat the cookie.
> I do not eat the cookie.

Past tense, regular verb:

> Mark learned his lesson.
> Mark did not learn his lesson.

Past tense, irregular verb:

> The dog dug a hole.
> The dog did not dig a hole.

Future tense, regular verb:

> I will earn money.
> I will not earn money.

Future tense, irregular verb:

> I will eat cake.
> I will not eat cake.

Regular	*Irregular*
Present	*Present*
I walk.	I eat the cookie.
I *do* not walk.	I *do* not eat the cookie.
Past	*Past*
I walked.	I ate the cookie.
I *did* not walk.	I *did* not eat the cookie.

RULE

Positive	*Negative*
verb (present)	do (present) + negation (not) + present form of verb
verb (past)	did (past) + negation (not) + present form of verb

Changing Active Declarative Sentences into Questions

Regular verb, present tense, active voice

> The boy learns.
> Does the boy learn?

Regular verb, past tense, active voice

> The boy learned.
> Did the boy learn?

Irregular verb, present tense, active voice

> The boy swims.
> Does the boy swim?

Irregular verb, past tense, active voice

> The boy swam.
> Did the boy swim?

Regular verb, present tense, passive voice

> The ball is chased by the dog.
> Is the ball chased by the dog?

Regular verb, past tense, passive voice

> The ball was chased by the dog.
> Was the ball chased by the dog?

Irregular verb, present tense, passive voice

> The target is hit by the arrow.
> Is the target hit by the arrow?

Irregular verb, past tense, passive voice

> The target was hit by the arrow.
> Was the target hit by the arrow?

Other transformations may be practiced following an outline of Menyuk (1964) which is given below in abbreviated form.

Contractions	He will be good.
	He'll be good.
Inversion	The toothpaste is here.
	Here is the toothpaste.
Relative questions	Where are you going?
	When are you coming?
Imperative, positive	Wash your hands.
negative	Don't eat my carrot.
"*ing*" form of verb	He is coming.
	I am going.
Using *do* and *did* as auxiliary verbs, positive and negative	I do like her.
	I do not like her.
	I did see him.
	I did not talk to him.
Reflexive	I cut myself.
	He wrapped himself in a white sheet.
Possessive	I am eating Mary's candy.
	I am reading Tom's book.
Conjunction	Peter is here, *and* you are there.
If conjunction	I'll give it to you *if* you want it.
So conjunction	He saw him, *so* he hit him.
Cause conjunction	He'll eat it *because* it's good.
Pronoun in conjunction	David saw the bicycle and he was happy.
Adjective clause	I have a dog *that is cuddly and fuzzy and pink.*
Relative clause	I don't know *what he's doing.*
Infinitive complement	I want *to play.*
Participal complement	I like *painting.*
Iteration	You have to drink milk to grow strong.
Nominalization	She does the shopping and cooking and baking.

The most difficult sentences to use correctly are those that contain dependent clauses denoting *causal relationships* ("I am happy *because* our team won"); *exclusions* ("Everyone was happy *except* John"); and *conditions* ("*If* our team wins, we will be happy".) As a rule, such sentences cannot be generated or transformed by children until they are seven and a half, eight, or even nine years old. As Piaget points out, the ability to understand causal relationships does not generally develop before this age level.

Teaching Language in the Classroom

The teacher's efforts to help children develop language skills (as well as other skills and abilities) must be guided by the maxim, "Human beings learn by doing." But it is not easy to ensure that every child in a large public-school classroom gets the necessary opportunities to express himself orally. "Sharing" and other activities that involve a large group of children are not suitable for developing verbal expression. No child has the opportunity to speak enough, and those who probably need to do so most may not talk at all.

Verbal expression is best developed when only two children or a very few children talk together. It is advantageous if at least one of the members already speaks good standard English.

The most important factor in encouraging a child to talk is the provision of an environment in which each child feels comfortable. A child who is insecure and fearful will not talk.

Some activities in which the children might be involved for the purpose of promoting language include puppet shows, acting with masks (see photo), role playing, using telephones (both real and play), discussing pictures taken or drawn by the children, forming committees for various purposes (e.g., to present some information to parents), dictating a story and recording it, and so on.

The combined use of oral and written language is highly important. If the teacher reads a story to a group of children, she should make the book available to them later; very often even very young children will repeat the story to themselves or to others, using the pictures as cues, and may be able to write a few key words under pictures that they draw themselves. Children who are first being introduced to formal reading instruction will enjoy dictating stories for the chalkboard, chart board, or typewriter, but as soon as possible they should write these themselves. Older children can be encouraged to report orally on various topics which are then written up in the form of a class newspaper. Examples of topics that might be used are television programs, food currently available at the market, a discussion with the custodian on how the classroom and play yard can be kept cleaner and prettier, the prevention of pollution and where to deposit materials for recycling, the programs currently available in city parks, and so on.

The teacher may elicit language directly by asking questions. The

more questions the teacher asks, the better the children learn and the more opportunities they have to express themselves verbally. Questions should be framed so that they do not always require the same type of answer. The vocabulary used must be understood by the children, and explanation may be necessary. Questions should not only require memory for facts, but should help students to clarify ideas, evaluate information, and draw inferences. Examples of questions that may elicit meaningful answers are: What do you know about it? What can you add to that discussion? What do you mean? Can you explain this? Are we assuming something? Can we assume anything? What could it be? What do you think could be the cause? Does this relate to something else? Can you combine these ideas?

Often the teacher can aid a child by stating an answer in the form of a question, in order to encourage him to talk. For instance, when the child replies, "I don't know" to the question, "Why is the Pacific less salty than the Mediterranean?" the teacher might ask, "Do you think this may have something to do with the free flow of currents? Could it be that it has something to do with the evaporation in that climatic zone?" and so on. Then the child should be called upon to explain *why* he chose a particular answer.

Regardless of whether the main approach to language teaching is through the regular curriculum supplemented by informal activities or through the use of more structured programs, the child's maximum progress will depend upon very careful records being kept of his mistakes in using language. The teacher is then able to direct the child into games or discussions in which he can correctly repeat the required form. Without keeping careful records the teacher cannot choose activities rationally and give the specific help that each child requires.

The ITPA, described in Chapter 10, has proved to be so helpful, not only for evaluation, but as a rationale for a model of remediation, that training procedures based on it have been developed by many people and in several countries. The suggestions in Table 7, based upon the ITPA, are excerpted from the language program used at the Frostig Center.

TABLE 7
Training Procedures Based on the ITPA

ITPA Subtest	Training Suggestions
Auditory Reception	Training auditory perception (Chapter 14) Answering simple yes or no questions a. Answering quickly (to improve attentiveness and speed of response) b. Answering in whole sentences and giving reasons for his answer Following directions or carrying out instructions a. Following instructions involving knowledge of prepositions b. Carrying out a sequence (to improve auditory sequential memory) Identifying words in a series which belong in the same category

TABLE 7 (Continued)

ITPA Subtest	Training Suggestions
	Identifying an action or object which is described; this exercise also helps the child's imagery
	Listening to stories or poems; retelling a story he has just heard
Visual Reception	Describing objects or pictures in books, catalogs, or encyclopedias
	Identifying objects and actions in the room, on the playground, in a film strip, on television
	Selecting particular objects or parts in a picture from a verbal description
	Describing an activity which is taking place, such as an action by another child, a science experiment, or a filmed episode
Manual Expression	Drawing, sculpturing
	Performing self-help activities, whenever possible accompanied by verbal directions
	Imitating animal movements
	Acting out a story told by the teacher or read in a book
	Acting out specific instructions, such as "Show me how you wash socks by hand and hang them on a clothesline"
Verbal Expression	Discussing, "sharing," debating, storytelling
	Describing an object; the teacher may guide the child by asking about specific attributes, such as color, material, size, purpose
	Telling all the uses the child can think of for a common object; he thus practices divergent thinking
	Formulating definitions
	Giving instructions to each other
Auditory Association	Completing an analogy orally
	Finding common characteristics; e.g., "A wigwam and a teepee are both ——————"
	Telling what word does not belong in a series and telling why
	Identifying absurdities and illogical relationships in sentences or paragraphs

TABLE 7 (Continued)

ITPA Subtest	Training Suggestions
Visual Association	Sorting objects and pictures according to functional association Describing tools and machines, and discussing their use Reproducing the movements of another person Classifying
Grammatic Closure	(See pp. 223–231)
Visual Closure	(See p. 256; see also discussion of training in figure-ground perception, Chapter 13.)
Auditory Closure	(See Chapter 14, p. 206; also Bush and Giles, 1969.
Sound Blending	(See Chapter 18, pp. 284–285 and 302.)
Auditory Sequencing	Playing a verbal "follow-the-leader" game in which each child has to repeat everything that has been said and to add a new item; e.g., "I went to camp and took my sleeping bag;" "I went to camp and took my sleeping bag and canteen;" and so on Supplying a word, number, or letter missing from a sequence Learning common sequences, such as days of the week, months of the year, common measurements, etc. Reporting his other activities in a temporal sequence Reporting the activities of a person in a story in a temporal sequence, or historical or scientific events in a logical sequence
Visual Sequencing	Copying sequences of beads, marbles, and so on Reproducing sequences from memory Copying and reproducing two-dimensional patterns Solving mazes Copying arithmetic problems from the board Spelling

Summary

Two principal themes have been emphasized in this chapter: the first part has been devoted to definition and discussion of the elements of language and the relationship of linguistics to the teaching of language.

The second part has been devoted to methods of training various language abilities—articulation, vocabulary, concept formation, syntax.

Because the ITPA evaluates so many different functions, a training program based on it will necessarily overlap the training in visual perception, auditory perception, integrative functions, and so on, discussed in other chapters.

Equally the exercises and activities suggested for language training and those for psycholinguistic training based on the ITPA overlap. This could not be otherwise because psycholinguistic training includes language training in the usual sense. Differences between the two are often only a matter of terminology—for example, receptive language is called "auditory reception" in the ITPA; correct syntax or grammar is termed "grammatic closure."

Other abilities evaluated by the ITPA are usually not classified as language abilities; visual reception is an example. But visual reception is not evaluated by any other test in the basic battery. Visual-perception tests cannot be substituted, because perception refers to a behavior on the automatic level and reception to the use of perceptual functions in conceptual processes.

The ITPA sequencing subtests and the exercises based on them are very valuable; children with learning difficulties frequently have deficits in memory for sequences. The ITPA is the only standardized test that taps the ability for memory of visual sequences, while the auditory-sequencing subtest of the ITPA is similar to the digit span forward test of the WISC.

WORKS CITED

Bereiter, E., and Engelmann, S. *Teaching disadvantaged children in the preschool.* Englewood Cliffs, N.J.: Prentice-Hall, 1966.

Bernstein, B. Social class and linguistic development: A theory of social learning. In A. H. Halsey, J. Floud, and C. A. Anderson (Eds.), *Education, economy and society.* New York: Free Press, 1961.

Bloomfield, L. *Language.* New York: Holt, 1933.

Bolinger, D. *Aspects of language.* New York: Harcourt, 1968.

Bricker, W. A., and Bricker, D. D. A program of language training for the severely language handicapped child. *Exceptional Children,* 1970, 37(2), 101–112.

Brown, R. In J. P. Hill (Ed.), *Minnesota symposium on child psychology,* Vol. 2. Minneapolis: University of Minnesota Press, 1969.

Brown, R., and Bellugi, U. Three processes in the child's acquisition of syntax. *Harvard Educational Review,* 1964, 34(2), 133–151.

Bruner, J. S. *Toward a theory of instruction.* New York: Norton, 1966.

Bush, W. J., and Giles, M. T. *Aids to psycholinguistic teaching.* Columbus, Ohio: Charles E. Merrill, 1969.

Chomsky, N. *Syntactic structure.* The Hague: Mouton, 1957.

Dawe, H. C. A study of the effect of an educational program upon language development and related mental functions in young children. *Journal of Experimental Education,* 1942, 11, 200–209.

Gleitman, L. R., and Shipley, E. F. A proposal for the study of the acquisition of English syntax. A grant proposal submitted March 1, 1963, to the National Institutes of Health.

Johnson, W., Darley, F. L., and Spriestersbach, D. C. *Diagnostic methods in speech pathology.* New York: Harper & Row, 1963.

Kirk, S. A., McCarthy, J. J., and Kirk, W. *Illinois test of psycholinguistic abilities.* (Rev. ed.) Urbana, Ill.: University of Illinois Press, 1968.

de Laguna, G. A. *Speech: Its function and development.* Bloomington, Ind.: Indiana University Press, 1927.

Lenneberg, E. *Biological foundations of language.* New York: Wiley, 1966.

Menyuk, P. Comparison of grammar of children with functionally deviant and normal speech. *Journal of Speech and Hearing Research,* 1964, 7, 199–221.

Menyuk, P. *Sentences children use.* Cambridge, Mass.: MIT Press, 1969.

Meyers, P. Q., and Hammill, D. D. *Methods for learning disorders.* New York: Wiley, 1969.

Osgood, C. E., and Sebeok, T. A. (Eds.), *Psycholinguistics: A survey of theory and research problems.* Baltimore: Waverly Press, 1954.

Rosenthal, J. H. A preliminary psycholinguistic study of children with learning disabilities. *Journal of Learning Disabilities,* 1970, 3(8), 391–396.

Shuy, R. W. Some language and cultural differences in a theory of reading. Paper presented at Preconvention Workshop of Psycholinguistics, International Reading Association, Boston, 1968.

Skinner, B. F. *Verbal behavior.* New York: Appleton-Crofts, 1957.

Staats, A. W., and Staats, C. K. *Complex human behavior.* New York: Holt, 1964.

Templin, M. C., and Darley, F. L. *The Templin-Darley tests of articulation.* Iowa City: University of Iowa Bureau of Educational Research and Service, 1960.

Torrance, E. P. Factors affecting creative thinking in children. *Merrill-Palmer Quarterly*, 1961, 8, 171–180.

Wyatt, G. *Language learning and communication disorders in children.* New York: Free Press, 1969.

16
THE
HIGHER
COGNITIVE
FUNCTIONS

The term *cognitive functions* refers to those functions that help us to understand the world around us; and includes perception in this book. The phrase *higher cognitive functions* refers only to thought processes. Understanding the world around us is a function of intelligence.

The Concept of Intelligence

Intelligence has been defined in various ways. Wechsler (1959) states that "intelligence is the aggregate or global capacity of the individual to act purposefully, to think rationally and to deal effectively with the environment." When intelligence is measured by an intelligence test, such as one of the Wechsler intelligence scales, it might be assumed that a person's score would indicate how effectively he can deal with the environment, but this is not always the case.

High scores on intelligence tests will not necessarily ensure smooth progress in school, but a lack of those abilities evaluated by the usual intelligence tests can be expected to retard school achievement. Among the psychological functions measured by intelligence tests are the cognition of facts, language, and the ability to pay attention, to form associations, to classify, to retain information, to comprehend, to solve problems, to reason, to perceive relationships, to judge, to choose correctly between alternatives, to visualize, to recall, to use language for the mediation (facilitation) of thought, and to manipulate graphic symbols. All these abilities are necessary for school learning.

For a long time there were educators and psychologists who believed that the intelligence was fixed—that a person's I.Q. did not change. Today all believe that intelligence tests evaluate abilities by scores that are the result of an interaction between inborn potential and environmental influences, and that therefore their results are subject to alteration. If the environment is optimum for the growth of cognitive functions, they will increase; if it is not stimulating, they will decrease.

The usual intelligence test provides a single score, a snapshot or composite based on the current state of the child's knowledge, language, and thought, whereas Piaget's concept of intelligence stresses the *processes* of mental operation and development. Piaget has differentiated four interacting factors that contribute to the intelligence that an individual has at his disposal: heredity, environment, social interaction (including language), and finally, personal drive to reach an equilibrium. This drive is directed toward achieving a balance between assimilation (perception and understanding) and accommodation (learning to adjust to and to use the environment). (See Chapter 8, Cognitive-Developmental Concepts). Both assimilation and accommodation are continuous processes that characterize all the contacts between the individual person and his environment.

Three of the factors that directly contribute to intelligence—the stimuli in the environment, the child's interest in learning (his drive to achieve a mental equilibrium), and the language and social activities in which he engages—can be influenced by the teacher.

What should the teacher do to make best use of these three factors? Partial answers to this question has already been given in earlier chapters: The school environment needs to be pleasant and adapted to the child's needs; the child must be made comfortable; the discrepancy between his home environment and the school should not seem overwhelming.

Our everyday experiences make us aware that thought is influenced by, and depends upon, our outer and inner environment, on diverse abilities and conditions, including, for example, memory, the words in which thought is clothed, our physical condition, our feelings, our goals and purposes. Children can not think well when they are unhappy or anxious or hungry, or when they see no purpose in what they are doing. The negative or positive alterations in their test scores reflect their increased or decreased ability to adjust to taxing situations—testing is usually a taxing situation in itself—as well as their increasing or decreasing ability to solve problems.

The positive changes observed in I.Q. do not therefore necessarily result from cognitive training; they may also reflect the influences of a child's relationship with the teacher or with his peers (Zigler and Butterfield, 1968), of the classroom atmosphere, and of any other circumstances that may have improved the child's mental health and well-being. Negative changes may equally well have been caused by emotional or health factors.

The teacher needs to promote social interaction and the use of language. Mental equilibrium will be achieved when the child's natural curiosity is satisfied, when he learns actively, so that both assimilation of new materials and accommodation can take place; or, in other words, so that he can understand and apply what he is taught.

Body movement and manipulation are indispensable to learning until the child is able to perform operations, such as proportionality, mentally, but this ability usually develops only toward the very end or rather at the completion of elementary school (from eleven to thirteen years of age) and even then, not in all children.

Piaget has stressed that development by interaction with the environment occurs on the child's own terms, given a rich environment from which he can select according to his interests and competence of the moment. The teaching suggestions made below might well be unnecessary if all children lived in a varied, stimulating, and caring environment, but such a situation unfortunately is all too rare.

An approach based on Piaget might advocate guided activity and experimentation during which the child learns to observe, to note down what he has observed, and to draw conclusions. A modification of a Piagetian approach is described in Aurelia Levi's work, which emphasizes classification and the perception and understanding of relationships. Her step-by-step procedures, which begin with equipping the child with perceptual skills and a store of concepts, are clearly and simply outlined in two papers (1965, 1966), and may provide the teacher with many suggestions.

Four Characteristics of Intelligent Behavior

Decentration

Piaget has suggested the term *decentration* for one of the main characteristics of intelligent behavior. Decentration has already been discussed in Chapter 8. It refers to the ability to shift one's point of view, to focus on several aspects of a problem simultaneously, and to relate these aspects. It is akin to what the psychologist and physician, Kurt Goldstein (1948), has called the abstract attitude. Brain-damaged persons and young children lack this attitude, and many children with learning difficulties have great trouble in acquiring it.

Children with learning difficulties need assistance in learning to shift attention and point of view. Training should begin at the sensory-motor level and include many activities that require the child to attune himself to the movements of others and physically cooperate with them. For instance, each time a child throws a ball to another child or catches one, he has to shift attention; he has to decentrate.

In visual-perceptual training, decentration is practised by means of exercises in figure-ground perception and the perception of spatial relationships. Decentration of thought is promoted by mathematical learning—for example, by attaining the concepts of one-to-one matching, seriation, reversibility, the commutative law, and so on—as well as through categorization exercises and through solving figurative and verbal-analogy problems.

In relation to developing the higher cognitive functions, the teacher can ask questions involving understanding of reciprocal and multiple relationships, such as, "Today is Carl's birthday. In one year he will have his seventh birthday. How old is he today?" or, "If Ann is older than Jerry, is Jerry older or younger than Ann?" Or, "Ethel is not my mother but a daughter of my grandmother. What relationship is she to me?" Children who have difficulty with such problems can often learn to solve them with the help of diagrams—though usually only after extended practice.

Discussion, role-playing, charades, drama, and symbolic play are all invaluable in developing decentration in communication and social skills.

In general, a teacher can help a child to decentrate by calling his attention to the various relevant dimensions of objects or situations. Encouraging the child to physically explore for himself and to manipulate objects, involves him in literally taking different positions with regard to them. At the same time, while the child explores in play or experiments or is involved in discussions with his peers, the teacher's verbal guidance and comments can lead him to see a situation from different points of view. "What did you observe when going to the park?" the teacher may ask. "And what do you think Bowser, Tony's dog, would observe?"

Verbal guidance is especially important for the child who seems unable to understand new and unusual subject matter or another person's point of view; in other words, the child with learning and behavior problems. For such a child the step-by-step progression suggested by the behaviorists may be insufficient to assure optimum progress. The teacher needs to point out the relevant dimensions of each task, be it the slant of a line in writing, the stress of a syllable in reading, or the reasons for a social custom or social change.

Formation of Schemata

Another basic characteristic of intelligence is that thought requires a schema or schemata. Piaget (1968, p. 15) says, "A 'schème' is that part of an action which is repeatable and generalizable in another action or operation; it is that part which is essentially characteristic of the action or operation."

The concept of *schema* has been discussed at various places throughout this book. A schema is a link formed by stimuli and responses: through repeated use the response becomes automatic (as when we write a letter or drive a car without having to consider how we do it). But in the use of thought, stimuli and responses can not always be linked and readily available. A stimulus can elicit various responses and chains of responses, and the problem-solver must weigh and choose one approach after another, keeping at the same time the original goal in mind.

The teacher's task is therefore twofold: first, to help the child establish a network of ready-made connections (schemata) that he can join to acquire more complicated skills; and second, to help him choose, evaluate, and rearrange his schemata to solve a particular problem. Well-learned sensory-motor skills are schemata (see the above example of driving). The child who has learned to tie a bow has acquired a schema for bow-tying; he will not have to think about the way to tie his shoelaces but will do it each day automatically.

Schemata are the building-blocks of thought; for instance, basic concepts are the schemata a child needs to manipulate his thought processes.

Schemata need not only to be built but also to be readjusted; this fact is often a stumbling block in adequate adaptation to a new situation. Rearrangement of schemata is best promoted by giving a child similar tasks in various circumstances. For instance, sorting (classifying) objects should be done according to various dimensions (size, color, shape, and so on). The schema (operation) of seriation is enriched and made flexible and adaptable when a child arranges in graduated order sticks according to length, shapes according to size, threads according to hue, solids according to weight, and so on. Sorting according to multiple criteria, as has earlier been pointed out, is a useful exercise in decentration.

Ability to Keep in Mind
Lengthy Chains of Thought

This is another characteristic of intelligence. This ability requires keeping facts in mind while at the same time judging their correctness. It can be developed through sequential activities that require the child to keep in mind a series of instructions. For example, the child can be required to carry out a succession of movements during a movement-education program. He can also be asked to repeat a story that he has recently read or which has been told to him; to solve oral and written word problems in mathematics, and to recognize and correct absurdi-

ties in narrative consisting of several sentences. The latter exercise also
helps the child to perceive relationships. The following is an example of
logical inconsistency (absurdity) in a story. The children have to point
out what is wrong with it. "John said, 'I can easily find out how many
cupcakes we need for our party. Every child in our class must have a
cupcake, and the teacher needs one too. We have twenty-four children
and one teacher, so it would be best to buy three dozen. Oh, that
wouldn't be enough.' " And so on.

Use of Models and Symbols
In Problem-Solving

A fourth characteristic of intelligence is the ability to use models
and symbols in problem-solving. One aspect of this characteristic is the
role of language, which will be discussed later when the relationship of
language to thought is considered. But not only oral and written language is used and taught in elementary school. Mathematical symbols
are also taught, as when the child learns to use graphs or to use the
symbols indicating more or less ($>$, $<$). Maps and other forms of symbolic representation are used in other subjects.

Coding exercises (discussed later) and the use of graphs, tables,
maps, and so on, help the child to become more efficient in the use of
symbols.

Educating for Intelligent Behavior

The relationship of thought processes to other abilities is an important
concern for the educator. Some of these relationships have been outlined earlier in the chapter on the developmental sequence.

Thought processes do not evolve independently of sensory-motor
functions, language, and perception. All these functions must be taken
into account in seeking to educate the higher cognitive skills. Thus
we return to the question of the interrelationship between thought and
speech, thought and perception, and so on.

For didactic reasons the authors of this book have discussed the
various psychological functions separately; but in the living human
being they are inseparably interrelated.

Movement, perception, and language all have implications for the
development of intelligence. Language and accurate perception facilitate thought. Movement makes possible the perception of temporal,
spatial, and causal relationships on which our understanding of the
world depends.

Movement, indeed, is often regarded as the royal road to all learning. Piaget and Bruner both suggest that in teaching new and difficult

concepts, movement (termed by Bruner, "the enactive mode") should precede the iconic (presentation through pictures and graphs) and that notation (the symbolic mode) should follow last. These procedures are particularly important in teaching mathematics.

The educator needs to be cautioned, however, that action is not always a necessary part of learning. Experiments (Devor & Stern, 1970) have indicated that static concepts can be taught by pictures quite as well as by action. *Processes* are learned by actions. Math should therefore be taught by action, because math teaches process. Movement is also involved in learning temporal and spatial concepts and concepts that denote relationships. But static concepts, such as a tree or a house, do not necessarily involve relationships and therefore do not necessarily involve elements of movement. Nevertheless the educator must always be aware that learning is an active, not a passive, process. The authors agree with Ginsburg and Opper (1969, p. 221): "Perhaps the most important single proposition that the educator can derive from Piaget's work and thus use in the classroom, is that children, especially young ones, learn best from concrete activities."

The Role of Representational Functions

Language, imitation, imagery, and symbolic play represent reality. Piaget (1962, p. 62) writes; "In its broad sense representation is identical with thought." The importance of imitation and imagery for the child's total cognitive development has been mentioned, but the training of these abilities needs further discussion.

Many children with learning difficulties are deficient in their ability to use symbolic representation, either in language or in their ability to employ imitation and imagery or in both. Children with severe difficulties in using imagery show their poverty of ideas in their play and in the perseveration of their behavior. They may engage in the same kind of activity day after day, making, for instance, the same kind of drawing with only minor variations. The teacher can help to eliminate such rigidity by encouraging gradual changes in the activity. She can, for example, suggest to the child that he use other materials, colors, backgrounds, accessories, frames, and so on in his drawings. Alternatively she might suggest a more radical change of activity. Probably both methods should be tried with the perseverative child, and the teacher should watch his reactions carefully to ensure that the changes she suggests are not too abrupt for the child to absorb, while being sufficiently rapid and demanding to promote optimum progress.

A third important approach in helping to develop a child's representational functions is perceptual training. Without adequate perceptual skills, a child's imagery can only reflect a distorted picture of reality. Perceptual training may develop imagery because it requires the child to attend to each part of a stimulus, as well as to the stimulus as a whole. Attention to both the parts and the whole is necessary for the formation of accurate visual images. The child should therefore be helped to pay attention to details, and should be given practice in both analysis and synthesis of patterns (Estes, 1970, pp. 10–11).

Verbal analysis on the part of both teacher and child will hasten success. The child needs to know what to observe and should learn to make statements concerning his observations. (See Chapter 13, on Visual-Perceptual Abilities.)

Mental imagery can be conscious or unconscious. It may be auditory, visual, or haptic;* it may involve taste, smell, sensation, temperature, or pain. The teacher may help the child to use imagery by encouraging him to express himself, first actively, and then by verbalizing his actions. The child, for instance, might be asked to jump as high as he can, then to close his eyes and imagine how it felt when he jumped; and then to describe what he did and how it felt. Or the child might be required to use imagery for visualizing changes in objects or events. According to the age and interests of the child, the teacher might ask such questions as "How do you think this picture would look with two trees instead of one and with a colored edge around it? Now draw it like that. All right?"

The Role of Language

Hans Furth (1970) has expressed the opinion that Piaget is probably the only great living developmentalist who is not of the opinion that language is a source of intelligence. Instead Piaget regards language as an important form of symbolic behavior. Whatever the specific relationship between language and thought may be, the importance of language for thought is undisputed.

In the classroom, the representative function of language needs to be emphasized in all its forms—oral, written and printed. When children working together talk about what they are doing, and record their activities in words, graphs, tables, pictures, and so on, they form mental representations that they can later retrieve. In other words, they organize their information and therefore understand it better. They learn and remember more of their classroom experiences than do the children who do not discuss their experiences. Written language, being

* Haptic refers to the perception of simultaneous stimuli from receptors in the skeletal muscles (kinesthetic) and in the skin (tactile). A child tracing velvet letters is receiving haptic input.

more permanent than oral language, should be used to record whatever the children are doing.

In the open classroom, which is to a significant extent based on Piaget's ideas, some of the functions of the teacher are to state the purpose and goal of each activity, to provide the child with adequate materials, to help him to arrive at a solution, and finally, to teach him how to note down his results.

Teaching Classification and Categorization

A most important skill, or to express it in Piaget's terms, a most important mental operation, is that of classification. Children begin to classify habitually—that is, they learn to think of things as members of groups—from about the age of seven. Piaget does not conceive of classification or any other operation as a single ability, but rather considers that each new operation is built upon a number of past operations in a hierarchical fashion. For example, before a child can classify an object on the basis of more than one attribute, he must be able to keep several ideas in mind simultaneously. The child who is younger than seven or even eight or nine years of age has great difficulties in considering two or more attributes simultaneously while classifying (logical multiplication); for instance, it would be difficult for him to sort a pile of objects into those that are large red, small red, large white, and small white. But if classification has been taught step by step, children are able to learn such skills at a much younger age (Sigel, Roeper, and Hooper, 1966).

Hierarchical classification is still more difficult than logical multiplication. Before the child can understand hierarchical classification (superordinate, coordinate, and subordinate categories), he must be able to understand class inclusion; that is, he must grasp the fact that if an object is a member of a class, then there is a class composed of members of which the object is one example. Once the child understands class inclusion, he will be able to grasp that inasmuch as both the dogs and the cats in a shelter are animals, there must be more animals than there are dogs in the shelter. Usually children above eight years of age are able to understand problems of class inclusion, and they should receive training in this skill. Excellent materials to develop classification skills are the Attribute Games (Education Development Center, 1966). The child first sorts objects, which is an easier task than working with figures or with concepts. The first step is to sort according to a single common attribute, such as color, for instance, separating all the red blocks from all the blue ones. Later the child sorts objects according to multiple attributes, such as size and color. Successive tasks include hierarchical classification and intersecting groupings.

Working with matrices also helps the child acquire logical multiplication (classifying according to multiple criteria) and to progress from the perceptual to the conceptual level.

For example, the child might be asked to fill in missing drawings in matrices. He might be given a sheet of paper on which clues,* such as those in Figure 1, are drawn and be required to draw in symbols to produce a final result like Figure 2.

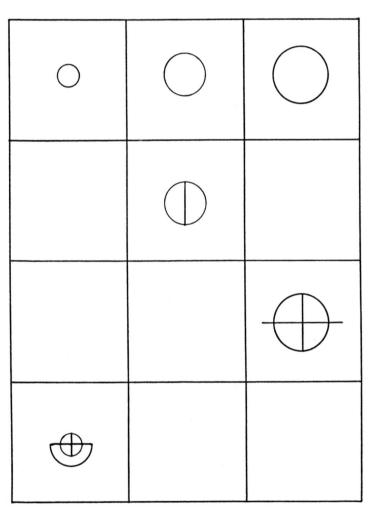

FIGURE 1.   Incomplete matrix

* The criteria are size, and the addition of a detail. If the child cannot draw the symbols accurately enough, he can choose the appropriate shapes from a selection drawn on pieces of paper, and place them on the grid.

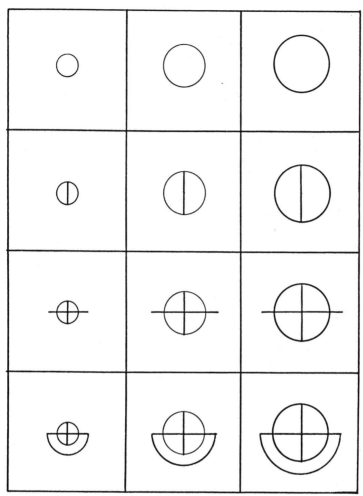

FIGURE 2.   Complete matrix

Wechsler's Model of Intelligence

The abilities tapped by Wechsler's Intelligence Scales can be influenced by the educative process. For instance, the ability to pay attention can be influenced (see the earlier chapter on educating sensory-motor functions). The degree of attention is of great importance for intelligence subtest results, as Binet pointed out as early as 1909. Another example of those abilities that can be trained which are reflected in intelligence tests is the ability to form associations, as, for instance, in learning new terminology.

A great amount of research is available indicating that Wechsler intelligence-test scores tend to go up with continuous adequate schooling—or at least stay at the original level—but that they decrease if the schooling is very poor or permanently interrupted (e.g., Hunt, 1961).

The three forms of the Wechsler test (WPPSI, WAIS, WISC) are similar in construction; they differ in detail only because they are designed for different age levels. In the following discussion, the Wechsler Intelligence Scale for Children (WISC) is used as a model. The reader will probably remember from previous learning or from reading Chapter 10 of this book that the WISC has twelve subtests.

Verbal Tests	Performance Tests
Information	Picture Completion
Comprehension	Picture Arrangement
Arithmetic	Block Design
Similarities	Object Assembly
Vocabulary	Coding*
Digit Span*	Mazes*

The following section does not present methods to teach the specific skills tested, but the broad characteristics of intelligent behavior that are tapped. These are abilities that are required and usually directly taught in any school program. All teachers impart information, teach the child to comprehend better what he hears and reads, develop arithmetical skills and vocabulary. There is therefore a direct correspondence between these abilities and the WISC subtests.

Verbal Subtests

ACQUIRING, STORING, AND RETRIEVING INFORMATION. Teaching consists to a large extent in imparting information. The child who has difficulty in learning new information needs to be carefully checked to discover in which sense modality he seems to learn best. Does he remember best by listening, by reading, by looking at pictures or a film, by writing?

Usually, information is remembered better when it is verbalized, regardless of the modality through which the child learns best. The child should be encouraged to say aloud what he has learned and, whenever possible, to write about it.

* Subtests marked with asterisk are optional.

A child who is to acquire information about the world has to be presented with an articulated sequence of topics. At each grade level new topics required by the public-school curriculum are introduced, but there should also be a branching-out into other related fields, depending on the child's interest.

Both the teacher and the child should record such information in a notebook. The teacher keeps the notebook in order to select from and review resource units. The child needs the notebook in order to review what he has actually learned.

Review is essential, but review must be interesting. Review may either add to a child's information or place it in a new light, in a new relationship; for example, the use of cotton could be discussed in relation to plant seeds, in relation to farming, in relation to the economy in other countries, and so on. Review can also be made interesting by a change in the form of presentation: by presenting a topic in game form (e.g., presenting phonics or number facts as a Bingo game), or having the children make presentations to the class, or having a child monitor his own progress. Children who have difficulties in acquiring or retaining information cannot be helped unless topics are frequently reviewed and related to each other.

DEVELOPING COMPREHENSION. The ability to comprehend is easily gauged in the classroom. The teacher who reads a story, explains how a pulley works, or discusses how the politics of a country are influenced by its economic conditions can readily observe whether or not the pupil has understood the topic.

Comprehension can be developed at the same time as information. If a child learns not only the facts, but the *why* of the facts, his interest and comprehension will increase. It is most important that the teacher asks questions that require a knowledge of underlying principles and that also require divergent thinking; e.g., finding multiple solutions to a problem. Factual questions such as, "What is the average temperature in Sacramento?" should not be as frequently asked as "thought" or "problem" questions, such as, "Would the temperature in Sacramento on most days in July be hotter or colder than in San Francisco? Why?" Such questions require the child to think about the different geographical features that influence the climate.

The study of history and of present and previous economic conditions, comparing various cultures in different parts of the world, and so on, provides many opportunities for guiding the children to developing comprehension, evaluation, and convergent and divergent thinking. Resource units are most helpful in preparing such lessons. Ample background material for various topics in the form of pictures, books, films, and other teaching materials should be on file, so that the teacher can easily find and assemble them.

Teaching a topic should be initiated by asking the children what questions they have to which they want answers. The teacher's answers to such questions might well be remembered without being understood. In order to enhance comprehension—assimilation in Piaget's sense— the teacher should therefore pose a question in return, How will you find out? and help the child to find and compile the information from various sources, and to observe and write down his observations.

The child with learning difficulties is often very concrete in his thinking (Serafica & Sigel, 1970). He needs much graphic and pictorial presentation to further his understanding, and he needs to manipulate and experience directly as much as possible. Films, pictures, simple reading materials, and visits to museums should be supplemented by direct manipulation, whenever possible.

For example, cooking can help children develop understanding of physical and chemical processes if they are encouraged to think about what they are doing. "Why does an egg become foamy when you beat it?" "Why does flour become sticky when mixed with liquid?" "Why can flour be digested after the dough has been baked?" are among the questions that might be posed to a child engaged in making muffins.

ENLARGING VOCABULARY. A child's store of words can be assessed by observation in the classroom. Vocabulary can be taught by the same methods and at the same time as information and comprehension are developed. Many children fail in solving verbal problems because they do not understand the words. Dictionaries (including a compilation of words and their definition made by the child himself) are often important aids in acquiring vocabulary. Children above the third or fourth grade may use a thesaurus as well (a simple thesaurus is very inexpensive). Children and teacher alike should look up definitions and synonyms. New terms should be practised in sentences.

Words are symbols, not signs. This means that one word often refers to a multitude of things: the word *tree* will represent all trees, not just a specific one. But a child learns to use words as symbols only gradually. The child with learning difficulties may remain tied to personal, subjective meanings of words he uses, a deficit which may not be evident so long as he uses only the most commonplace language. Words should be taught in various contexts and with varying shades of meaning.

Deficits in symbolic thinking lead to a great deal of confusion, misunderstanding, and bewilderment, because the child is unable to understand completely the words he hears or he himself uses words incorrectly. As a result he may withdraw from communication in order not to be disturbed by his confusion. Chapter 15, Developing Language Abilities, gives examples of how everyday words and the concepts for which they stand can be taught.

TEACHING MENTAL MANIPULATION OF NUMERICAL RELATIONSHIPS (*Arithmetic*). In the arithmetic subtest of the WISC, the child is asked to solve orally arithmetic word problems that are read to him. The most difficult problems he may also read to himself. The task requires accurate auditory reception, auditory memory, visualization, mental manipulation, the ability to keep several facts in mind simultaneously, and numerical ability (understanding numerical relationships).

The importance placed on this subtest is indicated by the broad range of abilities it requires, the fact that it consists of tasks required in school, and the fact that these tasks are often difficult for a child to accomplish. Arithmetical instruction can itself be an important means of developing the abilities required in the subtest, provided that the emphasis is placed on problem-solving. To understand numerical relationships requires both the learning and application of mathematical concepts. Concepts such as the equivalence of sets ($2 + 3 = 1 + 4$, and so on) should be taught both before and during the learning of computation. The mathematics curriculum described in a later chapter, sketchy as it is, provides an example of how a mathematics curriculum can be developed that will lead to the understanding of numerical relationships.

Mental manipulation and keeping several facts in mind simultaneously have already been discussed. Problems requiring these abilities for the mastery of numerical processes are found in every arithmetic textbook. It is suggested that a great many auditory and written word problems be used with children, and that auditory problems be illustrated with pictures, diagrams, graphs, or three-dimensional materials to aid understanding and to give practice in the use of symbols. Many diagrams and graphs can be culled from economic reports, magazine articles, and other such sources, as well as math books. The children themselves should draw pictures and diagrams. A child is helped to understand the verbal formulation of numerical problems better if he is required to verbalize numerical problems presented in pictures and to say what he is doing in using three-dimensional materials. For example, he might say: "Here is a picture of two umbrellas; here is a picture of four umbrellas. That makes—or adds up to—or equals—six umbrellas altogether." The authors agree with Piaget that specific mathematical vocabulary should be avoided until children have a clear understanding of the concepts to which they refer, in spite of the fact that the present trend requires early precise expression.

DEVELOPING PERCEPTION OF SIMILARITIES AND DIFFERENCES PRESENTED VERBALLY (*Similarities*).   The ability to think logically, to classify, and to shift one's point of view are tapped by the test.

To be able to perceive similarities and differences and to abstract common characteristics presupposes an ability to perceive relationships. This ability can be developed through teaching mathematics and through categorization exercises. Children who have difficulties in perceiving similarities and differences—which usually indicates difficulty with abstract thinking in general—should put the solutions to problems into words and write them down. This skill should be practised. As has already been mentioned, children should record information about a problem in figurative as well as verbal terms, using diagrams, graphs, and so on.

DEVELOPING MEMORY FOR AUDITORY SEQUENCES (*Digit Span*).   As Kass (1966) and others have observed, automatic functions are even more frequently deficient in children with learning problems than thought processes are. Children with learning problems typically have trouble with memory. They can't learn because they can't form associations and remember them to the degree that they become automatic. Johnny may know how to spell a particular word or be able to recite his multiplication tables today, but he may have forgotten them tomorrow; Jill seems unable to learn them in the first place.

Exercises for developing memory for auditory sequences are outlined in the ITPA program by Bush and Giles (1969). It should be emphasized that both verbal and numerical materials should be used in practicing auditory sequencing, and that the time between presentation of stimuli and recall should be varied as well as gradually increased. Responses may follow recall immediately in exercises that emphasize attention and memory span, while exercises that require an interval of a minute or so may be practiced more and more after the child has learned to pay attention. Remembering a fact much later—for instance, the next day—should also be practiced.

In memory exercises, particularly those in which recall is delayed, the child should be asked to look, write, trace, or hear what he is to remember. If a child has moderate to severe perceptual difficulties in one modality (vision or hearing, for example), that modality, if used, should be paired with one that is strong or the modality should not be used temporarily. For instance, a child with poor visual perception may learn to spell a word better if he hears and traces it with his eyes closed. (See p. 311.)

The digit span subtest requires the child to repeat numbers in the same order as he hears them (digit span forward) and also to repeat other numbers he hears in reverse order (digit span backward). The latter requires imagery and mental manipulation as well as memory. See pp. 170, 243–244 for discussion of training imagery.

Performance Subtests

The necessity for developing the various abilities tapped by the verbal section of the WISC (information, vocabulary, and so on) is obvious. But the significance for the child's development and education of such activities as completing a picture or copying a block design is less apparent. The reasons for including such activities in an intelligence test or in the curriculum are therefore given in the discussions of each subtest. Examples are also given of each ability tapped in the Performance section, because they are less familiar and therefore less easily observed than those of the Verbal section. The examples of training procedures can be used for purposes of evaluation as well as for training.

EVALUATION OF VISUAL DETAILS AS A FUNCTION OF MEMORY AND JUDGMENT (*Picture Completion*). Picture completion is the first subtest in the performance scale. Filling in the missing part of a picture requires memory for details, ability to scan, and the ability to perceive logical inconsistencies in a visual medium. All these abilities are important for learning, but are often lagging in children with learning difficulties. These skills can often be improved through the exercises mentioned in Chapter 13 (Visual-Perceptual Abilities) and the suggestions for training of "Visual Reception" and "Visual Association" of the ITPA (pp. 232–233). Some additional examples follow:

1. Before the children are shown a picture they are told what to look for. For example, the teacher might say: "We have discussed Egypt. On the picture that I will show you, you will see an Egyptian scribe. See if you can learn how he wrote from the picture."
2. One or more children dramatize an event, performing a scene without words. For instance, a person looks at a watch, walks impatiently up and down, goes repeatedly to the door, looks out, closes the door. The other children state what they have seen and draw conclusions about what it may have meant and what could happen next. Then they write the story.
3. A picture is shown to the children, who describe it verbally. Three other pictures are then shown, of which only one is identical with the first while the other two differ in their details. The children indicate which picture is identical and describe the changed details in the other pictures.

4. The children learn a specific fact in social studies or science; for example, that a campfire should not be built near logs or dry leaves or overhanging branches. They are then shown a series of pictures from which they are to pick out whichever one shows the campfire correctly made. They are asked to give a written or oral explanation for their choice, stating why they believe that this picture shows the correct procedures and the others do not.

UNDERSTANDING AND REMEMBERING SEQUENTIAL ORDER (*Picture Arrangement*). This subtest requires putting depicted events into a logical sequence. The pictures used are similar to those in comic strips.

Children slowly develop the ability to recognize, construct, and remember temporally and causally connected sequences; but many children have difficulty in perceiving and in differentiating between temporal and causal connections. Young children believe that events that occur in a temporal sequence are always causally connected. Even older children have difficulty in understanding that a succession of events is not proof that there is a causal relationship. Training in the perception of both temporal and causal connections needs to be included in the child's training of thought processes. It is an important skill for understanding past events, for instance, in studying history, as well as for evaluating the future consequences of actions and happenings.

Examples:

1. Arranging and then reading comic strips is an excellent method for developing the ability to understand the sequence of events illustrated by pictures. For this purpose, it is most helpful if the teacher possesses several sets of from four to eight pictures that are mounted individually on tagboard and covered with contact paper or laminated. The pictures could be cut from comic strips or drawn by the teacher herself—stick figures are quite sufficient. The child has to arrange the pictures in the order in which they will tell a coherent story; then he verbalizes the story and writes it down.
2. Sequences of pictures can also be made depicting the steps in a science experiment that the children have performed. The children put the pictures in the order in which the experiment occurred.
3. A series of pictures illustrating "experiments of nature" can be used for the same purpose. They might show, for example, the successive steps in which a valley is formed by water, ice, or wind erosion, or by the formation of mountains. The child places the pictures in the correct sequence and explains the sequence.

4. Instead of pictures, diagrams, flow charts, and maps can be used to illustrate what took place in a famous battle, how various species interact in establishing a natural balance, the steps of photosynthesis, etc.

5. A game "What will happen?" can be played to develop causal thinking. Tasks similar to the verbal tasks presented in the section on comprehension can be used.

6. Absurdities can be presented visually. For instance, a series of pictures might show the process of melting steel and forming ingots. For the last step, where the steel is poured into forms, three alternative pictures are given. One might show a man with a pitcher removing molten steel; the second, a man blowing into the steel as a glass blower does when forming a bowl; and the third picture would be correct. The child is asked to explain why the other two pictures could not be correct.

7. The child places sentences in the correct order, to form a story.

ANALYSIS AND SYNTHESIS OF VISUAL PATTERN (*Block Design*). The block design subtest requires assembling square and triangular surfaces to form other geometric figures. This task requires decentration and mental manipulation; the child must shift from the perception of a particular geometric form and manipulate shapes in his mind, so that a new form is created.

Poor ability to analyze and synthesize visual patterns may cause problems in such diverse tasks as spelling, learning geometry, reading maps and graphs, or following the instructions for making a dress. Assembling models or reading computer printouts may also prove especially difficult.

To develop pattern analysis, at first games and activities are used that require the reproduction of patterns with three-dimensional materials. A great variety of materials can be used, such as marbles, pegs, poker chips, which are set in boards with holes, slots, and so on; shapes made from wood, metal, and so on, may also be used. Many patterns of graded difficulty should be available for the child to copy. Creative work with the same materials should also be encouraged, the children developing their own patterns. The way in which the child works with these materials will indicate his ability to analyze and manipulate a pattern mentally. Later analysis and synthesis of patterns is done with two-dimensional and also with verbal materials, for instance, with anagrams. Many teaching aides of this kind are commercially available. Games that necessitate the visualization of changes in spatial relationships, such as chess, checkers, and Scrabble, can also be used.

DEVELOPING VISUAL CLOSURE (*Object Assembly*). Object assembly requires the child to assemble cardboard pieces to complete the picture of an object. Puzzles in which the pieces form logical parts (e.g., parts of a face or a machine) are commercially available, but the teacher can easily make her own by cutting pictures into parts that the child can reassemble by drawing conclusions about where they belong rather than by fitting their edges together. Jig-saw puzzles do not further the ability to relate details to the whole and should not be used.

By working on such closure puzzles and related materials, the child learns strategies for dealing with such a task as object assembly (e.g., a solution exists; the completed picture will be meaningful; the parts may be turned in different ways; and so on), and he also learns to expect success ("I can do it") and to work rapidly.

THE MAZE SUBTEST. The maze subtest requires planning, visualization, attention, and motor coordination. This is a timed test. Exercises to develop the abilities required have been described in various sections. Many children's magazines have pencil-and-paper mazes of varying degrees of difficulty; however, the present writers believe that these should only be used occasionally, and that primary emphasis should be placed on such activities as map reading, model-making, and other such tasks that the child frequently encounters at home or in school, and that require the same underlying abilities.

Enhancing the Ability to use Symbols (Coding)

As mentioned in the chapter on evaluation, the coding test requires the substitution of certain symbols for other symbols. Many children with learning problems have severe difficulties with this test.

A great variety of symbol substitution exercises should first be used in evaluating and training the ability to work with symbols. For example, the child might be required to substitute numbers for letters, and vice versa, or to use sequences of dots and dashes (Morse code), or substitute for each letter the previous letter in the alphabet (the word *come* would then be written *b-n-l-d*), or substitute for each letter a number that denotes its alphabetic postion multiplied by 3:

$$a \quad b \quad c \quad d \quad e \quad f \quad g \quad h$$
$$3 \quad 6 \quad 9 \quad 12 \quad 15 \quad 18 \quad 21 \quad 24, \text{ and so on.}$$

The above example shows how a coding exercise can be combined with academic learning, such as practice in the alphabet or the multiplication table.

Other exercises can be given in which the symbol pattern is not pro-

vided, and the pupil has to infer it. For instance, the child might be
asked: Can you add the missing third line to the sequence given below?

$$6 - 2 = 4$$
$$8 - 2 = 6$$
$$12 - 2 = 10$$

The child should then supply the line $10 - 2 = 8$.

Or he might be told, "Each sum or difference in the terms given
below represents a letter that is two more or two less than the letter
given. What word do the coded letters spell when put together?

$$u - 2; j + 2; m + 2; u + 2$$

The answer is "slow" (u minus 2 is s; j plus 2 is l; and so on).

Motivation for Cognition

Lack of cognitive growth is most often observed in children who seem
unmotivated to learn. In the healthy and happy child the meaning of
much that he learns has bearing for the future, and it is this aspect that
is the most important source of energy for cognitive growth. In all
normal children there is a drive toward the future that is not directed
toward any extrinsic goal. This drive toward being grown-up involves
a drive toward learning, because learning is a means of producing a
change in the self, in the direction in which one wishes to develop. This
is probably what is meant by the frequently heard term self-actualization. Learning should therefore be future-directed, not merely directed
toward a specific reward, an immediate pleasure, such as candy, or the
teacher's appreciation, or prospective benefits such as achieving a certain job or power or money. The need for self-actualization can be
observed. Children want to invent as well as to find out. They want to
clarify their impressions of the world and to organize what knowledge
they have about all aspects of living. They want to create what is for
them new knowledge and new combinations of skills, as well as to master the skills and knowledge transmitted to them. At the basis of the
drive for self-actualization is curiosity, the need for mastery, and the
desire to be like an admired grown-up.

Part of the economically deprived child's difficulty in being unmotivated for school work is that the adults whom he meets in his community are likely to be less schooled than he is to be, and the peer culture
does not regard school knowledge as an asset. But if the teacher can
win the child's trust and admiration, and become his model, then the
dull, disinterested nonlearning child may become interested and alert,
and make progress in school learning and his ability to solve problems.

WORKS CITED

Binet, A. Les idées modernes sur les enfants. Paris: Flammarion, 1909. (Trans. B. Holloway for Prof. R. Orpet, Department of Educational Psychology, California State College at Long Beach, 1972.)

Bush, W. M., and Giles, M. T. Aids to psycholinguistic teaching. Columbus, Ohio: Charles E. Merrill, 1969.

Devor, G., and Stern, C. Objects versus pictures in the instruction of young children. Journal of School Psychology, 1970, 8, 77–81.

Education Development Center. Attribute Games and Problems. Novato, California: McGraw-Hill, Webster Division, 1966.

Estes, W. K. Learning theory and mental development. New York: Academic Press, 1970.

Furth, H. On language and knowing and Piaget's developmental theory. Human Development, 1970, 13(4), 241–257.

Ginsburg, H., and Opper, S. Piaget's theory of intellectual development: An introduction. Englewood Cliffs, N.J.: Prentice-Hall, 1969.

Goldstein, K. Language and language disturbances. New York: Grune & Stratton, 1948.

Hunt, J. McV. Intelligence and experience. New York: Ronald Press, 1961.

Kass, C. E. Psycholinguistic disabilities of children with reading problems. Exceptional Children, 1966, 32, 533–539.

Levi, A. Treatment of a disorder of perception and concept formation in a case of school failure. Journal of Consulting Psychology, 1965, 29, 289–295.

Levi, A. Remedial techniques in disorders of concept formation. Journal of Special Education, 1966, 1(1), 3–8.

Serafica, F., and Sigel, I. E. Styles of categorization and reading disability. Journal of Reading Behavior, 1970, 2(2), 105–115.

Wechsler, D. The measurement of adult intelligence. Baltimore: Williams & Wilkins, 1959.

Wechsler, D. Wechsler adult intelligence scale. New York: The Psychological Corporation, 1947.

Wechsler, D. Wechsler intelligence scale for children. New York: The Psychological Corporation, 1949.

Wechsler, D. Wechsler preschool and primary scale of intelligence. New York: The Psychological Corporation, 1949.

Zigler, E., and Butterfield, E. C. Motivational aspects of changes in IQ test performance of culturally deprived nursery school children. Child Development, 1968, 39, 1–14.

PART V

Teachers are usually greatly concerned with a child's progress in academic learning. The achievement tests administered by the state or local school board are often the criteria by which the teacher's proficiency is judged.

A thorough discussion of methodology of teaching specific skills and subject matter is not a task of this book. Only a few of the methods will be discussed in regard to teaching the so-called 3 R's. They are mainly those which train basic abilities at the same time as academic skills are learned. Academic learning always involves the exercise of certain underlying abilities. The child who learns the measurement tables and understands them, has also practiced sequential memory and become aware of the reversibility of mathematical processes. (Three feet are one yard; one yard is three feet.) In undertaking various activities using measurements, the child also learns about conservation of liquids and about volume. He learns to translate his experiences with three-dimensional objects into pictorial presentation and then into notation.

The teacher who is aware of the abilities that a child has to acquire in order to progress optimally in academic learning will always keep in mind the possibility of a twofold purpose in the tasks she sets: the enhancement of the child's abilities as well as the improvement of his academic skills. Careful observation and testing whenever possible is necessary if the teacher is to be able to select the tasks and methods that will most benefit each individual child. She will also always be careful to use whatever teaching methods are most suitable for most children. She will, for instance, not merely tell a child that "three feet are one yard," but will see that he measures a yardstick with a foot ruler, verbalizing appropriately as he does so, "I must use the foot ruler three times to get the same length as the yardstick," and that he then writes down: 1 yard = 3 feet.

The methods and materials mentioned constitute only a fraction of the knowledge that the teacher will have to acquire during her years of teaching. It can hardly be included in three short chapters. But the teacher who understands the principles involved in choosing a method that matches the ability pattern of the child will learn to transfer methods used in teaching one skill to the teaching of another. To give another example, the teacher who understands the importance of visualization, planning, and mental transformation of images will not only ask a child to tell the time when the clock says three or four or five o'clock, but will also ask, "Can you show me the position of the clock hands two hours from now? What time will it be then?"

In many of the chapters we have given suggestions for further reading. We suggest for these next chapters that the teacher read very carefully Chapters 5, 6, and 7 of *Learning Disabilities* by Johnson and Myklebust (1967). These chapters give numerous excellent suggestions that can be applied directly to the classroom. As the text is illustrated, it gives many suggestions for making task cards for the classroom. As has already been emphasized, task cards are an indispensable aid to teaching academic skills to children with learning difficulties, because they enable the teacher to highly individualize the assignment. (See Chapter 11, "Programming").

Many other books and articles are also of great value, but in learning methods and techniques, it is more important to study a few books than to skim many. One cannot acquire methods solely by reading; they have to be tried out in the classroom and often adapted to the individual child.

WORK CITED

Johnson, D., & Myklebust, H. *Learning disabilities.* New York: Grune & Stratton, 1967.

17

PROBLEMS
IN TEACHING
BEGINNING
MATHEMATICS

In teaching mathematics, as in teaching all subject matter, success depends upon individualization, motivation, systematic teaching, and a careful working out of methodology. Some children learn math quickly and easily, but for those for whom it is difficult, no timetable should be set. Children should always be given the time they need to explore, to understand, and to remember. They will not feel that learning math is a chore and become discouraged if they are permitted to use a variety of objects and materials in learning. They will, however, need much guidance in developing each new concept, and the teaching of concepts must be explicit and detailed—no knowledge or understanding can be taken for granted. The method of teaching mathematics differs from that of reading, in that mathematics needs to be taught through body movement and manipulation of objects, so that it can be understood as denoting a change, as pertaining to processes. Two plus four equals six seems static to the child, an unalterable "given," a number fact. The child needs to discover that two plus four equals six refers to a process; that, for instance, when there are two children and four more come to play, a change occurs; now, low and behold, there are six children.

Only when the child performs or sees actions performed can he experience the flow of time which demonstrates that math deals with processes. The use of materials that he can touch and handle will also help to achieve that goal while motivating the child to explore and make discoveries. He becomes curious about what will happen, what he can find out.

Body movement is the ideal means by which a child can learn the basic ways in which time and space are related: Will it take *longer* to walk or to run? Will I arrive first if I am *faster*? I walk *around* the chair, and *then* I will crawl *under* the table. Is the table *high* enough? I will run a *straight* line *first* and *then* a *curve*.

The interplay between handling objects and materials and language must be continuous in the teaching of math. The meaning of mathematics cannot be perceived without applying math to many real and possible situations, and using language to mediate the processes. Word problems need to be used daily in practicing number facts and illustrated by action.

Material must be varied. This does not mean it has to be costly. Number is a universal attribute (Lamon, 1972). There are x number of cars in the street, x number of children in the school, x number of slices in a loaf of bread. There is 1 birthday cake with 7 candles, and 8 children ready to eat it. They need 8 plates and 8 napkins, and so on.

Measurement helps children understand mathematical processes. Measurement is the basis of all science. All cultures, including those at the very dawn of civilization, have developed units of measurement. The human body has frequently served as the standard for such units: an inch is the width of a thumb; a foot has kept its original designation; a yard is the distance from the fingertips of an arm extended on the horizontal plane to the tip of the nose (Capeland, 1972, p. 222).

Measuring with a piece of string is a valuable activity in learning about size. How big is Nora's waist? How tall is Max? How much higher is the table than the chair?

Integration into the Curriculum

As children grow older, math needs to be more and more integrated into the total curriculum—with science, social studies, and the other academic disciplines. It can be used to help in understanding other subject matter. For example, in discussing when the first trains ran in America, the children can learn how many years ago this happened, and what that length of time means in terms of human generations. The same is true in discussing other past events. What child would not be awed to realize the age of the oldest living organism—the bristle cone pine? Size comparisons can be made, for instance, in regard to dinosaurs, blue whales, and man. There again a surprise awaits the child who finds out how much bigger the blue whale is than the mighty *Tyrannosaurus rex*. Concepts of time and space can be illustrated with pictures or graphs that contribute to the child's knowledge of the world.

Mathematical Concepts

In developing his theory about thought processes, Piaget studied how children learn mathematics. From his findings, educators have developed new methods of teaching it. The following sequence of teaching mathematical concepts is only approximate. Many of the steps should be taught simultaneously. Certainly the more difficult applications in the earlier steps will be learned at the same time as later concepts are introduced. Handling the same three-dimensional material can help the child understand various basic processes. Total body movement will help him to experience sequences and relationships of size, space, and time. Observation and discussions will insure that he understands a particular concept. Each of these methods is necessary for the child to acquire a firm mathematical foundation.

1.   Before a child begins to work with numbers, he must learn to differentiate between such concepts as *more* and *less, higher* and *lower, wider* and *narrower, sooner* and *later.* Only by comparing and relating can he understand that number denotes units that can be counted, regardless of whether they are sheep, flowers, pebbles, time intervals (beats of the metronome or years), or energy (for instance, a child can understand that a 200-watt bulb uses more electricity than a 10-watt bulb). After the child can distinguish between *more* and *less* and other such concepts with the aid of three-dimensional objects, as well as through the use of body movement, he should use two-dimensional representations (pictures and diagrams) to illustrate the same concepts.

2.   To understand the concept of number, the child has to understand that the arrangement of a group of objects does not affect their number (conservation of numbers). Conservation is best learned by handling objects. Arranging and rearranging a number of objects and counting them repeatedly in different arrangements will give the child a firm grasp on number conservation. Block building can give much practice in spatial arrangement and rearrangement. Play with water and sand, pouring them into various containers, will help him acquire conservation of liquids; play with clay or Plasticine, conservation of mass. Fitting objects into slots, nesting boxes, and weighing are prenumber learning experiences that are invaluable in learning measurement and size relationships.

After the child has learned to observe changes in perceptual arrangements of three-dimensional objects, he does the same with representation of objects drawn on the blackboard. (An example of perceptual arrangement of three-dimensional objects would be to put three blocks next to each other in a row, stack three blocks vertically in a tower, and scatter three blocks in a larger area. The child would have to perceive all groups as having the same number.)

3. The child learns to arrange objects in an increasing or decreasing order in regard to some characteristic (seriation). For example, these blocks are ordered in relation to height. (See Figure 1.) Seriation means ordering in ascending order of one characteristic.

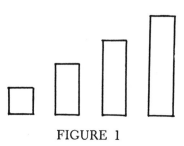

FIGURE 1

In learning to seriate, the child practices first with three objects that differ a great deal from one another in one attribute in an easily perceptible way, for instance, the ordering of number rods with one, five, and ten units. Intermediate steps are gradually added. Later the child learns to order objects according to less easily discriminated attributes, such as the number of sides in a figure, the intensity of shadings of a color, and so on. Ordering on the basis of a characteristic that is *less* perceptually dominant is more difficult, but such exercises help the child to learn to decenter. An example would be to have the child order the circles in Figure 2 on the basis of the number of dots.

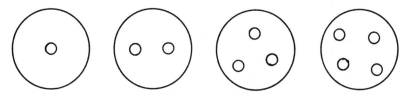

FIGURE 2

4. Piaget has pointed out that logical and mathematical thought processes are concerned with the same operations and need to be taught simultaneously. Conservation of numbers and reversibility are mathematic-logical processes that the child must understand before he can learn to work with numbers.

The following experiences are designed to demonstrate that a given amount of a physical substance remains the same if nothing is added or subtracted, although its perceptual appearance may vary (conservation). This learning may take place over several years, but the experiences and materials should be introduced at the kindergarten level or even before.

a. After the child has played with sand and clay, he will be ready to explore the concept of conservation of liquid more systematically. At first a given amount of liquid can be transferred from one container to another differing in height, width, and depth. As the child observes the perceptual changes in the liquid, he gains some understanding of proportion. The child can then be presented with two identical containers, each containing the same amount of liquid. He can proceed with one of them as above. If he makes a simple chart, he can be led to understand that the level of the liquid is proportional to two attributes of the container: height and width.

b. The concept of conservation of mass is introduced by the child's weighing pieces of Plasticine or clay, forming them into different shapes, and weighing them again. A balance scale should be used.

c. The concepts underlying conservation of length are introduced by manipulation of Cuisenaire, Montessori, or Dienes rods, so that the child understands that lengths of things can be measured by comparing the number of units. He will see that a rod with eight units is the same length as another rod with eight units, regardless of their position.

5. The child learns counting in sequence. Counting should be done at first with an action corresponding to what is being counted. Grasping is easier than pointing. A knob board is very helpful, since each knob is grasped while counting. (See Figure 3.)

6. While the child sorts objects according to size and learns to count objects, the child masters one-to-one matching, first with three-dimensional materials. If four girls are caught in the rain, they need four umbrellas. (See Figure 4.) If each child in a group of ten is given a can of juice, then ten drinking straws will be needed. First, objects, and then, later, pictures and diagrams can be used.

7. In this country, set theory is used very early in elementary school and even in kindergarten. The word *set* needs to be in-

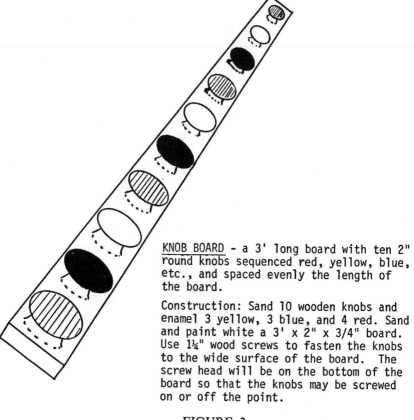

KNOB BOARD - a 3' long board with ten 2" round knobs sequenced red, yellow, blue, etc., and spaced evenly the length of the board.

Construction: Sand 10 wooden knobs and enamel 3 yellow, 3 blue, and 4 red. Sand and paint white a 3' x 2" x 3/4" board. Use 1¼" wood screws to fasten the knobs to the wide surface of the board. The screw head will be on the bottom of the board so that the knobs may be screwed on or off the point.

FIGURE 3

FIGURE 4

troduced by using it in the context of collecting and sorting activities, so that it becomes completely familiar. The child may sort objects, for instance, trees and birds, put a rubber band or loop around each grouping, and may be helped to say, "I have a set of three birds, and a set of two trees."*

Piaget (Hall, 1970) is quoted as saying, "Seven years would be perfectly all right for learning most operations of set theory because children have their own spontaneous operations that are very akin to those concepts. But when you teach set theory, you should use the child's actual vocabulary along with activity—make the child do natural things. The important thing is not to teach modern mathematics with ancient methods—you cannot teach concepts verbally: you must use a method founded on activity."

8. Young children may have difficulty in understanding the difference between ordinal numbers (first, second, third, and so on), which are based on ordering, and cardinal numbers (one, two, three, and so on), which are based on the number of objects in a set. For example, a child may count *one, two, three* correctly, pointing to each of the objects as he does so. When asked to give three objects, however, he may give only the one he has called "three," and maintain that the others are "one" and "two." Only verbal interaction between the child and teacher can help to clarify these concepts as he practices the two kinds of groupings: seriation (ordering) and equivalence (sets).

9. Sorting, seriating, and matching exercises need to be practiced in as many different contexts as possible, as they are the basis for all later arithmetical learning. Sorting develops the concept of cardinal numbers; seriating, of ordinal numbers; and matching, the idea that numbers are independent of the objects that are counted. The child who sorts, seriates, and matches objects also learns the concept of sets, of conservation of number, of equivalence and reversibility. In short, he learns to operate with numbers. He learns the concepts of addition and subtraction when he joins sets or separates them in his exploratory play. He sees that if a set of three is combined with a set of two, one gets a set of five; and if the set of two is removed, the set of three will remain (reversibility). He observes that he finishes

---

* The child should practice recognition of sets. If three to ten objects are put in a confined space, he should be able to recognize the number at a glance.

with the same number of cherries whether he takes two first and then three or three first and then two, and so observes the functioning of commutative property. As he joins several sets in various groupings, he also becomes aware of the associative property:

$$a + (b + c) = (a + b) + c$$

While sorting and working with sets, the child will learn to discriminate sizes and shapes. Manipulation with blocks and number rods will show him the relationship between length and number; for example, that a set of four cubes arranged in a row is longer than a set of three. (See Figure 5.) He will learn to to enlarge his spatial vocabulary with such words as *angle, opposite, slanting, vertical,* and so on.

FIGURE 5

10. The child learns to classify according to more than one characteristic (attribute) at a time; for example, large striped, little striped, large white, and little white squares can be grouped into four categories. (Figure 6.)

FIGURE 6

He learns to use matrices. A matrix, in mathematical terms, shows ordering according to at least two variables; Figure 7 shows a matrix in which the variables are size and the number of sides of the figures.

11. The writing of numerals is introduced after the child has learned basic number concepts. (For writing numerals, see Chapter 20.) Children need to practice recognition of numerals and their use as symbols. The late Florence Mateer, a former professor at Claremont College, used envelopes filled with small

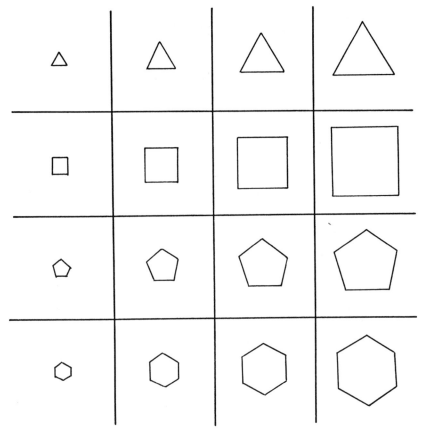

FIGURE 7

objects, drawings, numerals, and pictures. The child matches
each number and its corresponding numeral in four or six different ways, using the contents of many envelopes before proc-
eeding to the next number. In learning the concept of the number 2, for example, one envelope might contain two identical
objects and pictures of the paired objects. The child would have
to match the pairs of objects with their corresponding picture.
Another envelope might contain two identical pictures and the
numeral 2 for matching. Another envelope might contain several
pairs of different objects to be matched with the numeral 2. Still
another might have pictures—some of one, some of two, and
some of three objects; the child would have to match the numeral 2 with the correct picture. He would work in this way with
each number up to ten. (See Figure 8.)

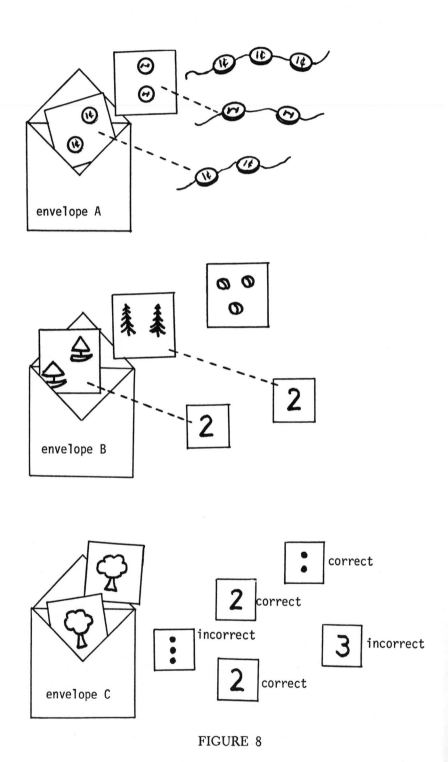

envelope A

envelope B

envelope C

FIGURE 8

12. The child becomes acquainted with numbers and numerals through twenty.

13. From now on, the child notes down in numerals any mathematical process in which he is engaged. He should also draw his own pictures to illustrate the process. Much practice may be needed until the child can count the elements in a set, and write the corresponding numerals. He also needs much practice in learning the concept of equality and in joining and separating sets. By manipulating and looking at objects, saying what they represent, and writing down their number, the child forms multiple associations.

Florence Sharp (1971) has emphasized that counting must be completely mastered before other math skills are taught, because all math skills are based on counting.

14. The child learns that counting means adding one.

15. The child learns counting by two, and the concepts of even and odd numbers. For instance, when jumping on the number line, he may count only when his right foot comes forward, so that he counts one, three, five, and so on.

16. The child learns that counting backward means subtracting one. He practices counting backward until it becomes completely automatic. Songs, such as "Ten Little Indians," can add fun to these activities.

17. The child learns to add two by skipping "one" in counting. He can use steps, number rods, classmates, or any other objects for this purpose.

18. The child learns to subtract two by skipping one, counting backward.

19. The child, by finding all possible arithmetic combinations of subsets in building a set (set equivalence), learns that every number can be understood as a sum of different other numbers (or partial sums) or as a difference. For instance, the number seven can be thought of as $6 + 1$, $5 + 2$, $0 + 7$, $3 + 2 + 2$, $1 + 2 + 3 + 1$, and so on; also as $10 - 3$, $9 - 2$, $8 - 1$. He notes this down. (This work should begin even before the child starts to write numerals, when he plays with rods and other objects, builds sets with blocks, and engages in other activities.)

20. The child learns to add and subtract by partial counting. When he does not know a number fact, he should not begin counting with the number one, but should begin to add one addend to another, or subtract from the minuend. For example, if he is to add two to three, he should not count "one, two, three, four, five," but should say "*three*, four, five," and then should write

and say $3 + 2 = 5$. In this way the fact can be fixed in the child's memory. The same applies to subtraction, of course, where the child needs to practice counting backward ($7 - 4 = 3$; 7-6-5-4-3-).

Subtraction is a very difficult concept. The child can learn it more easily when he reverses the direction of movement while counting his steps, jumps, or hops. The child should move in one direction while counting forward; in the other, while counting backward (subtracting). The number line has been found to be a most helpful teaching tool. (Number-line games are described in detail in Frostig, 1970, pp. 115–118.)

21. The child learns the number facts systematically, and practices them until they become automatic. Since he already understands the commutative property and reversibility, he can be shown that he need learn only half the possible number facts in addition, subtraction, multiplication, and division.

Number facts are taught in several ways simultaneously. First, they should be taught throughout the school day. We have six children at one table, and eight at another. How many children are there?

Another way of teaching number facts until they are automatic is by the "password" game. John cannot remember that seven plus eight equal fifteen. He must repeat this fact every time he enters the classroom, gets new material, or changes an activity. After he has learned the fact thoroughly, he gets another password.

Number facts can be practiced in many game situations. Almost all table games for children involve counting, and they can be adapted to teach specific facts. As noted above, the number line can be used as a basis for games.

Number facts need to be practiced orally, in writing, and with multisensory presentation; for instance, looking and saying, looking, saying, writing, touching and handling, looking, saying, writing. Again, it must be emphasized that activities are needed to make the learning of numbers meaningful.

22. The child learns to find how many more are needed. Here it is important to start the child working with number facts which he already knows and to work with three-dimensional objects as well as diagrams with related notations. He should match, then write, to find "how many more" are needed, and should apply his skill to everyday situations. We have nine cents to buy lunch cookies, but we need fifteen. How much more do we need? We have ten children in the room, but only eight sets of counting

sticks; the other children will get counting blocks. How many sets of counting blocks do we need?

23. After the child has learned the number facts through ten, he learns the decimal system.

Teaching Place Value, Expanded Notation, and Elementary Geometry

In working with numbers above ten, a great variety of materials will again prove helpful. The abacus and the number grid are indispensable tools. The child should always find the appropriate space for a number on the abacus or number grid; twenty-two means two rows and two beads, and so on. He should also construct the number with a strip or place value chart or similar materials. (Figure 9).

Only after the child understands place value should expanded notation be used. At first it should take the form: 22 is 20 + 2; 14 is 10 + 4. The form $2 \times 10 + 2$ for 22 should not be used with children with learning difficulties before easier versions are learned, because it combines two different steps.

The teacher needs to check to determine whether or not the concepts of *more than* and *less than* are understood with larger numbers also. The use of symbols, such as the symbols for an empty set or the symbols for *more than* and *less than*, should be avoided unless the concepts are very clear.

Only by using a variety of materials can the child proceed from a perceptual grasp to symbolization of the operations. The use of materials also helps the child to build up a store of concrete images and thus to visualize. Bruner (1966, p. 65) remarks that children taught in this way "not only understood the abstractions they had learned but also had a store of concrete images that served to exemplify the abstractions."

Elementary Geometry

As children engage in a great deal of building with blocks and using other toys, are familiar with eggs and egg-shaped objects, eat ice-cream cones, and so on, it is important that they know the correct names of these shapes. Adults are themselves frequently unaware of the correct name, referring, for example, to blocks that have the shape of a rectangular prism as rectangular blocks or even rectangles, and only calling the triangular prism a prism.

Children from five to six years old should be able to recognize and name most of the following solids: cone, ovoid, ellipsoid, sphere,

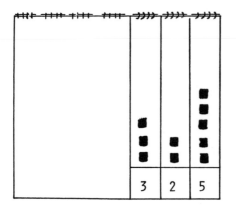

Strips, with sets and
numerals from 0-9, can
be flipped forward from
the back of the card to
form numbers from 0 to
9,999,999.

```
    3 0 0
      2 0
       5
  ---------
    3 2 5
```

```
  1 0 0,0 0 0
    6 0,0 0 0
     1,0 0 0
       3 2 5
  -----------
  1 6 1,3 2 5
```

```
  9,0 0 0,0 0 0
    1 6 1,0 0 0
        3 2 5
  -------------
  9,1 6 1,3 2 5
```

Flip-a-strip Place Value Chart
Available from Developmental Learning
Materials, 7440 North Natches Avenue,
Niles, Illinois 60648.

FIGURE 9

cylinder, cube, prism (triangular and four-sided) and pyramid (three- and four-sided). (See Figure 10.) When children are about six years

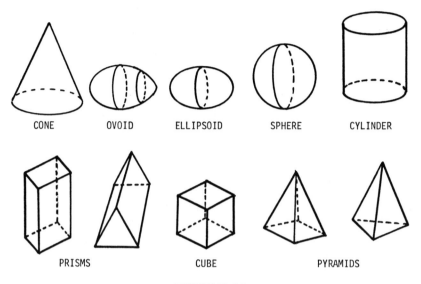

FIGURE 10

old, they should learn to match solids with two-dimensional drawings (circle with sphere; square with cube, and so on.) Parquetry sets, tangrams, and geoboards can be used for transforming plane geometrical shapes into other geometrical shapes; for instance, four equilateral triangles with a common point of origin form a square (Figure 11).

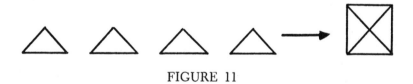

FIGURE 11

Playing with toys, such as the ones named, and measuring in the way described form a firm basis for the learning of geometry.

Remedial Methods

The sequence of activities that has been described touches only the essentials of the core program of beginning math instruction. It has not been possible to give here a full outline for teaching math in the elementary grades, nor can we describe remedial methods in detail, but we can discuss some of the problems that a child may encounter and some methods of overcoming them.

Rote Memory

One of the frequent difficulties encountered in teaching math is poor rote memory. Some children with learning difficulties may be able to understand mathematical concepts but unable to remember number facts. Automatization is very difficult for many children with learning problems. The teacher must get an oral response, as the child's answers on written tests may not indicate that he is resorting to counting rather than responding automatically.

Learning number facts often seems an overwhelming task to the child who feels he is faced with learning a hundred number facts for addition, an additional hundred for multiplication, and so on. But if he is shown the progress chart of number facts, he can see that by reversing each fact when he learns it, the task can be cut by more than half (see above, pp. 272). Other facts can be learned in a specific context before the child is required to learn his multiplication tables. For instance, if work with money (nickles and dimes) has preceded learning the multiplication tables—as it should—the child will already be familiar with the multiplication facts involving the numbers 5 and 10. If the two-times table has been equated with "doubling," then there are only twenty-one multiplication facts left for the child to learn, a feat that even a child with learning problems should be able to complete in a few weeks or at most a few months. (See Figure 12.)

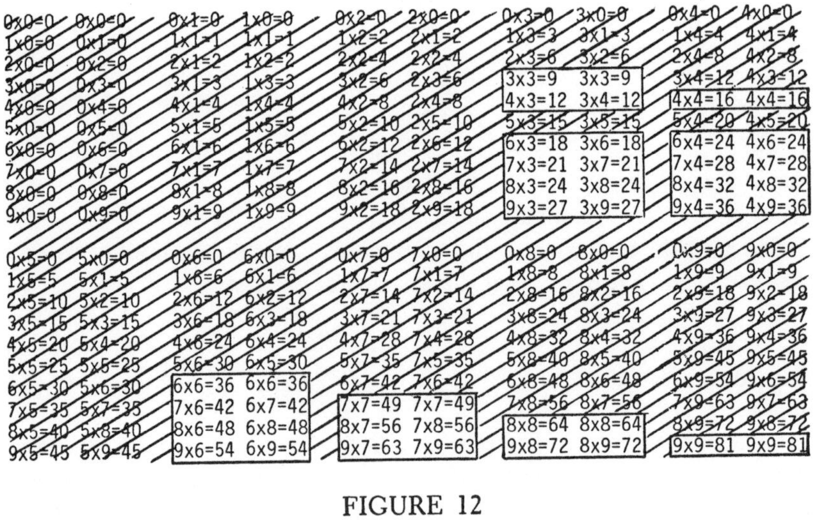

FIGURE 12

The above example of learning the multiplication tables shows that mathematics is made easier if the child is enabled to perceive patterns; that means the recurring sequences.

Eye-Hand Coordination

Visual-perceptual difficulties have a greater influence on the learning of mathematics than on reading because an understanding of visually perceived relationships is essential to mathematics.

If a child has difficulties with eye-motor coordination, he may skip an object or count one twice. Strauss and Lehtinen (1947, p. 155) describe a rod counting board. The knob board already mentioned is another version of teaching counting by grasping. When loose objects are counted, each object should be moved (for instance, across a ruler placed vertically in the center of the desk) in order to avoid errors.

Adequate eye-hand coordination is necessary for the accurate placement of numerals. It is equally important that numerals be legible because otherwise it is impossible to add, subtract, or undertake any other mathematical process without mistakes. When a child has eye-motor difficulties, he may need such aids as vertical lines to help him place figures correctly below each other. Elizabeth Freidus suggests using ruled paper and turning it so that the lines run vertically. Paper with grids, denoting the place for each problem, can also be used. For all children, much practice in writing and placing numerals is needed.

Writing exercises can be made pleasant. The child, for example, can be told to make something for the classroom, such as a calendar, or he can make a "Pair Tree." He writes one example very neatly on each pear without the answer. (See Figure 13.) The examples are so written that at least two examples have the same sum; for instance, $2 + 3$ and $1 + 4$.

Two or more children can play games with the "pair tree." One child finds the pairs; another gives the answer to the examples. The first child then hangs the pairs again on the little hooks on the tree. This gives added practice in eye-hand coordination.

Figure-Ground Perception

Poor figure-ground perception ability, and/or the tendency to perseverate (Strauss & Lehtinen, 1947), may cause a child to continue solving a series of numerical problems in the same way as the first one. If the first two problems have been addition (for instance, $3 + 4$ and

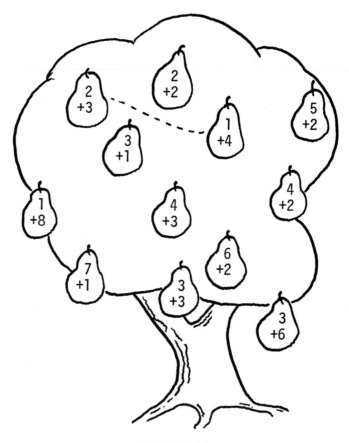

FIGURE 13

$7 + 4$), and the third is subtraction ($8 — 3$), the child may approach the third example as if it were $8 + 3$, and even continue to treat all the other problems on the page as if they were addition. For such children it is necessary to emphasize the signs by using different colors; by making, for instance, all the plus signs green and all the minus signs red, until the child no longer needs the additional cue.

Children with difficulties in figure-ground perception are especially handicapped when they begin to work with larger numbers with two, three, or more digits. They tend to lose their place in the step-by-step procedure of working out a problem. They also have particular difficulties in regrouping, in "carrying" and "borrowing." Similar difficulties occur in column addition, where the child may lose his place. In doing addition, it is wise for them to write down immediately the number to be regrouped; and when subtracting, to change the adjacent digit right away. The teacher may help by suggesting that the child place a small dot over each numeral as he deals with it.

Repeated regrouping in subtraction is very confusing for some children and should be practiced in small steps, first presenting a problem involving subtracting a one-digit number ($\frac{43}{-7}$), then a two-digit number ($\frac{43}{-17}$), then a three-digit number, but still only regrouping once, ($\frac{443}{-217}$), then with a four-digit number that requires regrouping twice, but not with adjacent digits, ($\frac{5443}{-617}$), then regrouping with two neighboring digits, ($\frac{443}{-266}$), and so on.

These steps should first be learned without using zero in the minuend, and then with zero.

Figure-ground difficulties cause even more confusion in multiplication and long division than in subtraction and addition, because the child becomes perplexed by looking at the many numerals on the page. It is sometimes helpful to provide the child with a small rectangular piece of paper with which to cover the numeral with which he has just worked, so that he will not use it again. Exercises with intersecting and hidden numbers may also be helpful. (See Figures 14, 15, and 16.)

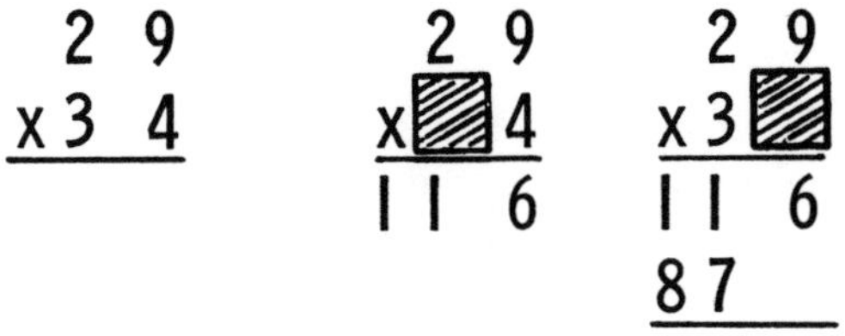

```
    2 9          2 9          2 9
  X 3 4        X ▨ 4        X 3 ▨
               I I 6        I I 6
                            8 7
```

FIGURE 14

Find and circle all of
the "59's":

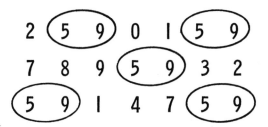

FIGURE 15

FIGURE 16

Perception of Number Problems

The following problems are identical; $\begin{smallmatrix}4\\+3\end{smallmatrix}$, IV + III, 3 + 4, three plus four, and four plus three, as well as the two problems pictured in Figure 17. But the child who has not achieved the concept of number,

FIGURE 17

or who has difficulties in perceiving the common elements in these problems, will suppose them to be quite dissimilar. The difficulty may be overcome if each problem is presented in a variety of ways.

Engelmann (1969) has pointed out that when a problem is written horizontally—(2 + 3)—the child must proceed from left to right; but when the problem involves two-digit numbers presented vertically, he has to work from right to left— $\begin{smallmatrix}24\\+3\end{smallmatrix}$ —and that this may contribute to his confusion.

Directional Position of Numbers

Children with difficulties in perception of the directional position of numerals tend to reverse them. The best way that the authors have found to avoid reversing numerals stems from an observation of Werner (1957), that children perceive letters and numbers physiognomically (i.e., the numbers remind them of something alive).

It is possible to make use of this perceptual attribute by telling the children that one and eight and zero are standing still; they are symmetrical (although in print, one is "turned to the left"): *1* 2 3 4 5 6 7 8 9 10. The *2 3 4 5 7 9* are turned to the left (these forms are either open to the left or seem to have their point of gravity toward the left), while the "ornery six" turns to the right (he must always have his own way).

Perception of Spatial Relationships and Imagery

The perception of spatial relationships may be the perceptual ability of most consequence for mathematical learning. Adequate spatial perception is necessary if the numbers on the page are not to look to the child like a wild jumble of marks. When perception of spatial relationships is inadequate, the confusion may be so great in trying to understand the chaotic appearing page that no energy is left for working with the numbers. Spatial imagery is necessary for perceiving the patterns that are basic to an understanding of the various number systems.

But most children in the beginning school years have poor perception of spatial relationships, because even in the so-called normal child this ability develops fully only at or after school entrance.

As has already been stated in this chapter, all children need to work continuously with three-dimensional materials. This is especially true of children with poor perception of spatial relationships.

Learning Concepts

Children with learning problems may have great difficulties in learning the concepts basic to mathematical thought, and in learning the words that denote them (*same, equal, similar, different, alternating, unit, more, less,* and so on.) Demonstration and practice with objects are essential and should be frequently repeated.

Concepts have to be clear before symbols are used. The child has to understand conservation of numbers before he understands the equal sign. He must have had a great deal of practice in comparing groups and understand the reversibility of processes, before he can use the symbols for greater than (>) and less than (<). Two objects, such as a pen and a book, might be used to teach the concept of different, and two pencils of equal length and color to illustrate the concept of sameness. The same concepts should then be illustrated by pictures, with words, with geometrical figures, and with numbers. Similar procedures involving concrete presentation and repetition in a variety of ways are necessary for teaching other concepts. Games, particularly those involving movement, are helpful for all children, and especially so when repetition is necessary and motivation may become a problem. Regular playground games provide many opportunities for using numbers to denote size, distance, and quantity. Taking turns, repeating an exercise, and keeping score require the use of both ordinal and cardinal numbers.

Visual aids should be used for all arithmetic games. A chalkboard, slate, feltboard, or magnetic board can be used both for giving directions and for translating movements into notation.

Suggestions for arithmetic games involving movement are given in *Movement Education* (Frostig, 1970). Other suggestions that may be helpful can be found in Chapter 16, "Education of Higher Cognitive Functions."

REFERENCES

Bruner, J. *Toward a theory of instruction.* Cambridge, Mass.: Harvard University Press, 1966.

Copeland, R. W. *How children learn mathematics: Teaching implications of Piaget's research.* New York: Macmillan, 1970.

Englemann, S. *Preventing failure in the primary grades.* New York: Simon & Schuster, 1969.

Frostig, M. *Movement education: Theory and practice.* Chicago: Follett Educational Corporation, 1970.

Hall, E. A conversation with Jean Piaget and Barbel Inhelder. *Psychology Today,* 1970, 3(12), 25–32, 54–46.

Lamon, W. E. *Learning and the nature of mathematics.* Chicago Science Research Associates, 1972.

Sharp, F. A. *These kids don't count.* San Rafael, Calif.: Academic Therapy Publications, 1971.

Strauss, A. and Lehtinen, L. *Psychopathology and education of the brain-injured child,* Vol. 1. New York: Grune & Stratton, 1947.

Werner, H. *Comparative psychology of mental development.* New York: International Universities Press, 1957.

18

MATCHING TASKS AND ABILITY PATTERNS IN TEACHING READING

Probably no aspect of education has been discussed more often or with greater fervor than the teaching of reading. Large sums of money have been invested in reading research here and abroad. Much time and effort has also been spent, but the controversy rages on. Reading problems are still estimated as affecting about 15 percent of all school children, 5 percent of all children being regarded as severely retarded in reading skills. In inner-city schools, the proportion is far higher; Cohen (1969) reports, for example, that by the third grade in schools on the Lower East Side of New York City, approximately three-quarters of the children score below grade level in reading.

The main controversy centers on the optimum way to teach reading. The principal methods advocated for public-school children have ranged from the alphabetic methods used by the *Horn Reader* at the end of the eighteenth century to a wide range of modern educational approaches, each of which has been hailed as best. With each one of these approaches there have been successes and failures (De Cecco, 1967, p. 176).

Whenever a problem seems to be unanswerable, there is the possibility that the problem has been incorrectly formulated. Perhaps researchers should not have asked, "What is *the* optimum reading method?" but "What is the optimum reading method for this particular child?" The choice of method will depend upon the specific characteristics of the individual child, the characteristics of the classroom, the community in which he lives, and the availability of such supplementary aids as resource rooms, volunteers, and teaching machines.

Difficulties in reading are very often caused by "developmental lags" in certain abilities (Gallagher, 1966), and these can be accessible to modification.

The first principle of correct reading instruction is therefore individualization. The second is motivation; the third and fourth, systematization and methodology.

Individualization

Most children have a preferred sense modality. If the vast majority of children are to be able to learn to read with ease, then reading instruction must be sufficiently individualized and varied to take each child's preferred sense modality into account. For instance, learning by phonics depends upon adequate auditory perception, but many children have disturbances in auditory perception and cannot discriminate among sounds. For these children, visual and kinesthetic methods often prove more helpful. Similarly, children with poor visual perception will learn better by methods stressing auditory perception. And children with disabilities in both auditory and visual perception will usually make more progress through a tactile or kinesthetic approach.* As a general rule, the teacher should emphasize the strong sense modality in teaching academic skills and subject matter, but at the same time he should train other abilities (Silver and Hagin, 1967).

The reader is warned, however, not to interpret these general guidelines as providing all the necessary information for selecting the optimum-reading method for a specific child. The importance of detailed analysis in evaluating children with learning deficits can be illustrated by two quite typical examples.

Difficulty in Sound Blending

Teachers find that though some children seem to learn sound-letter correspondence and even phonic rules with ease, and can sound out words letter by letter, *p-u-t* remains *p-u-t,* and the sounds are not blended. This difficulty occurs when the teaching of speech sounds is overstressed or when the child has specific reasons for difficulties in sound blending (Chall et al., 1963).

Any method of teaching that is unsuccessful should be dropped. When children cannot learn from a synthetic method (blending sounds into words), the phonic method must be abandoned, and an analytic (whole word) method tried. To assist a child in learning to blend sounds, the teacher might try presenting briefly words of two or three letters, pronouncing them as she does so. So brief a span of time prevents the child from reading the word letter by letter. Later the time of presentation might be further abbreviated and a commercial tachisto-

* Specific methods for these children are discussed later.

scope, teacher-made substitute, or Tach-Ex* used. New words can also be learned with the help of the Language Master,** which enables the child to see and hear a word simultaneously, while working independently of the teacher. When he has learned a word, the child should write it in *cursive* writing, whenever possible, and then reread it. After learning single words, the child should read phrases, then sentences aloud.

Difficulty in Associating Symbols and Meaning

Another difficulty occurs quite frequently. The child seems to read fluently; he shows no difficulties in any sense modality, has good intelligence, yet does not seem to understand what he has read. Most likely this child has established perfect sound-letter correspondence, but has failed to establish an association between the meaning of a word and its graphic representation. In this case, the child has the necessary decoding skills. The teacher's task is to help him to learn to extract meaning from his reading. First, it is necessary to find out if he grasps the meaning better when he reads aloud or when he reads silently; the more difficult mode (aloud or silent) is then dropped. The child is next given a few sentences to read. He turns on the tape recorder and hears the sentences, reads the same passage again without the recorder, then answers questions. If the questions are read to the child before he listens to the tape, his attention will be directed to the relevant information in what he hears and reads.

A child who has difficulty in associating symbols with their meaning should read only a sentence or two at a time, and he should be told to try to make a mental picture of what he reads. For example, if he reads, "I walked to school. I had books under my arm," he should try to imagine himself walking on the street a block away from school and "feeling" the weight of the books. The passages that the child reads should only gradually be lengthened.

It is essential that a child who is able to write should write a summary of what he has read at least once or twice each day, so that he is again obliged to associate the meaning with the printed symbols.

Individualization is necessary in teaching every aspect of reading because progress in reading can be hindered by deficiencies in any psychological function.

* Educational Developmental Laboratories, Inc., Huntington, New York.
** Bell and Howell, Chicago, Illinois.

Motivation

The second principle in teaching children to read is to motivate them as strongly as possible.

For principles and techniques concerning motivation, the reader is referred to the earlier chapters in this book on psychoanalysis, behavior modification, and humanism. In this chapter, motivation is discussed specifically in relation to reading.

By ensuring that reading meets the individual child's needs for information, directions, and emotional satisfaction, the teacher can provide an incentive for conquering the new medium and, at the same time, enhance the child's self-respect.*

These children enjoy reading in a warm comfortable atmosphere. (The "Reading Pit" at the Frostig Center.)

* Of course, an approach that emphasizes motivation does not negate the necessity for learning the alphabet, the sounds of letters, and so on.

Personalizing Reading

The incentives for learning to read will differ from child to child and from moment to moment. For example, Mary may be most eager to read Laura's letter; Mark may be interested in reading the instructions for his new model; Susan wants to read love stories. The most successful approach will take into account the individual child's interests and needs.

It has often been stated that television and radio satisfy children's curiosity in such a pleasurable way that they may find reading superfluous. It is therefore necessary to make reading a very personal affair if it is to be more attractive than television. Minority children, in particular, need to experience a personal meaning in schoolwork.

Personalization is especially important for those children, usually from a minority background, who fail in reading and in other school tasks because of a lack of confidence and self-respect. "To be successful, teaching must develop in the child a strong sense of personal worth." (Zirkel and Moses, 1970).

Motivating the Small Child

One method of making reading a personal experience for the child and enhancing his self-concept is to make use of sentences that reflect his own experiences.

An educator who has used this approach effectively is Sylvia Ashton-Warner (1963), who taught young Maori children in New Zealand. These children had not reacted well to the British school system because their customs, mores, and living conditions were far different, and their textbooks and other educational methods were therefore without meaning.

A somewhat similar approach has been used in the Tucson Follow-Through program (Maccoby and Zellner, 1970). The teacher led the group into reading by transcribing what each child said about his experiences. The teacher then showed the child what his words looked like in printing, and read them back to him, pointing out that as the words said something about the child, being able to read them might prove very interesting.

In both instances, success resulted from focusing on reading as a meaningful activity and from respect for each individual child. In psychoanalytic terms, reading was made *egosyntonic*; it was made pleasurable and fulfilling.

The three purposes of reading—for information, for receiving directions, and for emotional satisfaction—can not always be clearly differentiated. Information can arouse feelings. Instructions supply information. Literature that appeals to our emotions may also convey information or instructions. For the purpose of teaching and motivating a child, however, it is valuable to keep these three purposes clearly in mind in order to ensure that reading is regularly used for each purpose.

In British infant and elementary schools, reading and writing skills are used in an integrated fashion and applied to the tasks of daily life. A child, for example, may read a recipe, copy it down, and immediately use it; or he may keep a diary of his experiences in school and read it to his friends; or note down and read back the procedures and results of an experiment in science; or use a notebook to collect information from multiple sources and read it to the other children; and so on. By such means the child learns to use printed language to gain information and follow directions, and then derives emotional satisfaction from applying or sharing the result. Because the children work together and help each other, total failure is eliminated, and each child is aware of a purpose in what he is doing.

It will be clear from the foregoing that it is very important that reading and writing should not be restricted to the so-called reading period but should be used throughout the school day. Instructions and information should be given in writing as well as orally. For example, in conducting movement education the teacher could write the instructions on a large piece of paper or slate board. These instructions might at first be single words, such as *run, stop,* and so on, but later, short phrases and sentences might be used, such as "Take three steps," "Turn around," and so on. Similar opportunities for involving children in reading occur throughout the school day. And adequate provision should also be made for reading and writing related to expression of feelings.

Motivating the Older Child

The older child has often given up because of prior failure or personal difficulties with the teachers in authority or other social and emotional reasons. The question of motivation is therefore paramount in teaching reading to the older child. Older children need methods and incentives appropriate to their age level to enhance their pleasure and success in deciphering words. Crossword puzzles, Scrabble and similar games, typewriters, teaching machines, tachistoscopes, and other technological devices can be tried. Games are liked equally well by older and younger children.

With older children, especially those who are members of minority groups, it is also possible to use as a motivating force the history of their culture, its achievements, and the struggles of its members for better status. This desire should be fostered and met.*

Another potential motivating force, especially significant when working with an older child, is the child's liking for, and identification with, the teacher. (See Chapter 7, "Psychoanalytic Thought and Education.") A youngster who admires his teacher may want to learn to read in order to please her.

Emphasizing communication skills throughout the school day can prove as helpful in the higher grades as it does in the lower ones. Written instructions, appropriate to their reading level, to complete a sequence of tasks can be given to groups of youngsters working together. In movement education, for example, a large card might be shown that reads: "Take turns at throwing a beanbag into a circle. Start from five feet away. When the beanbag has landed in the circle three times, move back one foot. Continue until at least half in your group have reached a distance of ten feet. Then separate into two groups and take turns at throwing a ball over the net to each other." In math, written directions and printed word problems should be used daily.

In science and social studies, children should write information down and then read it over. They should keep permanent records of their achievement and frequently use their notes for review. Children should also be encouraged to find the information they need for their projects in books. It is very important to have in the classroom a variety of books, appropriate to different levels of reading skill, that contain information on many topics, including the sciences and social sciences.

The following examples illustrate how a group of adolescent non-readers were motivated to read by choosing subject matter appropriate to their particular circumstances.

The setting was a boarding school for delinquent girls from thirteen to sixteen years of age. The period of instruction was from January through June for one hour twice weekly. In the beginning the youngsters were told that they were going to learn about whatever most interested them. The word *reading* was avoided.

Reacting to the gloominess of their surroundings, the group decided to learn how to obtain and cultivate some plants. The youngsters determined not only to write for seeds, but also to make an illustrated booklet about the plants. At their request the teacher obtained a mail-order catalogue from which pictures could be cut, together with scissors, colored paper, and other materials. Reading was started by using the

---

* A step in the right direction has been taken by the Los Angeles school system, which has contracted with Scholastic Book Services to produce six mini-anthologies of Black literature.

matching method (Frostig, 1965). In other words, pictures were pasted in the booklet, and key words were written under them (rose, geraniums, tulips, bulb, seeds, money, package, and so on). Then games were played matching nouns with pictures. The teacher then introduced other words needed to form phrases and sentences, such as *"it"* (*it* costs), *"in," "the"* (planted *in the* spring), and so on; and gradually incorporated further vocabulary common to various preprimers, so that the girls would be able to write such sentences as "See the plants. They are red geraniums," and so on. The basic vocabulary was mastered in this way, through essentially a whole-word approach, integrated with a functional teaching of phonics.

After two months, the teacher decided to introduce some conventional reading materials. In order to avoid and overcome resistance, she asked the girls if they remembered how they had felt when they were asked to read a book in school when they were unable to read. They all recollected that it had been "awful." The teacher then inquired if they would like to prevent that experience happening to a child whom they loved, possibly a sister, or a cousin, or perhaps a child whom they themselves might have someday. The group indicated that they would indeed like to learn how to prevent failure in school. At this point the teacher introduced an advanced preprimer and said: "You have learned all the words in this book. Who would like to imagine that she is teaching a little child and is reading the book to her pupil?" One girl volunteered. She read the first story; and in a few minutes all the youngsters had read parts of the preprimer without making a mistake. In this way they discovered that they were able to read books after all, despite their former failure.

It was not possible to keep track of all the girls after they were released from the boarding school, but it was known that several had developed an interest in reading and made good progress in school.

Behavior Modification

For many children, learning to read is meaningful and reinforcing in itself, but a reading disability combined with traditional teaching practices sometimes condition a child to consider reading a detestable task. The child who has not been successful may well have lost all joy in reading. The teacher may then have to motivate the child by extraneous rewards or reinforcers, such as candy, stars, extra playtime, and so on. For further discussion of these approaches, the reader is referred to Chapter 5 on behavior modification.

Systematization

The third indispensable principle in teaching reading is systematization. By this we mean systematic presentation and systematic review carried on for a sufficiently lengthy period. (Of course, this principle applies to every subject, not only to reading).

Children, especially those with reading difficulties, need to practice decoding skills in reading until their responses are immediate and automatic. If the responses are not automatic, and the child has to work consciously at every sound-letter association, he will appear confused and "overloaded," and even well-learned skills will be disrupted (Bryant, 1965).

Systematic progression in learning requires specific attitudes and preparation on the part of the teacher. The teacher must be fully aware of the importance of knowing what has already been presented to the child. Step-by-step progress is necessary at any time, but especially during beginning reading. It is therefore a necessity for the teacher to take careful notes. Until the child has learned the first 250 words or so, the teacher should have a vocabulary list for each child, so that she can choose words for review and introduce new words as appropriate.*

A list of books that each child has read should be kept, so that no child will be assigned a book twice unless he requests it. The teacher also needs to note daily whether or not the child has used reading for the various purposes already discussed.

As the student progresses in reading, systematic review of vocabulary continues to be essential. Review can be made more stimulating and significant for the child if it is done in game form or if the child reads to the class what he has learned.

Necessary Reading Skills

To be systematic in her teaching, the teacher needs to teach, to integrate, and to review the skills the child needs for reading. The following lists may be helpful in ensuring that no skills are omitted.

1. **Decoding skills: perceptual skills**

    Visual perception of single letters.
    Visual perception of the sequence of letters.

* A vocabulary list may be kept in a book constructed and written by the child for himself. "The Child's Own Book" will be discussed later, in the section on reading techniques.

Auditory perception of speech sounds—consonant blends, dipthongs and digraphs.

Perception of sounds in a sequence and "word chaining." (See pp. 207–208, 302.)

Auditory perception of words in a sequence.

2. **Decoding skills: Recognition of phoneme-grapheme relationship**

Phonetic word analysis.

Structural word analysis.

Association of a whole visually perceived word, with the memory of spoken word and with its meaning.

Automatization of reading skills.

3. **Comprehension skills**

Understanding the meaning of a stated fact.

Understanding the meaning of a sequence of stated facts (paragraphs or story).

Making inferences and drawing conclusions.

Noting and remembering details in a story.

Carrying out an instruction.

Following a sequence of instructions (as in a recipe).

Appreciating reading; poems, story content, humor.

Finding specific information on a page (skimming).

Seeing cause-and-effect relationships.

Predicting outcomes.

Solving problems, including determining what information is needed.

Appraising information for validity and significance.

4. **Study skills**

Alphabetizing.

Knowing and using the various parts of a book (title, table of contents, index, glossary, etc.).

Using the format of the book (its arrangement into sections, chapters, paragraphs) as a guide to identification of the main ideas.

Classifying material under broader subject headings.

Using reference materials (telephone books, dictionary, encyclopedia, etc.).

Reading maps, graphs, tables, charts.

Using files and bibliographies.

Outlining and summarizing.

Methodology

Three principles of reading instruction have been discussed so far: individualization, motivation, and systematization. In the following section a fourth principle will be discussed in greater detail, namely, the correct choice of techniques.

In order to teach optimally all the necessary skills to all children in a variety of conditions, a variety of teaching methods have to be selected according to the needs of the individual child.* But one principle applies to all children: *reading, writing, listening, and oral language cannot be separated in instruction.* To be motivated, the child must experience reading as an extension of oral language that is needed for information, communication, and self-expression. Reading is therefore only one aspect of the total language program. There are many children even at the second-grade or third-grade level, who believe that to read means being able to recite the words printed in a book, without understanding that reading serves communicative purposes.

In the following sections an analysis is made of the skills required by a child in order to learn to read, and of the techniques that specifically promote each of these skills.** The abilities are discussed in the order in which they develop chronologically. The sensory-motor functions develop first and are discussed first.

Definitions

At this point a few terms that have not been previously used need to be defined. The term *linguistic* has a specific meaning when applied to a reading method. The meaning will become clear in the next few paragraphs when the characteristics of the three approaches most frequently used in teaching reading—the phonetic, the linguistic, and the whole-word approach—are examined.

The phonetic (synthetic) method begins with teaching sounds; sounds are synthesized into syllables, and then into words and sen-

---

* Vernon (1968, p. 14) states, "The best single means of prevention (of reading failure) is the adequate training of . . . teachers in the use of appropriate methods. . . . Since there is no general agreement as to a single universally successful method, it is advisable that teachers should be able to employ a variety of methods, materials and devices."

** An excellent comprehensive review of research, issues, and methodology in reading may be found in Bannatyne (1971), *Language, Reading, and Learning Disabilities.*

tences. In contrast, the whole-word, or look-and-say method, that relies on the visual channel, analyzes the whole word into its components for the purposes of spelling and for finding the rules for phoneme-grapheme correspondence. The whole-word method is therefore called an analytic method.

The linguistic method also uses whole words or syllables but follows a pattern in the presentation of letter-sound combinations. This method is much newer than the others. It resembles the phonic method in making the child aware of sound-letter correspondence and offering him a means of decoding; but it differs from the phonic method because it is not synthetic—words are not sounded out—and because it relies to a great degree on the visual perception of similar patterns among words.

Which decoding skills will be emphasized will depend on the method used. Learning phoneme-grapheme relations is usually developed through phonics. The phonic method includes teaching the alphabet, sounds, and rules for sound combinations. The phonic method teaches reading of vowels, of digraphs, blends, the silent *e* at the end of a word, and so on.

In the linguistic approach a child learns grapheme-phoneme correspondence and spelling by learning sound patterns, structural analysis of words (for instance, suffixes and prefixes), and structural analysis of sentences (syntax).* The linguistic method includes the teaching of punctuation, capitalization, and other rules relating to the written and oral structure of language.

The whole-word method is based on the fact that words are perceived as wholes; it aims to make word recognition automatic through over-learning. The use of flash cards, tachistoscopic presentation, phrase-reading cards, and so on, is emphasized by this method, but such materials can be used with the other methods as well.

Prereading Skills

A program teaching prereading skills (reading readiness) is usually introduced before any attempt is made to teach children to read in any systematic fashion. The prereading program usually includes at least the following skills: (1) learning to speak and to listen; (2) distinguishing letter forms from one another; (3) identifying letter sounds; (4) asso-

* Stern and Gould (1965) use the term *structural reading* to refer not to the teaching of reading through syntactical analysis, but to a method that builds on the child's oral language.

ciating letter sounds and forms;* (5) recognizing the sound of the letter in the context of the word; (6) writing simple words, usually in manuscript; (7) practice in the above skills.

As a rule, systematic vocabulary acquisition follows the initial work with sound and letter discrimination.

Many other prereading skills must be developed; for example, sensory-motor skills, especially laterality, discrimination of direction, oculo-motor skills, and many language and perceptual skills. Training in these skills should be given before the child begins to read, and continued for as long as required. (See Chapter 15.) Careful adherence to the education of basic abilities is especially important in developing the ability to read. Silver and Hagin (1960) conclude that optimum improvement can only be ensured if teaching methods are used that also improve the most deficient abilities.

Sensory-Motor Abilities and Reading

As we have discussed, sensory-motor training can influence a child's general functioning, and it can therefore be assumed to affect his ability to learn academic skills. (The reader may want to consult Chapter 12 dealing with sensory-motor training).

Movement can also be used to teach reading skills directly. Some suggestions for reading games involving physical activities are given in *Movement education* (Frostig, 1970, pp. 123-126).

In this section, however, we will not be concerned with movement education and its influence, but with three specific sensory-motor abilities that directly influence reading. They are ocular control, eye-hand coordination, and laterality.

Oculo-motor Skills

Claims and counterclaims have been made in regard to oculo-motor skills. Prechtl (1962), for instance, states that it is commonsense to conclude that erratic eye movements must retard reading ability, while in an eye-tracking experiment, Jones (1966) and her associates found that the ability of subjects to fixate and follow stripes on a slowly revolving drum did not correlate with reading readiness, and therefore concluded that eye-movement training is not indicated. Nevertheless, sufficient evidence has recently accumulated to suggest that eye move-

* Samuels (1971) found that letter-name training does not promote reading skills.

ment plays a significant role in reading, and that changes in eye movements can occur with training (Kephart, 1971).

It is best to begin training in eye movement before the child learns
to read. For examples of training exercises, see Frostig (1972), Kephart
(1971), and Getman (1962).

Nodine and Lang (1971) have demonstrated that eye movements
are not only a matter of learning to control the left-right progression of
the eye, but also of learning to bring eye movements under cognitive
control. Difficulties in scanning are therefore not only overcome by
training in the ability to progress smoothly from left-to-right, but also
by strategies that help the child to recognize whole words and to grasp
differences and similarities between words quickly. The child learns to
focus on those parts of words that provide the most important cues.

There is experimental evidence that the scanning strategies of older
children are superior to those of younger children. With increased
cognitive control of eye movements, the visual input is selected more
efficiently, and the child learns to attend selectively to the information
in the reading text. As his ability to read improves, so do his eye movements.

The diagnosis of erratic eye movements can be made by the teacher,
either by observing a child's eye movements directly or by using a mirror.
(See Figure 1.)

A child's mistakes may also betray erratic eye movements. He may
reread a word that he has read before or skip words or lines. For children

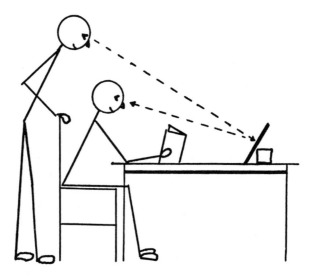

FIGURE 1.   Checking eye movements.

with these difficulties windows and markers and special exercises may be helpful.

The "window" consists of a stiff piece of paper with a slot large enough to expose one word, phrase, or line at a time, whichever is the optimum span for a given child. As the child learns to control his eye movements, his visual span may be gradually increased by enlarging the size of the window. (See Figure 2.)

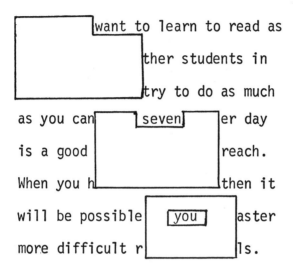

FIGURE 2.   Examples of various kinds of markers.

Some children have difficulty in moving from the end of one line of print to the first word in the next line. Exercises in making this eye movement can be done with the aid of specially lined paper. (See Figure 3.)

The "trailing pencil" (pointer) was regarded as indispensable by Strauss and Lehtinen (1947) and by Grace Arthur (1946). The name suggests that smooth eye movements will be more easily promoted if the pointer is used with a "trailing" movement. That is to say, it should slide smoothly across the page *marking the phrases*, instead of being jerked from word to word.

Tracking exercises should be used in addition to the use of markers and pointers.* (See Figure 4.) The following three exercises in tracking are independent of reading skills:

---

* Tracking exercises are also necessary for children who have difficulties in figure-ground perception, as will be discussed later.

FIGURE 3. Tracking exercises involving shifting
from end of one line to beginning of the next.

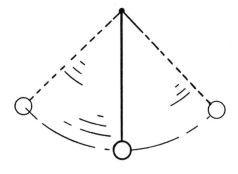

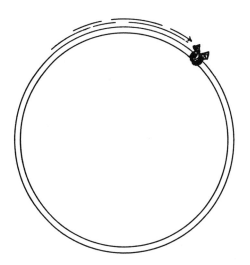

FIGURE 4.   Tracking exercises with pendulum and hoop.

1. The child follows a swinging pendulum with his eyes, without turning his head.
2. The child fixates on a ribbon tied to a turning hoop.
3. Most important is practicing left to right progression, together with the return sweep to the beginning of the next line.

Eye-Hand Coordination

Although the use of a pointer can generally be recommended, children sometimes resist this technique because of a difficulty in eye-hand or fine motor coordination. A child with difficulties in eye-hand coordination may also find it hard to copy from the board or from a book. Many exercises and games to promote eye-hand coordination have been developed by Kephart (1971).

Fine Muscle Coordination

Children with disabilities in fine muscle coordination are likely to have difficulty in writing, and in getting a book open at a certain page. They will be helped best by arts and crafts activities, by a step-by-step program for teaching writing, and by practice in finding a given page.

Laterality*

The importance of establishing laterality is another prominent issue about which opinions are sharply divided. Silver and Hagin (1960) believe that disturbances of laterality are nearly universal in children with reading difficulties; and Graubard (1966) found many cases of cross-dominance or unestablished laterality among poor readers. Others disagree. Flick (1966), for example, states that eye-hand dominance does not seem to be related to reading difficulties. Eisenson (1963) writes: "Some authorities feel that aphasic** children may demonstrate varying degrees of confused laterality. They consider this lack of cerebral dominance to be a causative factor of aphasia. However, there is as yet little evidence to support this latter contention." (Specific reading difficulty is usually considered a form of aphasia by authors who use this term.) Ayres (1965) found no relationship between laterality functions and those clinical syndromes she studied, focusing on the sensory modalities of touch, proprioception, and vision. She considered eye-and-hand dominance to be unrelated to perceptual motor functions in general.

In the majority of studies, eye-and-foot dominance and cross-laterality were not found to influence reading ability. This fact has been also observed by the present authors. Although cross-dominance (e.g., using the right hand consistently and the left foot consistently) is probably of no significance to reading success, mixed dominance (using right or left hand impartially) leads to directional confusion.

* *Laterality* refers to knowledge of the right and left sides of the body; *directionality* to the knowledge of right and left in space; and *dominance* to the preferred side of the body.
** Aphasia is a defect or loss of the ability to communicate by oral or written language or to comprehend it, due to neurological dysfunction.

The acts of reading and writing involve a progression from left to right. The child who has not established a preferred hand has no definite clue in deciding which side of his body is left or right. Directional confusion may therefore result and interfere with ability to read (Harris, 1970, p. 245).

Laterality can be tested with the Harris Tests of Lateral Dominance (1958). Observation can also reveal which hand a child prefers. Exercises to promote hand preference and also those that promote directionality are discussed in *Pictures and Patterns* (Frostig, 1972) and *Movement Education* (Frostig, 1970).

Auditory Perception and Reading

While many educators emphasize the importance of visual-perceptual skills in reading, others emphasize the importance of auditory perception.

The diagnostic procedures in cases of auditory-perceptual difficulties have already been discussed, and suggestions for specific remedial exercises have been given in an earlier chapter.

It has already been mentioned in regard to children who are handicapped in visual perception that they may learn to read in spite of their difficulty. This is also true of children with auditory-perceptual handicaps. The correlation between auditory-perceptual skills and reading is usually thought to be about 0.4.*

Phonic methods in reading should *not* be used exclusively with children with auditory-perceptual deficits.

Neither auditory discrimination training alone nor reading based solely on phonics is very helpful to a child with auditory-perceptual difficulties. This is due to the fact that the results of auditory-perceptual training seem to be more uncertain and achieved more slowly than those of visual-perceptual training. This was reported by Spache (1966) and has been found to be true by the present authors. Feldman and Deutsch (1964) also reported that they observed little effect of auditory-discrimination training in Negro children with reading difficulties. Because auditory training does not lead to quick success, it may cause some children to become unwilling to participate in reading at all. With children who resist auditory-perceptual training, it should as far as possible be used in the form of games.

* Stanchfield's research has shown that boys have more difficulty in auditory discrimination than girls; for example, boys took 3½ times as long to learn the *gr—cr* consonant blends (personal communication).

Auditory-Perceptual Skills Needed for Reading

The auditory-perceptual abilities that have the greatest significance for reading are discrimination of single sounds and of words, sound blending, perception of auditory sequences, and auditory imagery and memory. Auditory figure-ground perception difficulties may also influence reading, because they may cause a child to be distracted by normal classroom noises and also make it difficult for the child to become aware of the individual sounds in a word and of the whole word simultaneously.

Sound Discrimination and Sound Blending

In the experience of the authors, when a child has difficulty in discriminating speech sounds, or in sound blending, he should be taught to read by a predominantly visual or visual kinesthetic method, while training in discrimination of speech sounds must also be provided daily, but only for a few minutes at a session. Simple sound combinations that occur frequently may be taught directly. Rhyming games are helpful, but chaining is much more important. The term *chaining* is here defined as changing one sound successively to form a new word: *cat–can–man–mat–met,* and so on. The child should always indicate which letter has been changed and also read the new word.

Children with relatively severe and persistent problems in the discrimination of speech sounds may have a hearing loss in the high-frequency range. Audiometric examination is therefore indicated. A child with a hearing loss should sit as near as possible to the teacher and in such a position that he can watch the speaker's lips. The teacher should ensure that her face is turned toward the child when she talks and that her instructions are short, simple, and clearly enunciated. Many children with auditory-perceptual difficulties who have perfect hearing will also profit from such a procedure.

Whenever auditory perception is severely disturbed, and especially when complicated with articulation defects, the child's oral reading should be restricted, so that he does not make incorrect grapheme-morpheme associations. Silent reading is less affected. The oral reading of such a child should be carefully monitored. Culturally different children often have difficulties with oral reading because of their different dialects and also because auditory-perceptual disturbances are so frequent in this population (Deutsch, 1964).

The use of gross motor and locomotor activities can be a powerful tool in helping children with auditory-perceptual difficulties to learn to read, especially initially. For example, the child can be asked to carry out one-word instructions written on cards that are shown to him; e.g., run, jump, sit.

Auditory Figure-Ground Perception

It has been mentioned before that a child who can discriminate speech sounds, but who cannot read when the room is noisy, may have a disability in auditory figure-ground perception. The teacher might provide equipment with which earphones can be used, such as a tape recorder or a Language Master when these are available.

It is important that children have opportunities to read silently in a quiet room. Too often the only chance a child has for silent reading is when other reading groups are reading aloud. If he has difficulties in auditory figure-ground perception, he will not be able to understand what he is reading and may well lose interest.

Perception of Auditory Sequences

A child with difficulties in perception of auditory (temporal) sequences may reverse the order of sounds in words and the order of words when repeating a sentence or while reading. It is helpful for such a child to read silently to himself as the teacher reads a sentence aloud and then to read aloud the same sentence by himself.

The use of an oral-kinesthetic method may be helpful. The child is asked to look at the teacher's lips while she forms the sounds or words. The child then repeats the words and tries to be conscious of the movement of his lips. He is also made aware of tongue position. The child may put his hands on his throat to feel the movement of the larynx (in distinguishing the g sound from the k sound, for example).

Improving sequential memory through a combination of gross movement and speech may be used to help the child perceive sequences. For instance, the teacher may write a simple instruction on a card—"Hop three times" or "Write the word late," (and so on)—while the child watches (visual cue). The child reads the instruction, then follows the directions.

Some children learn to follow short sequences like those given above, but cannot grasp a sequence of events told to them in a longer paragraph or story. This difficulty is most probably caused by an inability to store and retrieve stimuli received through the auditory channel, though it may also be due to unfamiliarity with the concepts or the context in a particular narration. The teacher can help the child to understand and remember by making pauses in her narration, providing opportunities for the child to repeat what he has heard so far or to act it out.

Auditory Imagery and Memory

Reauditorization (auditory imagery) is important for all children, not only those with auditory-perceptual difficulties or those who cannot remember a sequence. But many children have difficulties in auditorization, and confuse sounds. Such children should always see the words that they are to learn—the teacher should never simply spell out a word orally.*

Practice in auditory imagery can be given by providing many opportunities for the child to hear something, and then to repeat it. It is helpful for most children with auditory-perceptual disabilities if they are also taught to visualize what they hear as an aid to memory. They are asked to close their eyes and picture how a word is spelled or what a sentence describes. Exercises in reauditorization and those in visualization should be given separately.

It is important to remember in teaching reading to children with auditory-perceptual problems to provide reinforcing visual, tactile, and kinesthetic cues. These children, even more than others, enjoy putting pictures in the "Child's Own Book." The use of rebus material may also be helpful, and color coding can be used for word analysis and synthesis. The use of linguistic readers can also be helpful, provided the child likes them; some children do not like them and "tune out" any reading in them. When that is the case, another book should be provided.

Since repetition and overlearning are particularly important when using a visual approach, whether linguistic or whole word, review is necessary in many contexts. In order to avoid boredom or fatigue, review should take the form of a game whenever possible.

Training in sound discrimination and sound blending have, of course, also been discussed in Chapter 14 on auditory perception.

Visual Perception and Reading

Behavioristic-oriented researchers and educators, such as Staats (1970), who view reading as a stimulus-response process, are greatly concerned with the visual-perceptual aspect of reading, because the child needs to be able to discriminate a stimulus before he can respond to it. These educators approach the teaching of reading by eliciting from the child

---

* Children with disturbances in *visual* imagery would not confuse sounds, which they perceive and remember in the correct order, but might make spelling mistakes that depend upon visual recall, such as "runing" for "running."

the correct response to a stimulus, and then reinforcing (rewarding) the response, so that the child will tend to give the same response to the same stimulus on subsequent occasions. They emphasize letter discrimination in beginning reading. Certainly the first step in decoding printed language is to perceive it visually: "Reading involves the visual perception of written symbols and the transformation of the symbols to their explicit or implicit oral counterparts. The oral responses then act as stimuli for a thoughtful reaction on the part of the reader . . . determined, in part, by the intent and the background of the reader and the nature of the materials" (Barrett, 1967, p. 15).

Correlation between visual-perceptual skills and *beginning* reading achievement has consistently been found to be in the low-moderate range—0.4 to 0.5 (Goins, 1958)—for unselected public-school children. This is not surprising in view of the fact that reading is a very complex perceptual, cognitive, and affective task. Dykstra (1967) has pointed out that readiness tests, intelligence tests, perceptual tests, personality tests, number tests, and teacher ratings all predict beginning reading achievement about equally well (with a Pearson point-moment correlation coefficient ranging from 0.40 to 0.70).

Many children with excellent perceptual abilities find learning to read difficult and others who have visual-perceptual disabilities have disabilities in other areas as well, any of which may contribute to reading difficulty. It is also true that many children with visual-perceptual deficits are often so proficient in other functions that they learn to read despite the handicap. Disabilities in visual perception and difficulty in learning to read should not be equated.

Nevertheless, children with lags in visual perception are likely to find learning to read more difficult and less pleasurable than their age-mates. In a cooperative research project with the University Elementary School, University of California, Los Angeles, the Marianne Frostig Developmental Test of Visual Perception was administered in July, 1962, to a group of twenty-five children between the ages of four and a half and six and a half. It was found that eight of the children had perceptual quotients (PQ's) in the lowest quartile (90 or below). For the next three months all the children were exposed to reading material but neither forced nor pressured to use it. In October, 1962, it was found that none of the children with a PQ below 90 had begun to read; and of the two children with a PQ of 90, one had not learned to read while the other read very well. Of the children with a PQ *above* 90, only one showed reading difficulties (Maslow et al., 1964, pp. 493–495).

When children with disabilities in visual perception are expected to learn to read, the stress resulting from the pressure to achieve despite such a handicap may result in emotional disturbances. This was indicated by the authors' own findings in another experiment. Among kindergarten and first-grade children rated by their teachers as the most poorly adjusted in the classroom, the vast majority were those with PQ's below 90 (Maslow et al., 1964, p. 492).

The correlation between scores on a test of visual perception and reading achievement becomes insignificant by about the third-grade level when the scores are obtained from an "average" classroom. However, children who have learned to read despite visual-perceptual disabilities will only have succeeded under abnormal stress, and may continue to be less assured and skillful readers than most children.

Krippner (1971) concludes from a study of 146 poor readers that "poor visual perceptual skills were the most common etiological factors in cases of reading disability, in the opinion of the clinicians making judgments." Belmont and Birch (1965) and Lovell and Gorton (1968) are among the many other research workers who have found reading disability associated with a general perceptual deficit, especially amongst the poorest readers.

Many culturally different and economically deprived children lag in visual-perceptual abilities. Lewis, Bell, and Anderson (1970) compared WISC scores of black and white children, all of whom were retarded in reading. No differences appeared on the verbal subtests, but black children scored lower on those subtests requiring visual-perceptual skills. This finding has direct implications for teaching these children. Fortunately they usually enjoy activities involving visual-perceptual training. Special techniques are necessary to transfer the perceptual skills they learn to the reading task (Frostig, 1972).

Disturbances in Figure-Ground Perception

A child with disabilities in figure-ground perception may have particular difficulty in analyzing a word. He may fuse letters (e.g., *clip* may be read as *dip*) or he may add, omit, or substitute letters. He may be unable to find a particular word on a page or to work on a crowded worksheet. If a child skips words or lines, loses his place and has to retrace his progress, the problem may be due to faulty figure-ground perception—though the cause may also be erratic eye movements, as we have already discussed earlier in this chapter.

The teacher can help the child with poor figure-ground perception to analyze words by having him form words with prefabricated or cutout letters (Figure 5), and by using color cues (see pp. 309–310). To give the child practice in focusing on relevant material despite distracting stimuli,

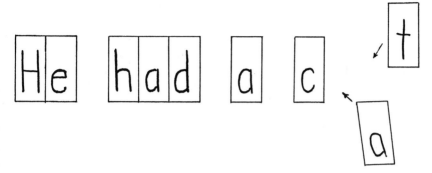

FIGURE 5.   Cut-out letters.

the teacher may write spelling or reading words that the child can read in intersecting fashion (Figure 6). Kinesthetic methods (tracing or writing) may also help him form the correct image of a word.

FIGURE 6.   Intersecting words.

In presenting new material, or in teaching certain skills that seem to present difficulties, the teacher must take a child's specific disability into account. For children with poor figure-ground perception, material in large print, such as that used for the visually handicapped, is helpful. When reference skills are being taught, these children may need specially prepared and simplified dictionary pages, a simple encyclopedia, and specially prepared maps with few stimuli. Their worksheets should be neat and uncrowded; "busy" workbooks should be avoided.

The teacher may use reading materials and exercises to help train figure-ground perception. For example, chaining may be used to train the child to analyze a word and focus on the changed letter. Or the child may be asked to find a particular group of letters in a word, a word in a sentence, an idea in a paragraph, and so on. Children with difficulties in figure-ground perception usually have difficulty in scanning.*

The teacher should never encourage children with reading difficulties to use the over-all shape of the word as a cue in word recognition. The shapes of words are of little value in helping children decode (Hochberg, 1968, pp. 56–57). For children with difficulties in analyzing words, using contour cues may lead to grave misreading; e.g., boy, dog, lay, and bag all have the same contour.

Disturbances in Constancy

A child with disturbances in this area may not recognize words that he already knows if they are presented in an unfamiliar style, and he may be unable to differentiate between letters of similar configuration; e.g., *n, r, h.*

The teacher can help the child by presenting familiar material (words and sentences) in as many forms, sizes, colors, and contexts as possible. The child can be helped to observe the details of individual letters if he uses a primary typewriter and preformed and cutout letters. When the child writes a letter, he should be encouraged to verbalize the motions that his hand is making; e.g., the child might say as he prints an *a,* "Around, up, down."

The linguistic approach can be helpful since the child is building from known patterns; e.g., r-*an,* c-*an,* f-*an,* and so on.

Disturbances in Perception
of Position in Space and Directionality

A child who consistently reverses and rotates letters beyond the age of seven may have difficulties in perception of position in space.** Children with laterality problems frequently show reversals.

Throughout the school day the teacher's instructions should give cues, so as to prevent such a child from making directional mistakes in reading or writing. For example, letters and numbers may be correctly

---

* Scanning is here defined as "rapid reading to gain a general impression . . . and . . . reading to find certain items or answers to specific questions. . . ." (Schubert, 1964).

** It should be emphasized that this symptom may also stem from another cause. A child may reverse *b* and *d,* for example, not because he cannot discriminate between them, but because he cannot remember which name or sound refers to which shape.

printed on his writing paper or attached to his desk so that he can continually compare them with his own work. He may need to write letters and numbers in grids (see Chapter 19) with a small cross drawn in each box to indicate where he should begin each letter or number. If he starts at the cross and does not cross the vertical boundary, it will be impossible for him to make a reversal. In reading, it is often helpful to provide passages in which the first letter of each word is colored as a directional cue. This may help children who read "saw" for "was" and "left" for "felt." For *b-d* discrimination, the mnemonic "bed" can be taught (the word has the configuration of a bed). (See Figure 7.)

Another method is to print the *b* with a solid circle (**b**-u-t) and to fade this visual cue out as the child recognizes the letter (b-u-t).

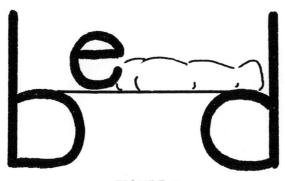

FIGURE 7

Disturbances in Perception of Spatial Relationships and Visual Sequences

Difficulties in this area may result in scrambled spelling, such as *s-i-t-r-n-g* for *string*.

Color coding has proved very helpful in teaching children with disabilities in spatial relationships to read. In the method used at the Frostig Center,* the same color is not used consistently for a particular sound.** Rather a change of color denotes a change of sound, with diphthongs and digraphs being written in the same color. Silent letters are stippled. (See Figure 8.) After the word has been analyzed by the use of color cues, it must be immediately presented also in a single

* Specific systems of color cueing have been developed by Gattegno (1963) and Bannatyne (1965), among others.

** Some teachers, however, print all short vowels in red and all long vowels in green as aids to learning.

EXAMPLES OF THE COLOR-CUE METHOD

cat   (each sound in a different color)

book   (oo, a dipthong, is heard as the same sound)

phonic   (digraphs are written in one color)

come   (silent letters are stippled)

The color cue method can be used for study of syllabification, prefixes and suffixes:

working

dis en chant ed

won der ful

FIGURE 8

color, so that the child can learn to synthesize the word. This last step is most important. If it is omitted, the child may not learn to spell the word or to recognize it when he sees it presented in black on white.*

* Color cues may also be used to teach structural analysis by using different colors for syllables, root words, suffixes, and prefixes.

Severe Handicaps in Visual Perception

Children with severe disabilities in visual perception may be helped to learn to read by "blind writing," which is an adaptation of the VAKT (Visual-Auditory-Kinesthetic-Tactile) method of Fernald (1943).

The teacher first writes the letter or word on the chalkboard at a height easily reached by the child. The child traces over the letter or word with closed eyes, the teacher guiding his hand. At the same time the teacher pronounces the letter or word slowly or describes the hand movement needed to form the letter ("up, around, down, and up"). After repeated tracings, the child can proceed without assistance. The child then writes the letter or word with his eyes open. Thus his relatively intact kinesthetic sense guides his deficient visual perception. The lesson has not been completed, however, until the child finds the word or letter in a book, reads sentences in which it appears, and then again writes it on paper. The child needs to transfer each newly learned skill from a special context to the regular classroom material.

Reading and Intersensory Integration

As the so-called normal child matures, his perceptions become more accurate and capable of finer discriminations within each sense modality (vision, hearing, and so on). Of equal importance is the child's increasing ability to integrate simultaneous inputs (stimuli) from two or more sense modalities. As Abravanel (1968, p. 1) puts it, he achieves a higher degree of "effective liaison" among the senses.

Such effective liaison is evident in almost every activity—dressing oneself, cooking, driving a car, picking flowers, even walking. Integration and association of perceptions from two or more sense modalities are particularly critical abilities in learning to read, because an association must be formed between visual stimuli (graphemes) and their auditory images (phonemes).

A number of studies have shown that integrative and associative functions are lagging in children who are retarded readers. See, for example, Birch and Belmont (1965), Kass (1966), and Beery (1970). Sabatino and Hayden's study (1970) is of particular interest because these writers tested children who were failing in elementary school with an extensive battery, including tests of general intelligence, language, visual and auditory perception, laterality and directionality, as well as tests of visual-auditory integration. Factor analysis of test scores showed that poor auditory-visual integration played a prominent role in learning failure at all levels, and occurred particularly frequently in younger children.

Because reading necessarily involves associative ability (grapheme-phoneme correspondence), methods of teaching reading to children who lag in this ability are chosen which make this correspondence easier. The i.t.a. (initial teaching alphabet) was designed to make a one-to-one correspondence possible between grapheme and phoneme in English (Downing, 1967). A recent survey (Warburton and Southgate, 1969) has reported that children taught with i.t.a. materials experienced fewer failures in reading than children taught by conventional methods. They also wrote more, and after transition to the regular alphabet, were superior in spelling and writing. I.t.a., however, encourages reading word by word, and some children later have difficulty in transferring to traditional orthography and spelling correctly.

Children with difficulties in auditory-visual integration may be helped best by kinesthetic (writing, or writing and tracing) methods. Kinesthetic methods form a bridge between the experience of an act extended in time, which occurs when we hear, and the experience of an act extended in space, which occurs when we see.

Whenever we say a word or read it aloud, we experience an act that is extended in time. The *v* at the beginning of the word *visual*, for instance, is heard before the *l* at the end of the word. But when we read silently, we usually take the word in at a glance, and all the letters seem to be perceived at the same time. The word is no longer perceived as extending in time but as extended in space. It may be that it is just this transition from a spatial dimension to a temporal one, and vice versa, that makes it difficult for a child to associate those words that he hears with those that he sees in print (Strauss and Kephart, 1949). The kinesthetic method helps to overcome this problem. When we write or trace a word, it takes *time* to write it; we perceive that a time span elapses while we are writing. We also experience a spatial dimension as we see the word extend itself from left to right on the page. Thus a word presented kinesthetically has both a temporal and a spatial dimension, which makes it easier for the child to connect the two experiences of seeing and hearing (Frostig, 1965, p. 579). VAK (Visual-Auditory-Kinesthetic) and VAKT (Visual-Auditory-Kinesthetic-Tactile) methods are variations of the kinesthetic approach (Fernald, 1943). In VAK, the child says the word aloud or subvocally as he writes it in the air; tracing is added when VAKT is used. Blind writing, a further variation, has been described above, p. 311.

Children with severe motor defects may be helped to form correct kinesthetic patterns by writing on the chalkboard, using stencils, tracing in grooves, or writing on resistant surfaces that form an impression such as clay, or with a sharp pencil on very stiff paper. Writing with the finger in paint is even more effective.*

Other methods designed to develop a child's lagging ability to associate auditory and visual stimuli include using the tape recorder or Language Master (so that the child hears what he is reading), shadow reading,** and choral reading. All of these methods ensure that the child receives simultaneous input from both auditory and visual channels.

The reader is again reminded that no single method is effective with all children. Children who suffer difficulty in associating auditory and visual stimuli may profit from a variety of methods. For example, as we have mentioned, reading aloud, generally required to enable the teacher to monitor the child's performance, provides many children with auditory and oral kinesthetic feedback that helps them learn grapheme-phoneme correspondence. But for some children with auditory-perceptual deficits, reading aloud is difficult and disturbing. The teacher's observation is the main basis for determining which method is appropriate for which child.

We recommend that the teacher compare each child's ability to comprehend paragraphs of similar difficulty after he has read one aloud and the other silently. If a child understands better when receiving auditory feedback, he may learn better by reading aloud in a group or with a tape recorder, and so on.*** But if he understands better when reading silently, emphasis on writing methods may be helpful. The child's preference and his performance under various conditions are very important clues.

It is most important for all children with associative difficulties to learn new patterns of grapheme-phoneme correspondence step by step, with much overlearning. It is also important that they read a great deal, so that overlearning can occur.

Writing also promotes the learning of grapheme-phoneme patterns, as the child learns the invariant relationships of letters and groups of letters with their sounds.

* It is essential to guide the child's hand when he learns to write a new word or letter (See chapter on writing).

** In shadow reading, the teacher reads with the child. When the child is reading confidently, the teacher allows her voice to fade away to a shadow; whenever the child falters, the teacher's voice comes in more strongly with the word in context and maintains the pace. At all times the child both sees the printed words and hears them pronounced correctly.

*** The goal of being able to read silently for meaning should be kept in mind; these children may need much overlearning and progress slowly step by step from simple short passages.

Grapheme-phoneme correspondence is also called spelling-to-sound predictability. A child who learns to read well is more likely to form useful spelling patterns, whether or not he can state any rules of spelling.

Learning to read through spelling has been suggested by Gibson (1949, pp. 437–442) and her associates, among others. The child does not learn a sound-letter correspondence, but a sound-spelling correspondence. For example, he learns to spell na*tion*, sta*tion*, peti*tion*, and so on; he will then be expected to recognize the vocal equivalent of *tion* in new words. This method is similar to the linguistic method; however, the initial approach is through writing, rather than recognition of visual patterns.

As noted earlier, all children should be constantly aware of the communicative purposes of reading; they should also learn grapheme-phoneme correspondence, and they should practice word-attack skills until they become automatic. Spelling, reading, and writing should therefore always be taught together, with constant shifting between reading and writing, and with continual·practice throughout the school day. Kephart (1972) states that writing skills need to be taught before reading. The authors believe that writing (including spelling) should at least be taught simultaneously with reading (as part of decoding).

Methods for Simultaneous Deficits in Auditory and Visual Perception

Children with perceptual difficulties in both modalities are severely handicapped in adjusting to environmental demands, including learning to read. Intensive training in both auditory and visual perception should be conducted concurrently, with a major emphasis on keeping the children motivated, because many tasks are arduous and discouragingly difficult for them.

The most effective teaching method will probably be a kinesthetic or a tactile method. An example of the latter is to "write" a letter or word to be learned with the eraser end of a pencil on the palm of the child's hand or on his back. The child pronounces the letter or word as he feels it. If he misses, the teacher repeats the procedure. When he has identified the letter or word correctly, the child writes it (at first with the teacher's hand guiding his). This method helps the child to perceive and visualize the word or letter. Usually after one to three weeks the teacher can discard the method, as the child will have learned to make a visual image of the letter or word without this step.

Difficulty in Working with Symbols

When the difficulty in working with symbols is severe, a labeling or matching method has to be used in conjunction with a highly controlled vocabulary.* To understand the value of the matching (labeling) method in reading, we have to remember that reading is a form of language, and that many of the difficulties in reading are the result of difficulties with language, rather than with reading difficulties specifically. For a young child, a word is a property of an object rather than its signifier. The matching method makes use of this earliest connection between word and things. The child is taught the object-word connection before he understands the symbolic meaning of the word.

Usually just two words are taught at first. They are cut out from an old workbook, and placed in an envelope fastened to the back of a page, ready to be matched with the pictures pasted on the front of the page. This process is later reversed. When the child can match the words and pictures with ease, the same two words are used again on the next page with a new third word added. All three words plus a fourth word are then used on the third page, and this system continues to be maintained. The matching can be repeated indefinitely since the material to be matched is always available. The child should switch frequently between matching words with pictures and matching pictures with words. After several words have been taught, they should be joined in as many ways as possible to form simple phrases or sentences. The word *run* and *Billy* can be written, "Run, Billy," or "Billy, run," or "Run, Billy, run!" for instance.

This method is, of course, limited by the fact that only words for concrete objects or depictable actions can be matched with pictures. Conjunctions and other parts of speech, such as *the*, *to*, and *and*, which exist for the purpose of organizing language, cannot be illustrated; they are gradually added to the illustrated words so that phrases and sentences can be formed. These words have to be learned by repetition, but at first only in the context of phrases or sentences in which their function is clear.

The labeling method has been found of particular value in teaching children suffering from specific dyslexia or more pervasive defects, such as moderate to severe mental retardation. The process requires careful preparation by the teacher, but usually need not be maintained for an extended period. When the child has learned to match from nine to

---

* The descriptions of the matching method and the highly controlled vocabulary are adapted from Frostig, M., Corrective reading in the classroom. *The Reading Teacher*, 1965, 573–580.

twelve words, he will very likely indicate that he has developed the ability to visualize words and will no longer need the help of pictures. Other children probably learn to auditorize and learn to read by forming auditory images.

The matching method has been used with success in treating deaf and hard-of-hearing, aphasic children, children with severe reading difficulties, and those who have speech disturbances.

For children with severe difficulties in expressive speech, matching words with objects or pictures is not only the method of choice in learning to read but also in learning to talk (McGinnis, 1956).

Children with difficulty in the use of symbols also have difficulties with number concepts and mathematical signs, such as $\div$, $=$, $<$ $>$, and so on. Such children have difficulties with abstract concepts denoted by symbols, particularly spatial or temporal concepts expressed in specialized notation, such as Σ or S. These functions may even be lagging in adults with otherwise good intelligence, who may therefore have difficulties in learning advanced mathematics or statistics.

Difficulties in Memory

All books designed for children who are just learning to read use a vocabulary that is controlled to some degree, new words being slowly introduced with frequent repetition. But in teaching children who have learning difficulties, this process needs to be refined. In preparing such children for reading a preprimer, for instance, it is advisable for the teacher to first compile original books for the children, using the same vocabulary that is used in the preprimer. The teacher thus has control over the pace at which vocabulary is accumulated, and can eventually provide each child with encouraging success when he tackles the printed book.

The teacher writes in the right upper corner of each page of the child's book the words that the child has learned in the order of their original presentation. The words also appear on the page in story form. As soon as the child knows a few words, this presentation is made in as lengthy units as possible—phrases, sentences, and finally paragraphs— rather than in the individual words or two-word phrases that necessarily characterize learning by the matching method. Emphasizing larger word units avoids chopped and relatively meaningless learning, which lessens interest and fails to instill a feeling for the structure of language.

One or two new words should be introduced daily, and repeated daily for a sufficient period of time to insure overlearning. The list of words in the upper corner constitutes a record of the sequence. If a word is missed, the teacher can go back to the page on which this word was first introduced and review the succeeding pages. When necessary, a page is prepared without new vocabulary for the purpose of review. It is helpful to give the child familarity with reading different kinds of print by composing the reading matter in the book from words cut from old textbooks, newspapers, and magazines, as well as from words written by hand in both manuscript and cursive writing. Illustrations can also be gathered from a variety of sources or can be made by the children themselves.

Proper names, which occur at this stage in most preprimers, are best omitted because they are not common vocabulary and because it is best to first let children tell stories about themselves. The appropriate proper names can be introduced when the rest of the vocabulary has been learned and the child is about to read the preprimer. When the child has learned to read one book in this way, he should learn to read others in a different series at a similar level, before progressing to the vocabulary and stories of the next level.

Other commercially available books may be used in addition to primers and preprimers in such a way as to insure sufficient repetition of each word. Such books usually have a highly controlled vocabulary and a great deal of repetition, but as with all commerical books, some words are repeated many more times than others. Before giving these books to the children, therefore, all words that are likely to cause difficulty should be written on flash cards and learned beforehand. Words missed by the child in reading the book should also be written on flash cards or listed on a chart and taken home by the child for review.

Beginners' books may also be used to develop other reading skills. A list of printed questions concerning the text can be prepared, glued to cardboard, and inserted in a pocket on the last page of the book. These questions help the child to develop certain areas of reading comprehension or reading skills, such as finding a certain piece of information on a page, finding the main idea of the story, finding a word that rhymes with a given word, and so on.

Teaching reading by the use of a highly controlled vocabulary can be adapted to work with both the usual basic readers and individualized reading programs. Ensuring adequate mastery of the vocabulary beforehand greatly enhances the probability that the child will enjoy what he reads and will acquire increased motivation.

The Child's Own Book

Reference has already been made in this chapter to the Child's Own Book. The Child's Own Book can be used with any method the teacher chooses. It provides a format for practising reading skills in a way that is flexible and has meaning for the child.

Estes (1970, p. 92) states, "It is well established that the availability of learned associations is strongly influenced by the frequency with which they have been activated. . . . The substantial success claimed by recent Russian writers for their programs of education of the mentally retarded in their 'auxiliary schools' is attributed to an important extent to the use of *'the method of modified repetition,'* that is, the instigation of repetition and rehearsal in varied contexts, and the establishment of connections between material learned in school and practical activities carried on outside."

The use of the Child's Own Book* permits the teacher to use the child's own interests and experiences in teaching reading skills systematically and with much over learning. Because it is made especially for, with, and even by the child, the material is both individualized and personalized. The child's special ability patterns can be taken into account (e.g., for a child with disabilities in figure-ground perception, only a few words or sentences may be written on each page, and the words may be color-coded.)

The teacher helps the child actually to make his Own Book by providing construction and writing paper and helping him choose his favorite color for the covers, and staple the papers together. A photograph of the child on the cover helps to bolster the child's self-concept. (A drawing, however inadequate, labelled with the child's name, can serve the same purpose.)

The teacher and the child discuss together what is exciting and important to the child. The teacher will have to be creative in guiding the story so that it remains significant to the child but is expressed in a vocabulary that the teacher carefully controls. It should be chosen mainly from the preprimers in standard reading series, but express the child's thoughts and interests. "Special" words will therefore be included. A boy fascinated by engines might want the word *generator*, for example, and would be especially proud of his ability to recognize the word.

The speed at which new words should be introduced depends on the individual child. It may range from one word in one or two days to about four words a day. The teacher should introduce the new words to the child by the method best adapted to his ability pattern. She should insure that he writes the word. A little later, he may be able to write sentences using the words in *his* book.

In summary, the Child's Own Book is a highly effective and adapt-

---

* This approach, together with others described in this chapter, is demonstrated in the film, "Preventing Reading Failure," produced at the Frostig Center.

able method of helping the child to learn, taking into account his cognitive and emotional needs. It combines the advantages of experience charts, Sylvia Ashton-Warner's organic method, and of a highly controlled vocabulary.

Summary

Causation and symptomatology in reading difficulties are usually multiple. Treatment should be concerned with ameliorating the underlying deficits while using the child's best abilities for learning new academic skills and subject matter.

The frequency of visual-perceptual and auditory-perceptual disturbances and their relationships to difficulties in beginning reading and to emotional disturbance warrants special attention to these deficits. Certain aspects of motor development also directly influence reading skills and are therefore of concern to the reading teacher. Of special significance are ocular-motor functions, laterality, and fine motor coordination.

Other factors that may contribute to reading difficulties are poor association between visual and auditory input, and poor memory for visual and auditory sequences. These disabilities may require special treatment also.

Most reading specialists suggest a multisensory approach. Reading requires spatial perception, and Bannatyne (1966) and Semmes (1966) have concluded that spatial perception involves the integration of visual, kinesthetic, vestibular, and auditory stimuli. This fact may explain the effectiveness of multisensory methods. It is equally important to integrate general language training with the teaching of reading because reading is but one form of verbal communication.

The use of kinesthetic methods, much practice in oral language, and amelioration of underlying deficits are the most important avenues in teaching reading to children with learning difficulties. But none of these will be truly effective without the key factor to ultimate success—motivation. Methods must be used that arouse in a child the desire to read.

WORKS CITED

Abravanel, E. The development of intersensory patterning with regard to selected spatial dimensions. *Monograph of the Society for Research in Child Development*, 1968, 33 (2, Serial No. 118).

Arthur, G. *Tutoring as therapy*. New York: Commonwealth Fund, 1946.

Ashton-Warner, S. *Teacher*. New York: Simon & Schuster, 1963.

Ayres, A. J. Patterns of perceptual-motor dysfunction in children: A factor analytic study. *Perceptual and Motor Skills*, 1965, 335–368 (Monogr. Suppl., 1–v20).

Bannatyne, A. D. The colour phonics system. In J. Money & G. Schiffman (Eds.), *The disabled reader*. Baltimore: Johns Hopkins Press, 1965.

Bannatyne, A. D. Verbal and spatial abilities, and reading. Paper presented at the First International Reading Association Congress, Paris, France, August 1966.

Bannatyne, A. D. *Language, reading and learning disabilities: Psychology, neuropsychology, diagnosis and remediation*. Springfield, Ill.: Charles C Thomas, 1971.

Barrett, T. C. Goals of the reading program: The basis for evaluation. In T. C. Barrett (Ed.), *The evaluation of children's reading achievement*. Newark, Del.: International Reading Association, 1967. Pp. 13–26.

Beery, J. Matching auditory and visual stimuli by average and retarded readers. Optometric Weekly, 1970, 61, 93–96.

Belmont, L., and Birch, H. G. Lateral dominance, lateral awareness and reading disability. *Child Development*, 1965, 36, 57–71.

Birch, H. G., and Belmont, L. Auditory-visual integration, intelligence and reading ability for school children. *Perceptual and Motor Skills*, 1965, 20, 295–305.

Bryant, N. D. Some principles of remedial instruction for dyslexia. *Reading Teacher*, 1965, 18, 567–572.

Chall, J., Roswell, F., and Blumenthal, S. H. Auditory blending ability: A factor in success in beginning reading. *The Reading Teacher*. 1963, 17, 113–118.

Cohen, S. A. *Teach them all to read. Theory, methods, and materials for teaching the disadvantaged*. New York: Random House, 1969.

De Cecco, J. P. *The psychology of language, thought, and instruction*. New York: Holt, 1967.

Deutsch, C. P. Auditory discrimination and learning: Social factors. *Merrill-Palmer Quarterly of Behavior and Development*, 1964, 10, 277–296.

Downing, J. *Evaluating the i.t.a.* London: Cassell, 1967.

Dykstra, R. The use of reading readiness tests for prediction and diagnosis: A critique. T. C. Barrett (Ed.), *The evaluation of children's reading achievement*. Newark, Del.: International Reading Association, 1967.

Eisenson, J. Disorders of language in children. *Journal of Pediatrics*, 1963, 62, 20–24.

Estes, W. K. *Learning theory and mental development*. New York: Academic Press, 1970.

Fernald, G. M. *Remedial techniques in basic school subjects*. New York: McGraw-Hill, 1943.

Flick, G. L. Sinistrality revisited: A perceptual motor approach. *Child Development*, 1966, 37, 613–622.

Frostig, M. Corrective reading in the classroom. *The Reading Teacher*, 1965, 18, 573–580.

Frostig, M. *Movement education: Theory and practice.* Chicago: Follett Educational Corp., 1970.

Frostig, M. Visual perception, integrative function, and academic learning. *Journal of Learning Disabilities*, 1972, 5, 1–15.

Frostig, M., and Horne, D. *Pictures and patterns; and, Teacher's Guide to pictures and patterns.* Chicago: Follett Educational Corp., 1972.

Frostig, M., and Maslow, P. Reading, developmental abilities, and the problem of the match. *Journal of Learning Disabilities*, 1969, 2, 571–574.

Gallagher, J. J. Children with developmental imbalances: A psychoeducational definition. In W. M. Cruickshank (Ed.), *The teacher of brain-injured children: A discussion of the basis of competency.* New York: Syracuse Univ. Press, 1966. Pp. 21–34.

Gattegno, C. *Words in color.* Chicago: Learning Materials, 1963.

Getman, G. N. *How to develop your child's intelligence.* Luverne, Minn.: Research Press, 1962.

Gibson, E. J. *Principles of perceptual learning and development.* New York: Appleton-Century-Crofts, 1969.

Gillingham, A., and Stillman, B. W. *Remedial training for children with specific difficulty in reading, spelling, and penmanship.* 7th ed. Cambridge: Educators Publishing Service, 1966.

Goins, J. T. *Visual perceptual abilities and early reading progress.* Chicago: Univ. of Chicago Press, 1958 (Suppl. Educ. Monogr. No. 87).

Graubard, P. S. Psycholinguistic correlates of reading disability in disturbed children. Presented at the American Psychological Association, New York, September 1966.

Harris, A. J. *Harris tests of lateral dominance.* (3rd ed.) New York: The Psychological Corp., 1958.

Harris, A. J. *How to increase reading ability.* New York: David McKay, 1970.

Hochberg, J. In J. F. Kavanaugh (Ed.), *Proceedings of the Conference on communicating by language: the reading process.* Washington: Government Printing Office, 1968.

Jones, M. H., Dayton, G. O. Jr., Dizon, L. V., and Leton, D. A. Reading readiness studies: Suspect first graders. *Perceptual and Motor Skills*, 1966, 23, 103–112.

Kass, C. E. Psycholinguistic disabilities of children with reading problems. *Exceptional Children*, 1966, 32, 533–539.

Kephart, N. *The slow learner in the classroom.* (2nd ed.) Columbus, Ohio: Charles E. Merrill, 1971.

Kephart, N. C. The bases of the reading process. Presented in a workshop, "The Problem Reader," sponsored by the Cache LaPoudre Chapter, Council for Exceptional Children, Fort Collins, Colorado, January 15, 1972.

Krippner, S. Research in visual training and reading disability. *Journal of Learning Disabilities*, 1971, 4, 66–76.

Levin, H. In J. F. Kavanaugh (Ed.), *Proceedings of the conference on communicating by language: the reading process.* Washington: Government Printing Office, 1968.

Lewis, F. D., Bell, D. B., and Anderson, R. P. Reading retardation: A racial comparison. *Journal of Reading*, 1970, 13, 433–436, 474–478.

Lovell, K., and Gorton, A. A study of some differences between backward and normal readers of average intelligence. *British Journal of Educational Psychology*, 1968, 38, 240–241.

Maccoby, E. E., and Zellner, M. *Experiments in primary education: Aspects of project follow-through.* New York: Harcourt, 1970. Pp. 15–16.

Maslow, P., Frostig, M., Lefever, D. W., and Whittlesey, J. R. B. The Marianne Frostig development test of visual perception, 1963 standardization. *Perceptual and Motor Skills*, 1964, 19, 463–499.

McGinnis, M. A. et al. *Teaching aphasic children.* Washington, D.C.: Volta Bureau, 1956.

Nodine, C. F., and Lang, N. J. Development of visual scanning strategies for differentiating words. *Developmental Psychology*, 1971, 5, 221–232.

Prechtl, H. Reading difficulties as a neurological problem in children. In J. Money (Ed.), *Reading disability: Progress and research needs in dyslexia.* Baltimore: Johns Hopkins Press, 1962, Pp. 187–194.

Sabatino, D., and Hayden, D. L. Psychoeducational study of selected behavior variables of children failing the elementary grades. *Journal of Experimental Education*, 1970, 38, 40–57.

Samuels, J. Letter name versus letter sound knowledge in learning to read. *Reading Teacher*, 1971, 24, 604–608.

Schubert, D. G. *Dictionary of terms and concepts in reading.* Springfield, Ill.: Charles C Thomas, 1964.

Semmes, J. Hemispheric dominance: A possible clue to mechanism. Paper presented at the meeting of the American Psychological Association, New York, 1966.

Silver, A. A., and Hagin, R. A. Strategies of intervention in the spectrum of defects in specific reading disability. Paper presented at the American Orthopsychiatric Association Annual Meeting, Washington, D.C., March 1967.

Silver, A. A., and Hagin, R. A. Specific reading disability: Delineation of the syndrome and relationship to cerebral dominance. *Comprehensive Psychiatry*, 1960, 1, 126–134.

Spache, G. D., et al., A longitudinal first grade readiness program. *The Reading Teacher*, 1966, 19, 580–584.

Spalding, R. B. *The writing road to reading; a modern method of phonics for teaching children to read.* New York: Whiteside and Morrow, 1962.

Staats, A. W., Brewer, B., and Grass, M. C. Learning and cognitive development: Representative samples, cumulative-hierarchical learning and experimental longitudinal methods. *Monograph of the Society for Research and Child Development*, 1970, 35 (8, Serial No. 141).

Stern, C., and Gould, T. S. *Children discover reading: An introduction to structural reading.* New York: Random House, 1965.

Strauss, A., and Lehtinen, L., *Psychopathology and the education of the brain-injured child.* Vol. 1, New York: Grune & Stratton, 1947.

Vernon, M. D. *Backward readers.* London: College of Special Education, 1968.

Warburton, F. W., and Southgate, V. *i.t.s.: An independent evaluation.* London: John Murray & W. R. Chambers, 1969.

Witty, P. A. (Ed.), *The educationally retarded and disadvantaged.* Chicago: National Society for the Study of Education, 1967.

Zirkel, A., and Moses, E. Self-concept and ethnic group membership among public school students. *American Educational Research Journal*, 1970, 8, 253–265.

19
TEACHING HANDWRITING

If children are to do well in their academic subjects the importance of learning to write can scarcely be overemphasized. Spelling, for example, needs a great deal of review, and spelling words have to be written. In math a child must be able to write not only numerals but also verbal accounts of the problems he has solved and the observations he has made.

Learning to write easily and legibly is critically important for children who cannot learn to read except by a kinesthetic method—either Visual-Auditory-Kinesthetic (VAK) or Visual-Auditory-Kinesthetic-Tactile (VAKT). Writing is also highly important for children with difficulties in using expressive language, and for those with memory defects or auditory deficits. By providing opportunities for guided practice in a highly motivating situation, the teacher can help the child to learn to express himself in writing, and by so doing, improve all of the child's language abilities.

The most important use of writing, however, is as a tool in learning to learn. As mentioned earlier, note-taking should be a regular feature of the classroom from the elementary grades on, and should not be restricted to high school and college. At all age levels, the ability to review one's own thoughts and expression on a subject makes assimilation of new facts, skills, and concepts more thorough. Moreover, children with learning difficulties often have deficits in memory. The short sentences the child writes—or the pictures he draws—can serve as memory pegs making recall easier.

First Steps in Learning to Write

Written language requires a relationship with inner language (thought) that is different from the relationship between oral language and thought. The beginning of writing is therefore often difficult, even when the child has no difficulty in forming the letters. Nevertheless, like language, writing is learned more easily if started early. Montessori

324

(1965) states that the best time to begin instruction in writing is from four and a half to five years of age. According to Kephart (1971), writing should be taught before any systematic reading instruction is initiated, an opinion that the authors share.

In teaching writing, the same principles hold as in teaching reading, math, or any other skill or subject: individualization, motivation, systematic teaching, and a careful working out of the methodology.

Some children have no difficulty in learning to write. The teacher can give them a model to copy, with or without explanation of how the letters are to be formed, and the children will do quite well. Some children need much verbal guidance. For instance, the teacher might say, "When you write the letter *d* be careful to make the downward stroke vertical," and then she may illustrate how a vertical stroke should be done. Other children may first need to work with a great number of prewriting exercises.

Among children with learning problems are some who are unable to control and guide their movements well enough to use any tool skillfully, and therefore have difficulty in using a pencil. These children may need exercises for developing coordination and strengthening the muscles involved in grasping a pencil correctly. Spring clothespins can be used for this purpose. The child squeezes the pins to open them and then places them around the edge of a cardboard box. Stories can be devised to make the activity more interesting, with the child "building cages for a zoo" (paper or small three-dimensional animals may be put in the box); or he can make a safety fence for a pool, or form a corral, or circus ring, and so on.

For the preparatory exercises, the child should use a crayon. Crayons with semicircular cross sections are much easier to hold than round or hexagonal crayons and will not roll from the desk. Writing on the board with chalk can also be introduced at this point.

The steps in learning to grasp a pencil or crayon correctly are as follows:

1. The child grasps the crayon with his fist closed around it, and is told to pretend he is stirring a pudding, cereal, or some such. He should stir counterclockwise with a whole arm movement.
2. When the child has learned to make the circular movement with ease, he is shown how to move the three fingers around to the back of the crayon and to hold the crayon between thumb and pointer (index) finger.
3. The child moves the crayon slightly up and down with his thumb and index finger, while keeping the other three fingers relaxed behind the pencil.

4. The child moves his thumb and index finger down nearer to the point of crayon and again practices control by wiggling it.
5. The child relaxes the grip with his thumb and index finger and allows the crayon to rest against the middle finger in the correct position.

After the child can use the crayon, he is given a pencil. Individualization is again necessary. Many children do not write well with the usual primary pencils because they are too thick for a child's hand. Each child should try out both a primary and a regular pencil and say which he prefers. The teacher should also observe how the child handles both pencils. Sometimes a child rejects the thick primary pencil only because he feels such a pencil is childish; in this case, too, it is important for the teacher to make the child feel comfortable.

The grasp on a regular pencil can be improved if an eraser of the kind that is usually slipped over the end of a pencil is cut in half horizontally and the lower part pushed down near the pencil point. This forms a grip that permits a more correct and relaxed grasp of the pencil.

Premanuscript Exercises

Children should first practice the elements of letter formation—circles, lines, curves, and combinations of curves and straight lines—with finger paint on large sheets of paper, if that is possible, and then continue the same activity on newsprint or old newspapers with paint and paint brush. A starting point for each pattern should be marked on the paper, and the teacher should verbalize the direction and shape of the strokes, e.g., "Up, over the candlestick, and down." If a child has difficulty in forming the shape, the teacher can first guide his hand, then gradually relax the guiding pressure.

Those children who are able to use a pencil or crayon can then practice parts of letters as indicated by the premanuscript exercises shown in Figure 1.

Manuscript Letter Formation

Similar letters are taught together, but *b* and *d* should not be taught in succession as they are so easily reversed. For the same reason *c* is inserted between *p* and *b*. The letter *q*, another letter of roughly the same configuration, is taught much later, together with *u*.

These exercises are guides for the teacher to use.

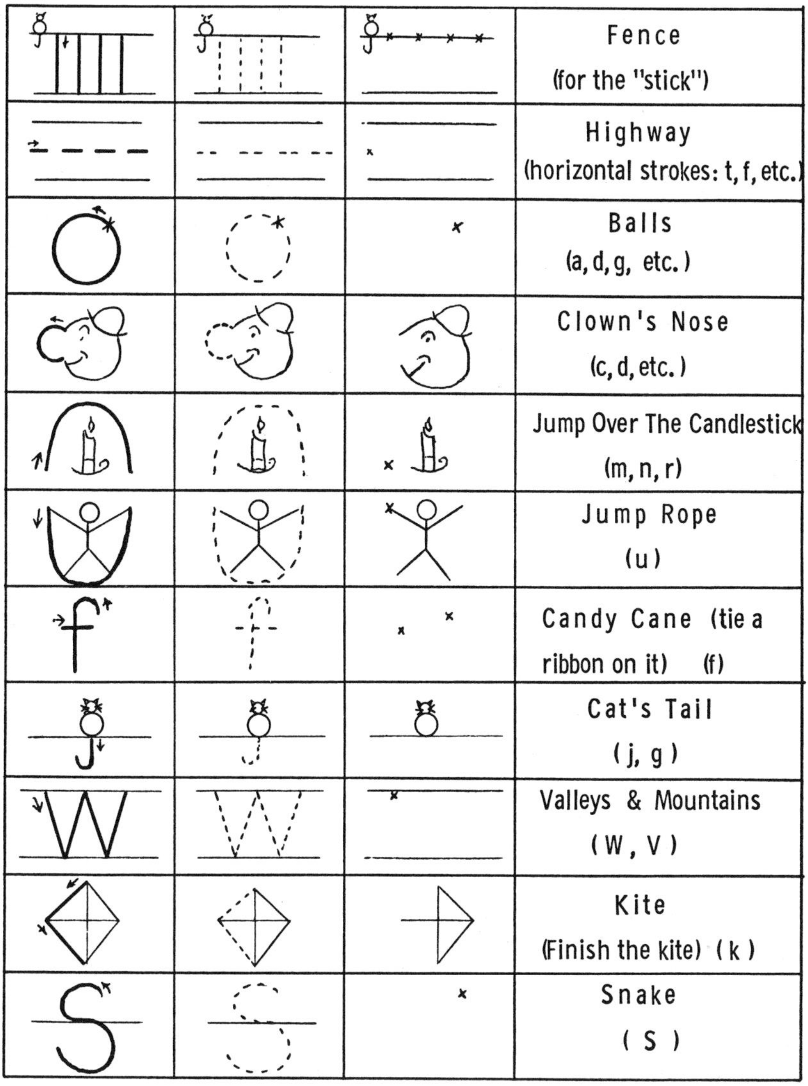

			Fence (for the "stick")
			Highway (horizontal strokes: t, f, etc.)
			Balls (a, d, g, etc.)
			Clown's Nose (c, d, etc.)
			Jump Over The Candlestick (m, n, r)
			Jump Rope (u)
			Candy Cane (tie a ribbon on it) (f)
			Cat's Tail (j, g)
			Valleys & Mountains (W, V)
			Kite (Finish the kite) (k)
			Snake (S)

FIGURE 1. Premanuscript exercises.

Groups of letters should be taught in such a way that each letter develops more or less from the preceding one as in Figure 2.

The letter s is taught in such a way that it crosses small horizontal marks drawn on the paper to show that it consists of two curves, which open (face) in the opposite directions (as shown in Figure 1).

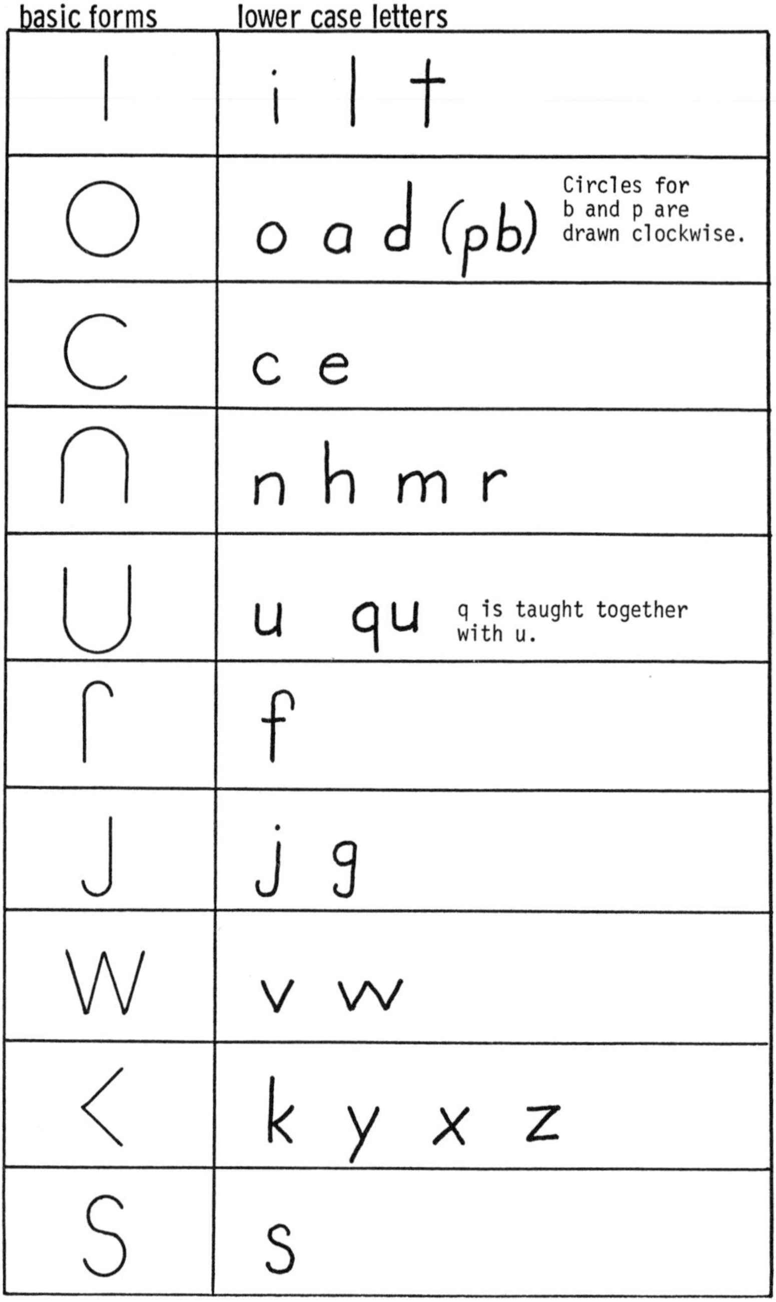

basic forms	lower case letters	
I	i l t	
O	o a d (pb)	Circles for b and p are drawn clockwise.
C	c e	
∩	n h m r	
U	u qu	q is taught together with u.
ſ	f	
J	j g	
W	v w	
<	k y x z	
S	s	

FIGURE 2

Children should practice making letters, as well as letter parts, by using finger paints or paint and brush on large sheets of newsprint or old newspapers.

Many children, however, need a stronger tactile feedback to monitor their movements. Before or at the same time as using finger paint, they may be helped to form letters correctly by tracing with their fingers letters made from sandpaper, felt, velvet, or clay. The haptic (kinesthetic and tactile) feedback provided from tracing soft, warm materials seems more effective for many children than tracing sandpaper letters; the teacher has to be guided by the child's response. Writing with a knitting needle on a surface of clay or Plasticine* also provides strong haptic feedback; the resistance of the material enhances awareness of muscle movement and also makes random, impulsive movements more difficult.

When a child has mastered the form of one or two letters, he can learn to write them on a large sheet of unlined newsprint. The teacher marks the point at which he starts to write the letter in order to orient him on the page and prevent reversals, and also verbalizes the direction in which the pencil or crayon moves. ("Down, up, and right around. There's your *p*!"). Verbalization while writing makes the task more interesting and assists in memorizing the formation of the letter. Verbalization also helps the child to perceive the letter shapes and the differences between them. The child can be told, for example; "Look, the *n* and *h* are different, because *h* has a longer downward stroke than n"; or, "*w* is like 2 *v*'s together."

After the child has succeeded in writing a large letter on newsprint, he learns to write it in a grid. The starting point for the letter is marked in each "box" of the grid, and the child is told that his letter must not cross the vertical lines. Compliance ensures that there are no reversals. (See Figure 3.)

Reduction grids can then be used, to help the child form letters correctly on a smaller scale. Such grids can easily be improvised by folding the child's sheet of paper in half (or having the child do it), then requiring him to write the letter in the top half; again folding the paper, then writing the letter in one quarter; and so on; reducing the size of the letter by approximately a half with each fold.

At the lower grade levels, it is a rare class in which all the children are comfortable in writing on the same kind of ruled paper. The classroom should therefore have available many kinds of writing paper, varying as to width between the lines, the type of line used to indicate letter proportion (stippled or colored guidelines), and shading (again

* A rolling pin can be used to flatten the dough, clay, or Plasticine.

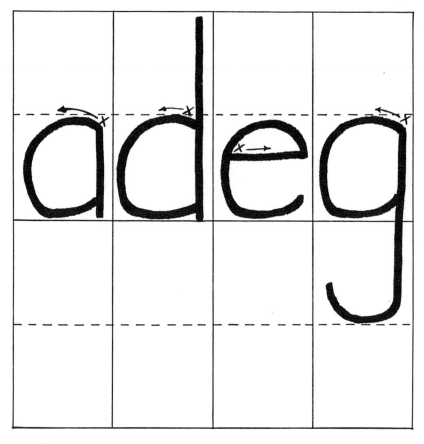

FIGURE 3

to indicate correct letter proportions). It is sometimes helpful for each child to have his own folder of writing paper.

Children with severe visual-perceptual disabilities are sometimes unable to perceive the whole Gestalt (form) of letters. It is helpful to give such a child cutout forms to glue together on a piece of paper. The teacher will need to have available cutouts of circles, curves, half circles and straight bars.

Capital Letters

In manuscript, capital letters are taught by juxtaposing each capital letter with a small (lower-case) letter.

In many school systems the capital letters are taught first, but capital letters are used much less than small letters, and it is therefore suggested that they should be taught afterward. Another reason for this procedure is that the small letters correspond more closely to most of the letters printed in the child's reader, and he can therefore associate reading and writing more easily.

Cursive Writing

Many authorities—among others, Kephart (1971), Cruickshank (1961), and Strauss and Lehtinen (1947)—recommend teaching cursive writing before the child learns to print. One reason is that the flow of cursive writing helps the child to establish smooth left-right progression and avoid reversals; another is that cursive writing helps the child to experience words as wholes, an advantage that outweighs the advantage the similarity of manuscript to book print affords. Cursive writing is also quicker, less laborious, and helps to establish spelling patterns.

Although children in regular classes are often required to learn manuscript writing first, they should not begin with cursive writing later than the second grade. The optimum time differs from child to child. The teacher will probably want to individualize and not have all children in her class begin either manuscript or cursive writing at the same time. But learning cursive writing should not be delayed because the child writes poorly in manuscript.

In introducing cursive writing, the child's needs for mastery (ego needs) can be used to motivate him. The teacher might say, for example, "This is the grown-up way of writing, the way most mothers, fathers, and teachers write. Now you can learn to write that way, too."

Precursive Exercises

Precursive exercises are designed to introduce basic cursive-letter forms in a pleasurable way, so that academic work involving writing will not be associated with failure. As with manuscript, the exercises may subsequently be used to warm up for cursive writing. For children with writing difficulties, component forms are introduced before letters. Each precursive component is introduced by rainbow tracing* on the board with colored chalk or on paper with a crayon. It is often helpful for children with severe eye-motor coordination problems to trace with a finger or a stylus on clay.

* "Rainbow tracing" refers to tracing over and over the same lines in different colors.

The precursive exercises should be accompanied by verbalization emphasizing the rhythm of the stroke. This accompaniment should appeal to the child's imagination. Here are some examples (Figure 4):

1. Hills and Valleys: Let's go *up* the hill and *down* to the valley, *up* the hill, *down* the valley, *up*, *down*, etc.

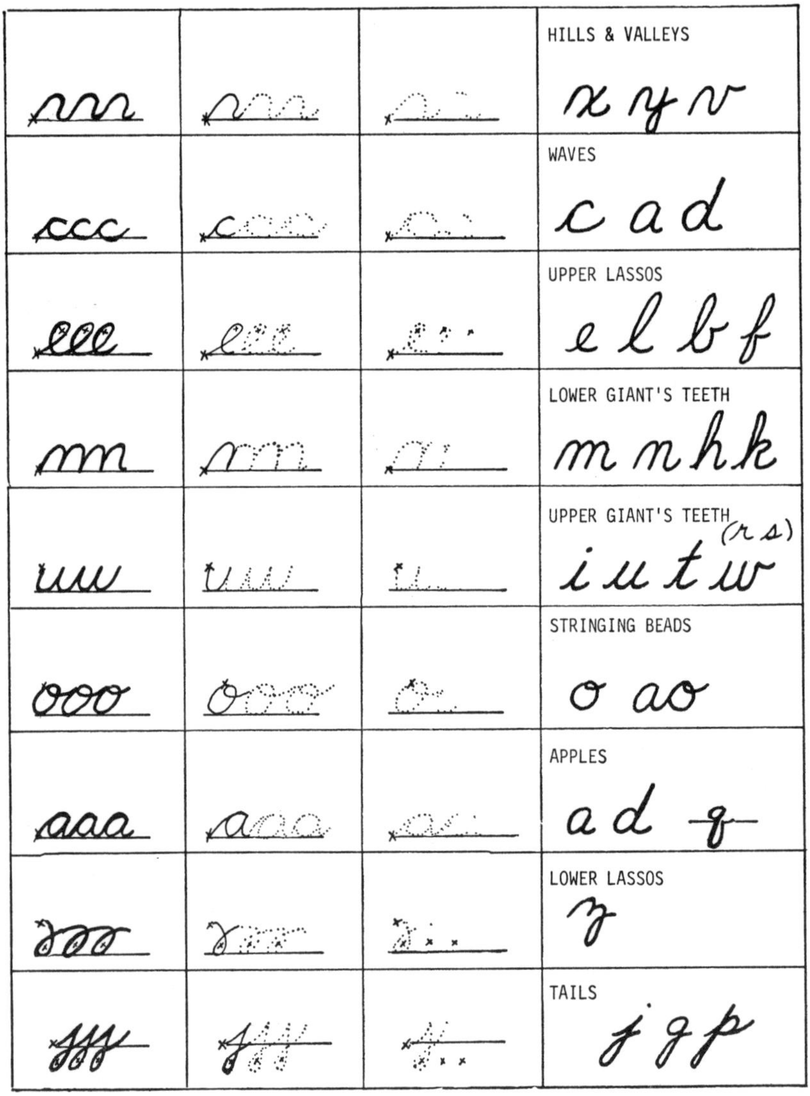

FIGURE 4. Precursive exercises.

2. Waves: The surfer's wave goes *up* and breaks, *up* and breaks, etc.

3. Lassos (x represents a steer): Go up and lasso the steer, go up and lasso the steer, etc.

4. Giant's teeth: Here are the giant's teeth. Can you tell which are the uppers? Which are the lowers? Why? How would he look if he had cavities? That's right, there would be spaces. Let's make the giant's teeth, and let's make sure to leave no spaces; we don't want him to have cavities. Say: upper—upper—upper teeth; lower—lower—lower teeth.

5. Stringing beads: String the beads, bead and string, bead and string, etc.

6. Apples: Around, up and swing, etc.

7. Tails: Up and loop, up and loop, etc.

After the child has learned the letter form, size reduction guides can be used to help him write the letter in the correct size. As with manuscript writing, each classroom should have available many types of writing paper which vary in regard to line width and type and number of cues to indicate letter proportions.

Cursive Letter Formation

If the children have already learned to write in manuscript, they are shown that cursive writing is essentially only a method of joining the letters they have already learned. The child is told that some letters have to be changed so that they can be joined. The change may consist of having the letter "stretch out his arm" to reach the next letter, or of adding a loop because that makes writing faster.

All cursive letters are compared with the manuscript letters, and the change in certain letters has to be carefully explained. For example, the letter *e* has no corners when written in cursive.

Whenever the teacher notes that the child has trouble with cursive letters which differ greatly from manuscript letters, she can let the child use a form which is more similar to manuscript. This is called joined manuscript writing. In most letters the change is minimal and does not disturb the flow in writing.

The use of color and directional arrows and X marks to indicate starting points may reinforce the direction of movement. The degree to which these are used depends on the degree of difficulty that the child is having.

Order in Which Letters are Taught

Teaching cursive letters in the sequence suggested for manuscript writing ensures that only one new form is introduced at a time, and that in general the easier letters are taught first. This sequence is recommended for children with learning problems. The child learns the precursive form first and then the letters containing that form.

Learning to Write Words

Joining each letter should be introduced on the same day that the child achieves proficiency in forming the letter at a reduced size. The words formed should be those that the child has already learned to read.

Children with learning difficulties are often unable to read or copy words in cursive writing because they do not perceive that the letters that compose the word are letters that they have already learned.

The teacher can facilitate this perceptual decentration by drawing slanting lines between the letters, and holding a pencil along each line so that the child can perceive the individual letters (Figure 5). The child then practises writing the words himself, at first exaggerating the distance between the letters.

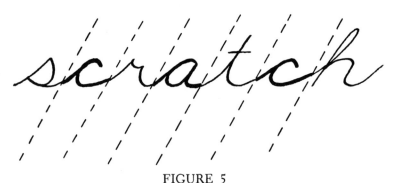

FIGURE 5

Teaching Spacing

Some children have difficulty in spacing words. They should be told to put the index finger of the nonwriting hand at the end of the word and to leave the same amount of space before writing the next word. They may make a dot where the next word will begin. Usually this exercise is necessary for only a short time—a few successive days at the most—before the child acquires the habit of correct spacing.

Remedial Training

Exercises in Directionality

Many children have problems with directionality.

The following exercises are helpful for all children, but especially necessary for children with directional confusion.

1. The children begin directionality training on a gross motor level, using both arms.

    a. The child starts with his hands at the sides of his body. He raises and lowers his arms as the teacher says: "Up, down. Up, down."
    b. The child stands with his arms stretched out in front of his chest. He moved them out to the sides and back to the central position as the teacher says: "Out, in. Out, in."
    c. The child makes the same movements according to the instructions: "Up, down, out, in," but using only the hand that he will use for writing.

    These are the directions the child will use in learning to write letters. "Out" will be to the left for a left-handed youngster, to the right for a right-handed youngster. "In" will be in the opposite direction in each case.

    Verbalization during these and the following exercises is very important as a reinforcement to the motor act of writing. The teacher says, "Out, in, up, down," as the child makes the movements. As soon as possible, the child verbalizes himself. Internalized verbilization facilitates the motor act of writing.
2. The children then draw on the board using their dominant hand. A mark coinciding with the midpoint of the child's body is made on the board with chalk. The child stands in front of the board, places his chalk on the midpoint and draws lines rhythmically to and from the point in the following directions: up, down, out, and in.
3. Children with visual perception problems may have great difficulty relating directions on a vertical surface to directions on a horizontal surface.

    a. Learning must be directed toward understanding that:
       1. "Up" on a vertical surface is *away* from the body on a horizontal surface.

    2. "Down" on a vertical surface is *toward* the body on a horizontal surface.

A method of overcoming this difficulty is to have the child draw a chalk line up and down continuously on a vertically held blackboard, slate, or paper pinned to a firm surface. The writing surface is gradually tilted downward until it is horizontal, while the child continues to draw the line and verbalizes the direction of the line ("up, down").

When the board is flat, the child will perceive that "up" is the direction of a stroke away from the body, "down" toward it.

    4. The midpoint of the body in relation to the writing paper on the child's desk is different for the left-handed and right-handed child.

Children with specific difficulties can be helped if the teacher selects remedial steps from those that have been discussed, and intensifies, prolongs or adapts them to each individual child's needs. For instance, Max may need to write on clay because his lines are wobbly; John, who cannot perceive the whole form of the letter, may need to assemble precut forms; Mark may need to write in grids because otherwise he reverses letters.

The problem of remedial teaching becomes more difficult with older children. Children in the third and fourth grades may consider these approaches childish, and more modification may be required.

One of the most useful methods to help older children learn to write with a good even flow is tracing, and the child will usually cooperate if he is told that tracing will help him to obtain speed and ease in writing and thus dispel the disagreeable feelings that he currently experiences when writing. But tracing should only be used extensively after the child has mastered the basic form of the letter.

In tracing cursive writing, letters of about half to three-quarters of an inch are used at first, and later the size is somewhat reduced. The child is given thin paper to place over the letters, which he then tries to trace with even strokes, without taking the pencil off the paper. If he prefers to do so, he may trace part of the time to the accompaniment of music (earphones should be available, so that he will not disturb other children). Tracing words is of help. A child who had been diagnosed as having agraphia (neurologically based writing difficulty) was supposed to enter a special class because he could not learn to write. He traced the spelling words in a third-grade speller, in which the words were printed quite large in cursive writing. He worked on this and similar tasks during one summer, and was able to learn to write.

The diagnosis of agraphia was reversed after this period, and he was able to keep up with the regular class.

A tracing method using templates can be used to help children acquire good eye-hand coordination. In the middle and upper grades, the geometrical figures traced with the templates need to be made more interesting by superimposing and intersecting various figures. The child can later color these figures to make an abstract design.

Lettering with stencils is another method of improving eye-hand coordination and fine muscle control. Older children can prepare writing sheets for younger children with ruler and pencil. They can decorate notebooks with cutout geometrical figures, and draw with pencil, compass, and ruler in beginning geometry. All these activities are appropriate writing preparation for children at older age levels.

Helping with the tasks necessary to keep the classroom running smoothly can promote eye-hand coordination. Children can set the table neatly for lunch or snack, pour their own or each other's drinks, make simple toys in which hammer, nails, bolts, and screws are used. A child can be put in charge of the bulletin board and required to put up the materials neatly. Children can send each other letters or drawings and invitations to play outside or meet during lunch. Such activities obviously have value in terms of social development as well as eye-hand coordination.

WORKS CITED

Cruickshank, W. M., et al. A teaching method for brain-injured and hyperactive children. Syracuse, N.Y.: Syracuse University Press, 1961.

Kephart, N. C. The slow learner in the classroom (2nd ed.). Columbus, Ohio: Charles E. Merrill, 1971.

Montessori, M. Dr. Montessori's own handbook. New York: Schocken, 1965.

Strauss, A., and Lehtinen, L. Psychopathology and the education of the brain-injured child, Vol. 1. New York: Grune & Stratton, 1947.

CONCLUSION

The purpose of this closing section is to restate the goals that were initially set and the approaches needed to achieve those goals.

The main purpose of this book has been to set forth the theoretical considerations and the educational procedures that may help to prevent and remedy classroom problems. These aims—prevention and remediation—are not new. The common characteristic of the great educators of the past—Montessori, Aichhorn, Fernald, Pestallozi, Froebel, Itard, and Seguin, among others—has been their intense dedication to the children they wished to help and their refusal to give up, even when intervention seemed hopeless.

Thousands of teachers today, like the great professional educators of the past, are rescuing untold numbers of children from lifelong dependency, delinquency, and despair. Their investment of patient work, skill, and energy will help not only the children and their families, but also the larger society. In monetary terms alone—and unfortunately this is often considered the one standard of measurement—such commitment saves considerable tax money because it assists children to become independent and well-adjusted adults. (It is hoped that those who dignify the calling of teacher will receive both recognition and commensurate salaries.)

The knowledge that a teacher needs to be optimally effective comes from a variety of sources, of which the most important are the children themselves. This book records some of the lessons its authors have gratefully learned from children and their parents, and from the communications of scholars and other educators in books and talks. It is hoped that this book will in turn impart some knowledge that will be of value.

Classroom problems often arise because a child lags behind his agemates in one or several basic abilities. A major portion of this book has therefore been devoted to a discussion of the training of abilities and of the teaching methods that match a child's tasks to his basic ability patterns.

But learning difficulties also arise from a sense of despair and futility

338

that affects even young children. The question of optimum motivation has therefore also been emphasized. It has been discussed from several vantage points: the importance of maintaining and utilizing children's natural curiosity, of helping them appreciate their own culture, and particularly, of encouraging them to take on social responsibilities. A child who experiences the pleasure of planting seeds in a box in his classroom and sharing "the produce" with his classmates, for example, will be far more likely to find fulfillment in learning than if he merely reads that a farmer grows plants.

This book has also been concerned with far-reaching educational goals. Education can teach children to feel for others and to exercise the imagination necessary to foresee the consequences of their actions, even if the consequences will not affect them directly or may occur at some far-off point in time or space. It is hoped that education will assist children in acquiring a sense of meaning and purpose in life and that it will help them to use whatever intelligence they have in making decisions and formulating constructive plans in pursuing their own goals, as well as helping others to pursue theirs.

Most of all our culture needs to educate children so that they will undertake and support whatever is constructive and creative. The blight in our cities that stares at the visitor in the form of abandoned boarded-up buildings, neglected remnants of once lovely parks, and unsafe streets will be changed less by urban renewal than by an alteration in people's attitudes. The poverty in Appalachia and other rural areas will not be remedied by alms. People must first *care;* they then can evaluate various possible solutions and act.

An understanding of common human needs and a concern for the survival óf civilization must be developed in every child. Wars, destructiveness, and murder can only occur when man no longer takes thought, when he is no longer able to evaluate the emotional, social, and physical consequences of his behavior.

Concern for the over-all goals of education has caused the authors of this book to include a section on four trends in modern thought which give their stamp to education—behaviorism, humanism, psychoanalysis, and cognitive-developmental psychology. These trends have their roots in a variety of fields—psychology, medicine, philosophy—but they can all contribute to education.

When a child has difficulty in meeting the demands of the educational system, the position taken in this book is that it is necessary to analyze his difficulties in the specific task and his pattern of psychological abilities to find out what his basic deficits are. Medical diagnosis has not been discussed extensively, because it is not helpful for a teacher to learn about causation and diagnostic procedures if appropriate methods of prevention and remediation are not the direct result. A diagnosis of brain damage, epilepsy, neurological dysfunction, character disorder, psychotic reaction, and so on, gives little indication to the teacher as to the appropriate classroom treatment for a child.

Etiological diagnosis summarized in a label may also lead to a one-sided view of the child's difficulties and therefore to one-sided remediation. A child diagnosed as having neurological dysfunction may initially have had a most satisfactory home environment, but his hyperactivity may eventually lead to rejection on the part of his family, which in turn may intensify his maladjustment. Thus a physician seeing the child at a later date might diagnose him equally correctly as having an "adjustment disturbance of childhood." In reality both diagnoses are correct, but both are incomplete.

In many children, interaction between constitutional factors—accidents of illness and injury—and negative experiences at home and at school seem to trap them behind a barrier offering no way out to success and happiness. The child caught in this self-feeding cycle of adverse circumstances may finally be abandoned by all who have contact with him—parents, school, and community. Sometimes, however, so-called miracles do occur, and a helping hand reverses the process—usually when someone ignores whatever label has been attached to the child and tries instead to help by every available means.

The authors hope that this book will be of some practical benefit to our readers in their task of educating children, especially children with learning and behavior problems. Above all, we hope that it conveys our conviction of the importance of our emotionally and intellectually challenging common task. The basic issues discussed are not only significant for the education of children with learning difficulties but for all children and for the future conduct of our society and the well-being of mankind as a whole.

The Chinese ideogram for *thought* combines the ideogram for *head* with that for *heart*.

INDEX